A Glossary of
NORTH INDIAN PEASANT LIFE

A Glossary of NORTH INDIAN PEASANT LIFE

WILLIAM CROOKE

Edited, with an Introduction, Notes and Appendices by

SHAHID AMIN

DELHI
OXFORD UNIVERSITY PRESS
OXFORD NEW YORK
1989

Oxford University Press, Walton Street, Oxford OX2 6DP

New York Toronto
Delhi Bombay Calcutta Madras Karachi
Petaling Jaya Singapore Hong Kong Tokyo
Nairobi Dar es Salaam
Melbourne Auckland
and associates in
Berlin Ibadan

SBN 0 19 562209 X

Typeset at Taj Services Ltd., Noida. U.P. 201301
Printed at Rekha Printers Pvt. Ltd., New Delhi 110020
and published by S. K. Mookerjee, Oxford University Press
YMCA Library Building, Jai Singh Road, New Delhi 110001

Contents

Editor's Preface

This is an enlarged edition of an important late-nineteenth-century compendium on the north Indian countryside. It is a work which is not really in the public domain—I have been able to locate only one extant copy in a library in Lucknow. But this is not the only reason for bringing William Crooke's work out in print: his Glossary of 1879 demands attention irrespective of its rarity. The importance of this text was underlined by the celebrated author of an analogous work on *Bihar Peasant Life* six year's later in 1885. In the Introduction to that classic 'discursive catalogue', George Grierson acknowledged that he had followed Crooke 'very closely . . . and in many cases had not scrupled to use his very words . . .'. It is hoped that this edition of Crooke's Glossary will aid a fuller understanding of rural north India, past and present.

The text of Crooke's 1879 Glossary is here printed in its entirety, with a few modifications. I have retained the original spellings of place names but simplified the transcription of Indian words. The chapter headings and the subdivisions are Crooke's, but I have arranged the book into numbered paragraphs. The Index lists all the Indian words found in the book, indicating the paragraphs where these can be located. I have also added several appendices to the original Glossary along with a dozen illustrations. Finally, the sources cited by Crooke in the margin of his original text have been collated in the Bibliography.

As regards the transcription of Indian words, the long vowels *ā, ī, ū* have been indicated where these occur at the beginning or in the middle of a word. I have, however, dropped this diacritical mark for the last letter of a word, as such vowel-endings tend invariably to be elongated. Thus *hal* (plough) and *hāl* (the iron rim of the wheel) are distinguished, but *jua* (the yoke) appears without an accented *a*. I have also refrained from burdening the vowels '*e*' and '*o*' with diacritical marks, as in the majority of the Hindustani words used in the book these represent elongated vowel sounds.

I have not attempted to distinguish between hard and soft consonants—this would have resulted in the text being pockmarked with dots and other such excrescences. Thus the word for both 'presents from the bridgegroom's house' and 'pulses in general' is represented by the same three letters (*dal*). Of course the '*d*' of the former is much harder (as in the English 'do'), but no diacritical allowance is made for such phonetic differences.

A book such as this could not have been put together without the help of several individuals. I wish to record my gratitude to Shri Jagannath, without whose typing expertise Crooke's text would have remained unpublished. I also wish to acknowledge the help I received from the following: N. C. Saxena, Rajendra Bahadur and Jagjivan Rupainwar introduced me to the records and printed materials at the Board of Revenue, the UP State Archives and the Secretariat Library in Lucknow. In Delhi I have to thank the librarians and the staff of the Nehru Memorial Museum, the National Archives, the Central Secretariat Library, the Ratan Tata Library and the St Stephen's College Library. And specially Richard Bingle and Shabana Mahmud of the India Office Library, London. The British Library and the Museum of Mankind, London, allowed me easy access to their collections. Rajiv Kumar and *janab* Vidya Prakash Sahab in Lucknow, Habib Ahmad in Gorakhpur, and Heather Joshi, David Page, David Hardiman and Dinesh Bhugra in London very kindly provided hospitality. In Deoria Begam Qamar Jahan Chishti agreed to play the part of my 'native informant'. My parents helped me with ethnographic materials; Jawahara lightened the dreary work of proof-reading. Khan Masood has saved me from numerous errors. For those which remain the OUP and I will have to share the blame.

My thanks go to Gautam Bhadra, Dipesh Chakrabarty, Bernard Cohn, Veena Das, Deepak Mehta, Sanjay Nigam and Savyasaachi for commenting on earlier drafts of the Introduction. I also wish to thank Moonis Raza for arranging for the computerized compilation of the Index. I am grateful to the Indian Council of Social Science Research for supporting research on this project in England. To Muzaffar Alam I am deeply indebted for several rounds of discussion and for his translations from Persian.

Ranajit Guha has been a constant source of ideas and criticism for the past fifteen years: I say *shukriya* to him once again.

I wish to thank Ravi Dayal and the Oxford University Press, Delhi, for making this book possible.

And, finally, Bano for prodding me all along: *jhulani ke dhakka bariyaar baate na . . .*

Delhi
3 February 1989

Shahid Amin

Materials for a Rural and Agricultural Glossary of the North-Western Provinces and Oudh

by

WILLIAM CROOKE, B.A.

Bengal Civil Service

Published by authority of Government for circulation to officers of the Revenue and Agricultural Departments.

(Seal)

Allahabad
North-Western Province and Oudh Government Press
1879

Editor's Introduction

This Glossary was compiled by a relatively young colonial civil servant in the late 1870s. William Crooke, Assistant Magistrate at the east UP district town of Gorakhpur, was not quite thirty when the *Materials for a Rural and Agricultural Glossary of the North-western Provinces and Oudh* he had put together was officially circulated within the provincial bureaucracy. This Glossary was intended to be a draft document. The idea was to enlarge the quantity of 'accessible information' within it by 'local enquiries', correct its entries and ascertain the areas in which 'special words are used'. The procedure suggested was to 'mark . . . with red ink' in the copies circulated 'the words used in each district'. The final product was to be a 'fairly complete Rural and Agricultural Glossary' with the assistance of the 'many officers' to whom the prototype, or rather the proto-text, was being circulated.[1]

There is evidence that the provincial officialdom in the Revenue and Educational departments responded to these directions. Their replies, however, are not available where one might most expect to find them. In the William Crooke Papers, now preserved in brittle condition in the Museum of Mankind, London, there is a packet entitled 'Notes for a Glossary of Indian Terms' which contains not the corrections 'marked in red ink' but titbits of a very general nature.[2] In the event, the revised and enlarged Glossary was never published, and even of the 1879 *Materials*, to my knowledge,

[1] See Crooke's Preface, reprinted herein, p. xliii; *Journal of the Asiatic Society*, 1924, pp. 147–8, Obituary Notice by G. A. G [rierson]. Crooke's *Materials* is referred to herein as the Glossary.

[2] William Crooke Papers, MS. 127, Museum of Mankind, London.

only one copy remains in the provincial capital of UP. In a sense, therefore, the present volume is the revised and enlarged edition of this lost text.[3]

Crooke's Glossary, which forms the core of the present volume, contains a wealth of very useful information about the north Indian countryside. What we have here is not just a welter of facts, obeying no other logic than the rule of the English alphabet; the text is organized to a plan and follows a detailed system of classification. A pioneering *systematization* of colonial knowledge about the everyday life of the Hindustani peasant, it neatly divides the rural world into the realms of field, household and workshop.

I

In his 1879 *Materials* Crooke incorporated the information that the colonial state—in the process of ruling, policing and taxing—had gathered till then on the north Indian artisans and peasants. The scholarship involved ferreting out indigenous words from readily available gazetteers, settlement reports, extant glossaries and Hindustani dictionaries. Crooke supplemented these sources (listed in the Bibliography) with his own administrative experience as a district officer in Gorakhpur, and classified the 5000-odd words and phrases in terms of an elaborate schema which has been retained in the present edition. Crooke's role as author was more important in arranging the words, not in discovering them. His contribution as a greenhorn *junt-sahib* (the Assistant or Joint Magistrate of local parlance) lay in imposing an authoritative order on a large number of rustic words and phrases. Once the entries were assembled in columns, big and small, the task of the local functionaries was confined to checking and correcting them. The analogy with census operations is deliberate:

[3] Crooke did, however, publish a dictionary—*A Rural and Agricultural Glossary for the N.W. Provinces and Oudh* (1888). Despite the similarity of its title to the present volume, the two books are quite different from each other.

the systematic counting of heads and the arrangement of agricultural terms were both part of the same late-nineteenth-century movement from a descriptive to a classificatory representation of colonial India.[4]

Crooke's text is an important link in a long chain that stretches from the newly-discovered Persian Glossary of 1781, through Elliot and Wilson's arrangements of Revenue and Administrative Terms (1845; 1855), to Carnegy's *Kachahri Technicalities* (1877), culminating in Grierson's *Bihar Peasant Life*.[5]

The earliest revenue glossary of the colonial period, for whose discovery and translation we are indebted to an unpublished work by Syed Hasan Mahmud of Baroda University, was compiled in Bengal by one Khwaja Yasin 'Ājiz', erstwhile *mutaiyana* of the *muhtasib* of Delhi. Khwaja Yasin was a learned man of the old regime and there was a certain piquancy in his choice of a *nom de plume* (*ājiz*=helpless) which reflected the harassed and unsettled conditions of his times. 'Ājiz', a *mansab* holder of 500 and of a *jagir* worth 4 lakh *dams* annually, needed protection from both *āfat-i-samāvi* and *āfat-i-arzi* (heavenly and earthly calamities), which he poetically

[4] The best general discussion of the construction of 'official' knowledge of colonial India is to be found in the writings of Bernard S. Cohn. See specially, 'Notes on the History of the Study of Indian Society and Culture', and 'The Census, Social Structure and Objectification in South Asia', in Cohn, *An Anthropologist among the Historians and Other Essays* (Delhi, 1987). See also Cohn, 'The Past in the Present: India as a Museum of Mankind', paper presented to the conference on 'Poetry and Politics of Representations', The Smithsonian, Washington, Sept. 1988.

[5] H. M. Elliot, *Supplement to the Glossary of Indian Terms, A–J* (Agra, 1845); John Beames, ed., *Memoirs on the History, Folk-lore, and Distribution of the Races of the North Western Provinces of India: being an amplified edition of the original Supplemental Glossary of Indian Terms by the late Sir Henry M. Elliot* (London, 1869; reprinted Osnabrük, 1976; Delhi, 1985); H. H. Wilson, *A Glossary of Judicial and Revenue Terms* (London, 1855; reprinted, Delhi, 1966); Patrick Carnegy, *Kachahari Technicalities* (Allahabad, 1877); George A. Grierson, *Bihar Peasant Life* (Calcutta, 1885; reprinted Delhi, 1975).

invoked in an arresting Preface to his work.[6]

Such a glossary, containing an alphabetical arrangement of 'many of such Arabic, Persian, and Hindi words that have found vogue in the languages spoken in Delhi, Calcutta, Dhaka, Patna and others [written] at the behest of Mr. James Grant, may God perpetuate his glory...',[7] may not have materially aided the Company as revenue collector. James Grant fulminated against the 'collusive chicanery of native agents, in withholding official intelligence from their new masters, and fraudulently converting the use of such knowledge, to their own private emolument at the public expense', and this required other than purely administrative solutions.[8] The writing of historical narratives on the landed wealth and 'finances of Bengal' was one such strategy for gaining access to that immediate past which was being denied the English

[6] Syed Hasan Mahmud, 'Yasin's Glossary of Revenue Terms: Edition, English Translation, Annotation and Analysis', Ph.D. thesis, Jamia Millia Islamia, New Delhi, 1984. The Preface to this manuscript reads in part: 'Panegyrics to the *Āmil*, the plough of whose tender love has rendered the *raqbās* (areas) of the people the nursery of *jins-i-kāmil*, and the cultivation of the land (*arāzi*) of faith and conviction, by the *belcha* (spade) of His guidance weeded out the grass of doubt and unbelief . . .', pp. 113–14 of Hasan Mahmud's translation. Yasin's 'flowery' Preface is here articulating the code of medieval Persian and Arabic scholarship wherein the Almighty's attributes are invoked in terms of the subject and tenor of the work concerned. Thus, in a 'Dictionary for the Wanderers', Allah and Mohammad are praised in terms of their lexicographic control, while a collection of the letters of Aurangzeb invokes the blessings of God by using the metaphors of *imla* (dictation) and *insha* (its representation in writing), two central terms associated with such literature. I am most grateful to Muzaffar Alam for discussing medieval prefaces with me, and for locating and translating the material discussed in this note. See Badruddin Ibrahim, *Farhang-i-Zafan-goya wa jahan-poya*, ed. S. A. Bayevsky (Moscow, 1974); *Ruqqat-i-Alamgiri* (Kanpur, 1273 AH); Ziauddin Barani, *Tarikh-i-Ferozshahi*, ed. Sheikh Abdur Rashid (Aligarh, 1957).

[7] Hasan Mahmud, 'Yasin's Glossary', p. 114.

[8] Cited in Ranajit Guha, *An Indian Historiography of India: a nineteenth-century agenda and its implications*, Deuskar Lectures, Centre for the Study of Social Sciences, Calcutta (Calcutta, 1988), p. 5.

by Bengal revenue specialists.[9]

Ranajit Guha regards this withholding of official intelligence by wily Indians, and the resultant anger and fear of the *Company bahadur*, as just one aspect of that 'ethnological encounter' which marks the setting up of a colonial state. The English attempt 'to historicize the Indian past in order to have access to it' was situated within this early resistance, put up by *mutassadis, amils* and *qanungos*, to the erection of the basic edifice of colonial rule in late-eighteenth-century Bengal.[10] Another strategy for apprehending the immediate past and the present was for a James Grant to coax a Yasin 'Ājiz' into displaying his specialist knowledge of the revenue world of north India.

As the colonial state dug deeper into Indian soil, the access of English officials to the Indian countryside also increased. Natives might still have provided the expert information, but it was the sahibs who wrote it up. Early-nineteenth-century descriptive accounts of the Company's territories were very often the creation of individual authors. The most notable of these was by Buchanan-Hamilton, who has left behind fat accounts of the parts of south and north India which he toured between 1802 and 1813.[11] By the 1830s, enthusiastic administrators were compiling district lists of local terms. However, it was in the 1840s that the idea of an Imperial Glossary was mooted at the highest level in London. The Court of Directors resolved in August 1842 'to adopt measures for forming a Glossary of words in current use in va-

[9] Guha, Deuskar Lectures, Lecture I, *passim*.

[10] Ibid., p. 12.

[11] See Francis Buchanan, *A Journey from Madras through the Countries of Mysore, Canara and Malabar* (London, 1807), 3 vols; Buchanan's writings on several districts of Bengal, Bihar and parts of eastern UP are brought together in Robert Montgomery Martin, ed., *The History, Antiquities, Topography, and Statistics of Eastern India* (London, 1838), 3 vols. An Indian reprint of the above is available; Buchanan's volumes on the south Bihar districts have also been recently reissued by Manohar Publications, Delhi. See also Cohn, *An Anthropologist among the Historians*, pp. 152–3.

rious parts of India, relating to the administration of public business in every department...'.[12] In the exercise of power, Englishmen could not afford to do away with Indian words. On the contrary, 'documents relating to the administration of the government' were 'thickly studded with terms adopted from the vernacular languages of the country...'.[13] A Handbook of *all* the relevant Indian words was an administrative necessity for everybody, from provincial bureaucrats to Members of Parliament—so argued H. H. Wilson, Boden Professor of Sanskrit at Oxford and the Company's librarian in London. Wilson's plan of first producing a prototype glossary in the India House, and then having it corrected and augmented in the colony, was a failure:

> Many of the lists came back blank; of several the leaves had not been cut; in the far greater number, a mere pretence of doing something was displayed by the insertion of a few terms neither novel nor important; . . . Several of the native officers . . . misapprehended the object of the collection, and admitted a copious collection of words which had no *peculiarly official significance*.[14]

With the 'one honourable exception' of a major new contribution from UP (Elliot's *Supplemental Glossary*), Wilson

[12] Preface, p. iii, in H. H. Wilson, *A Glossary of Judicial and Revenue Terms and of Useful Words Occurring in Official Documents relating to the Administration of the Government of British India from the Arabic, Persian, Hindustani, Sanskrit, Hindi, Bengali, Uriya, Marathi, Guzarathi, Telugu, Karnata, Tamil, Malayalem and other languages*. Compiled and Published under the Authority of the Honourable The Court of Directors of the East-India Company by H. H. Wilson, Librarian to the East-India Company and Boden Professor of Sanskrit in the University of Oxford (London, 1855; reprinted, Delhi, 1966).

[13] Ibid., p. i.

[14] Ibid., p. iii (emphasis added). See *Glossary of Indian Terms for the Use of the Various Departments of the Government of the East India Company* (J. & H. Cox Bros., Printers to the Hon. East India Co., n.d.). The copy in the Central Secretariat Library in New Delhi has the year 1885 wrongly embossed on the spine. The format, 4–5 entries on the left-hand side of the page, with a space left blank 'for suggestion and additions', and the eccentric orthography, suggest that this is one of the copies of the draft glossary circulated by Wilson in the 1840s.

had to rely perforce on existing materials for his mammoth project. His *Glossary of Judicial and Revenue Terms and of useful words occurring in official documents*, published in 1855, was offered as an Imperial Handbook for civil servants. Its design was pan-Indian, its concerns official. The administrative focus of this *Glossary* is evident in Wilson's exclusion of 'ordinary Dictionary terms', and the way in which he constantly refers his readers back to colonial legal codes where 'useful words' are either recognized or derecognized.[15]

H. M. Elliot's *Supplemental Glossary* for the North-Western Provinces was also meant for official use, but his list of 'the tribes, the customs, the fiscal and technical terms' encompasses facets of the rural world which an exhaustive compilation of 'useful words', such as Wilson's, was bound to pass over.[16] Another agricultural glossary, compiled in 1839 by E. A. Reade, the Collector of Gorakhpur, attempted to list terms in vogue at the district level (see Appendix G).[17] This archaic list is not without its interest: Elliot relied on it for many of his terms, and William Crooke, Assistant Magistrate of Gorakhpur, copied in turn from Elliot without being aware of Reade's Glossary—which, incidentally, still lies in a corner of the District Records Room of that town.

Elliot's work is important in that it was the first attempt at cataloguing castes in an official glossary.[18] John Beames, edi-

[15] See, for instance, the entry under *Chauki*: 'Station of police or of customs, a guard, a watch, or a place where they are placed.—Beng. Reg. iv. 1795. ix, x. 1810. xvii. 1816 etc.'. For a derecognized term (*vide*, 'Reg. xiv. 1807, cl. 14'), s.v. *Bharai*. For Wilson's defence of a general exclusion of all non-technical terms, see his Preface, p. xviii.

[16] The first edition of Elliot's *Glossary* is not easily available. It was a bit of a rarity even in Crooke's time; Crooke used the amplified edition prepared by John Beames. Reprints of this 'bestseller' are available in India under three different titles!

[17] The entries under *angwār, angwāra, bīsar* and many others are common to Reade, Elliot and Crooke, indicating the influence of the Gorakhpur Glossary of 1839. In his 1844 Preface, Elliot acknowledged this influence.

[18] Richard Saumerez Smith, 'Rule-by-record and rule-by-report: complementary aspects of the British Imperial rule of law', *Contributions to*

tor of a revised edition of the *Supplemental Glossary*, carried the trend further. By the late nineteenth century—the time of Risley and Ibbetson—the administrative knowledge of castes had become a specialized colonial art: a whole new set of tribes-and-castes series was projected and published. Crooke was to produce his own four volumes on the castes of UP in 1896.

The significance of Elliot's effort also lies in another direction: it created a field, encouraging others to report rustic terms. The raw materials for Crooke's Glossary were, in other words, being assembled. The *Gazetteer of Muzaffarnagar District* (1875), for instance, devotes a separate section to rural vocabulary. The model was H. M. Elliot: 'Sacks or baskets called *akaia* in the glossary is here *mānchi*. A pair of grain bags used as a pannier termed *akha* in the glossary are here *khurji*. The word *ara*, with the meaning of cross-ploughing, is in this district the second ploughing... . A pair of plough oxen, called in the glossary *goin*, are here called a *jot*.'[19] Just as Elliot's *Glossary* only covered the letters A to J, so did the Muzaffarnagar notice confine itself to the first twelve letters of the English alphabet!

Incomplete as some of the information in individual reports was, there is no denying that the 1870s and 1880s witnessed a noticeable spurt in the collation and codification of colonial knowledge on Indian society.[20] This was the time of the Divisional Gazetteers, the Final Settlement Reports,

---

Indian Sociology (xix: 1, Jan.–June 1985), special issue: 'The Word and the World; Fantasy, Symbol and Record, ed. Veena Das, p. 171.

[19] *Statistical, Descriptive and Historical Account of the North-Western Provinces of India*, iii, pp. 473–4; cf. pp. 27–31; 513–21. See also the 'Glossary of the Principal Vernacular Terms', appended to vols. I, III and IV of the series.

[20] Cf. the essays of Bernard Cohn cited above. For a detailed study of the codification and enforcement of one such piece of specialized knowledge about 'criminals by birth and caste', see Sanjay Nigam, 'A Social History of a Colonial Stereotype: the Criminal Tribes and Castes of Uttar Pradesh, 1871–1930' (University of London, Ph.D. thesis, 1987).

the regular decennial Censuses. The exhaustive district-wise Settlement Reports, also of this period, were not just revenue handbooks. They were meant to document the progressive integration of Indian agriculture into the national and world economies, 'assess' the increase in revenue that the district could *now* bear, and evaluate the generally beneficial effects of British rule on the countryside. These Settlement Reports operated within the domain of rent and revenue; in his 1879 Glossary Crooke endeavoured to create a distinct rural and agricultural sphere.[21]

From the viewpoint of 'discursive catalogues' of rural life, the significance of Crooke's text lies in its prototypical character and in its subsequent appropriation by George Grierson for his classic work on the Bihar peasantry.[22] Not only the 'general system and arrangement', but also hundreds of words and entire sentences, are common to the *Materials* and *Bihar Peasant Life*: Grierson seems to have incorporated Crooke's work so completely as to have almost consumed it.

It was not just their respective glossaries that were so similar; between themselves the two civil servants had annexed large portions of the intellectual and spiritual worlds of the peasants of northern India as their field of specialization.

[21] It needs to be borne in mind that a glossary of this kind was not *merely* a linguistic exercise. It was an instrument for establishing control over a regional agrarian economy, just as it drew for its information on official reports which documented this historical movement. An argument could be made which seeks to demonstrate the context of agricultural glossaries in far greater detail than attempted in this introductory note. I am here more concerned with the organizing principles of Crooke's Glossary rather than establishing its functionality. The best general discussion of the context of colonial UP agriculture still remains Elizabeth Whitcombe, *Agrarian Conditions in Northern India: vol. I: the United Provinces under British Rule, 1860–1900* (University of California Press, 1971).

[22] George A. Grierson, *Bihar Peasant Life. Being a Discursive Catalogue of the Surroundings of the People of that Province, with many illustrations from photographs taken by the author* (prepared under the orders of the Government of Bengal) (Calcutta, 1885; reprinted Delhi, 1975), esp. pp. 1–2 and footnote on p. 2.

Both were graduates of Trinity College, Dublin, and had joined the Indian Civil Service in 1871, along with Vincent A. Smith and four other students of the same institution. Smith, who served for a term as Collector of Basti district, went on to become a prolific writer of Indian history—specimens of his Victorian prose processed into bazaar notes are still assiduously committed to memory by students in UP and Bihar. Crooke and Grierson were not expressly concerned with our history, being more interested in India's timeless past. Grierson concentrated on the popular literature and languages of eastern UP and Bihar, and went on to conduct the monumental Linguistic Survey of India. Crooke, on the other hand, concentrated on ethnographic themes and produced valuable work on the tribes and castes and popular religion of north India.[23] These different orientations in their research interests corresponded to a difference in the two scholar–collectors' style of gathering and processing native information. According to an official notice, Grierson's delight 'was to hear of some orally current song or poem, to get it written, to find if possible, an existing manuscript, to trace its tradition or authorship and date, and with any available help of local pandits or experts to establish or translate its text.'[24] Crooke, for his part, after eighteen years of uneventful career—he was to retire as a District Officer—found his anthropologist's bench in Mirzapur district. Here, to quote from an obituary notice by a kindred spirit, Crooke could 'even better than in other districts that he administered, find means to search into the minds of a primitive population and

[23] *An Ethnological Hand-book for the N. W. Provinces and Oudh* (Allahabad, 1890); *The Popular Religion and Folk-lore of Northern India* (London, 1896), 2 vols; *Tribes and Castes of the North-Western Provinces and Oudh* (Allahabad, 1896), 4 vols. Most of Crooke's writings are now available in Indian reprints.

[24] 'George Abraham Grierson, 1851–1941', by R. W. Thomas and R. L. Turner (Obituary Notice), from the *Proceedings of the British Academy*, vol. xxviii, p. 11.

into the civilisation of the remoter parts of India . . . .'[25]

It was during his career at Mirzapur that Crooke stepped in as Richard Temple's successor to edit *Punjab Notes & Queries*. This 'monthly periodical, devoted to the systematic collection of authentic notes and scraps of information regarding the country and its people', was renamed *North Indian Notes & Queries* and published by Crooke from Allahabad from 1890 till his retirement six years later. By throwing open its columns beyond the missionary, the planter and the collector to the local informant lower down the *sarkari* ladder, the editors encouraged a distinct type of ethnographic description of colonial India. The ethnological information supplied by bilingual Indian subordinates had certain set obsequious motifs woven into it, but there was no doubting the belief in a common anthropological mission. The joint endeavour was to capture a particular aspect of the indigenous society before it was swept away by the winds of colonial change.[26] Thus, while conveying the belief, prevalent among east UP women 'that all infant girls represent the seven sisters of the godess Bhavani',[27] an important native informant was to pause and invoke the blessings of the new Bhavani, Queen Victoria! 'These names differ in different parts', Grierson's informant cautiously notes, and goes on to add:

[25] 'William Crooke, CIE, Litt. D., FBA, 1848–1923', Obituary Notice by Richard C. Temple, *The British Academy* (London, 1924), The British Library, London.

[26] Cf. Denzil Ibbetson's memorandum for guidance in collecting Ethnological Notes, 1882: 'I would remind you that no notes can possibly be too fragmentary or too trivial to be worth sending me . . . We in India have an inexhaustible store-house of facts at our very doors, and unequal facilities for ascertaining and recording them. Every year sees some of the existing material disappear under the powerful solvent of contact with western thought and appliances of civilisation. . .'. Cited in H. H. Risley, *The Tribes and Castes of Bengal: Ethnographic Glossary*, II (Calcutta, 1891; rpt. 1981), appendix 3, pp. 187–8.

[27] These are '1. Durga, 2. Kali, 3. Chandi, 4. Phulmati, 5. Chamariya, 6. Shitla, 7. Bhanmati'.

I have given the names I heard from my grand-mother who is, as it were, a living dictionary of all popular beliefs and superstitions. My former master's [i.e. Crooke's] Introduction to the Popular Religion and Folklore of Northern India owes a good deal to that old mother. With her perhaps will die away in my family all the superstitions; for the younger women have become so intelligent through the grace of learning imparted to us in the schools and colleges set up all over the country by the beneficent English rule that even the women who come in our contact [*sic*] do not escape enlightenment we have received through the blessings placed in our reach by *Queen Victoria.*[28]

Only after this flattering declamation on the beneficial effects of English rule on Indian superstition could the interrupted description of the *Chohri-khilāna* rite continue.

The invocation to Queen Victoria occurs during the course of a long manuscript titled 'The Domestic Ceremonies of the Eastern Districts of N.W.P. and Oudh', now preserved at the India Office Library, London. Full of ethnographic minutiae, the text is marked by the absence of the name of its writer; for some reason the native informant refrained from identifying himself as the author. Having conventionally absented himself, the informant chose to insert his name in the margins of the text, within parentheses. In the passage cited above he draws attention to himself via the name of his 'former master', William Crooke. A different stratagem is employed in another section—'The Christening, or the Ceremonies of giving a name to an infant'—of the same manuscript. Here the information proffered is that the child is named on the eleventh day, and the title 'Sarma' or 'Varma' or 'Gupta' or 'Das' is 'affixed to his real name', depending on whether the infant is born into a Brahman, Kshatriya, Vaishya or Shudra household. After this, we read in the margin:

[28] (Emphasis in original): 'The Domestic Ceremonies of the Eastern Districts of N.W.P. and Oudh', entry under 'Chohri Khilāna', Grierson Papers, MS Eur. E 223, India Office Library, London.

Examples of this be met with in every page [*sic*] of the ancient Sanskrit works but in the present day you will hardly find instances of this old Hindu custom being practised in Northern India. We, the Brahmans now-a-days add to our names, the distinguishing titles of our clans, as *Ram Gharib Chaube*. The Kshatriyas seldom assume the title of Varma. The Vaisyas in N.W.P. and the Punjab have totally forgotten *their* title. The Sudras . . .'.[29]

Pandit Ram Gharib Chaube, a prolific ethnographer from eastern UP, is here both identifying himself as informant-author and offering his name as an illustration of the disjunction between prescriptive 'ancient Sanskrit' texts and 'present-day practices', a fracture brought about by the rule of Queen Victoria and a long line of Europeans stretching all the way back to Vasco da Gama! Functioning as invocations to the power of British rule in India, such statements seem to impede the flow of ethnographic description; on a second reading they make sense as tell-tale signs: we are looking at chips of colonial ethnology gathered by a Ram Gharib Chaube for a Crooke or a Grierson. A destitute Chaube ('I pray . . . to my Crooke family . . . to send a morsel of bread from their table'), describes a finely-embroidered cloth (*chikan*) to William Crooke, now in retirement:

The cloth by needlework becomes the reverse of *chikan* (i.e., soft), yet the name is given to it possibly according to the custom of the country [of calling things by the wrong name], which finds vent in the following couplet of Baba Kabir Das, the weaver philosopher who flourished during the reign of *Sikandar Lody*, the Emperor, *whose reign is famous for the fact that the first European ships came to India during his reign.*[30]

The 'late Pandit to William Crooke' and 'Assistant, Linguis-

[29] Ibid. Entry under 'Christening, or the ceremony of giving a name to an infant'.

[30] Appendix B: 'On Cloth and the Clothes of the Natives of Eastern United Provinces', para 749 (emphasis added). Chaube cites the well-known couplet: *Chalti ko gāri kahai, bane dūdh ko khoya; Sahi ko bahi kahai, yeh suni Kabīra roya.*

tic Survey of India'—as Chaube styled himself—[31] is here straining to find the precursors of English rule in sixteenth-century India. Again, in a perceptive discussion of *ek-ranga-saris* (see para 739, Appendix B), he manages, by recalling one of Crooke's pronouncements, to denounce the appearance of low-caste women as 'really exciting laughter [rather] than pity in the hearts of all thinking men'.

Chaube had, according to one account, become a workaholic by 1899 and was 'driven to insanity by the lack of adequate recognition'.[32] But personal quirks aside, Indian informants never missed the opportunity to harp on the theme of 'progress'. Evidence of 'change' was sought by them in the everyday life of their countrymen. It therefore comes as something of a surprise that both Crooke and Grierson appear to have wilfully ignored many signs of change in the north Indian countryside.

Grierson toured parts of the province with a camera for his *Bihar Peasant Life*. He published some of his photographs and underlined the difficulty in taking them. Clearly, the task of photographing natives and their appliances was not an easy one in the 1880s.[33] His illustrations of the bullock-cart, the country boat, flour and oil mills, and a contrived 'fashion

[31] Chaube wrote to Crooke on 14 December 1900 (Crooke Papers, MS. 139): 'I value your worship's name so much that whenever I write an article for any periodical like Journal of the Asiatic Society of Bengal, Journal of the Anthropological Society of Bombay etc., I always subscribe [*sic*] myself as late Pandit to William Crooke Esq. ICS (retired) and thus keep your worship's name always before the learned public of India'. See, for example, Chaube's article in the *Journal of the Anthropological Society of Bombay*, iv: 6 (1897). See also, *Bhasha Vigyanankur, wa kuch bayan apne desh ki juban ka jise Pandit Ram Gharib Chaube, Assistant, Linguistic Survey, India ne nij desh ke balakon ke labh ke liye likha* (Patna: Khadagvilas Press, Bankipur, 1899).

[32] Chandrashekhar Shukl, *Ramchandra Shukl: jeevan aur krititva* (Varanasi, samvat, 2019), pp. 95–6. I am extremely grateful to Dr Ramchandra Tiwari of Gorakhpur for drawing my attention to this source, and for once again placing his library at my disposal.

[33] Grierson, Preface, p. 4.

plate' showing eleven Biharis in various states of dress, were all meant to be novelties. Here was native life as it *really was*.

However, when Grierson stumbled upon improved cane-crushers in village after village in the Sadr tahsil of Patna district, he did not bother to use his camera. He lamented the fact that not one of the traditional country mills 'was in a fit state for a photograph to be taken of it'. An indigenous appliance—the mortar and pestle *kolhu*—could not be photographically reproduced. Grierson also 'apprehended' that his 'description . . . will be of little else than antiquarian interest', yet devoted the next six pages to identifying the parts of the *kolhu* and the operatives who worked it. On a rough count, he listed over one hundred and fifty terms associated with the wooden mill, and proffered, by contrast, only one term (*kal*) for the 'English-made iron crushing mill'.[34] Besides *kal*—a generic Hindi term for 'machine'—not a word was said about the twin-roller cane-crusher which was being supplied by the sugar planters of Bihia.

It is equally noteworthy that Crooke's Glossary gives no indication of the adoption of English words by peasant speech. Just as they had adopted Persian terms, local dialects must have been peppered with peasantized English words. Several examples come to mind, for instance, from Bhojpuri: *tīsan*=station; *bumpulis*=(from) bamboo place, an enclosed privy; *gāng* (from) gang, a side (in a game), a faction in a dispute. All these words were a part of the Bhojpuri dialect by the 1870s.[35] But there is no indication of this sort of naturalization in the Glossary. It would have been perfectly feasible for a Crooke or a Grierson to have catalogued several

[34] *Bihar Peasant Life*, pp. 50–6 and *passim*. For a discussion of the improved iron-crusher sold by the European sugar planters of Shahabad district in Bihar, see Shahid Amin, *Sugarcane and Sugar in Gorakhpur: An Inquiry into Peasant Production for Capitalist Enterprise in Colonial India* (Delhi, 1984), Appendix A.

[35] My own favourite, '*otiyar*', an adaptation of the nationalist 'volunteers', is of later date. For *gāng*, see J. R. Reid, *Azamgarh Glossary* (Allahabad, 1881).

such terms connected with, say, the railways. But not even passing mention is made; in fact the railways do not figure in the section titled 'Appliances used in the conveyance of goods and passengers'. Predictably, that portion concerns itself with the country cart, the bullock and pony carriages, and the country boat.

Perhaps the reason why English-based terms were excluded was that these were not illustrative of indigenous rural life. But this is a questionable assumption. The native or the rustic may have names for objects that he does not possess. Trousers, by all accounts, were not common wear, yet in the east UP countryside the Azamgarh peasants had slang words for them, according to one of Crooke's informants. One such word, *padgaunj* was obviously adapted from *pad*=foot and *patloon*=pantaloons. Another, *gorānw*, had a more interesting etymology, for this particular feminine noun (from *gor*=foot) had 'the rope by which cattle are tied up by the foot' as its primary meaning.[36] If *rēl* and *tīsan* could find no place in provincial glossaries, *padgaunj* and *gorānw* could hardly be expected to qualify.

But why did Crooke and Grierson neglect changes in the material and mental world of the peasant? Personal predilections apart, was not the zeal of late-Victorian colonial ethnography itself predicated upon a notion of 'progress'? Stability within the world of its objects is no doubt essential for any Handbook: 'When change reaches a certain pace, reference work becomes impossible'. This insight by William Reddy, offered apropos a discussion of commercial dictionaries compiled before and after the French Revolution, also suggests why such works, even when out of date, keep getting reproduced. They go unchallenged because only the emergence of another discourse can enable a wholesale rearrangement of all the details.[37]

[36] S.v. *padgaunj* and *gorānw* in *Azamgarh Glossary*.

[37] William M. Reddy, 'The Structure of a Cultural Crisis: Thinking about cloth in France before and after the French Revolution', in Arjun

A slightly different perspective may be offered on Crooke's Glossary: the presentation of the material culture of the peasantry is here informed by a prior notion of the changelessness of the physical world of the Indian peasant. The Glossary has a lot to say about implements, crops, animals, and even insects—objects which are fashioned or which grow but which do not essentially change. With Crooke the emphasis on the *production* process has the effect of putting *exchange* relations in parenthesis. There is much more here on *dhān*, less on *chāwal*; the cane crop receives detailed consideration (pp. 106–8), whereas *gur* and *rāb*, the commodity form of this valuable crop, are noticed only in passing (paras 150, 505).[38]

Within such an arrangement the moneylender or the manufacturer has no assigned place. This leads to paradoxical results. To take an example, the implements used in the sugar manufactory get listed but the sugar refiner (*khandsāri*) goes unnamed. The *rāb*-producing peasants, especially in central UP, were closely tied to the *khandsāris*. From the mid nineteenth century refiners intervened much more directly in the production of raw sugar by demanding *ras* or cane juice from peasants. They converted fresh cane juice into *rāb* in their temporary boiling sheds (*bels*).[39] Crooke refers to the *bel* as the 'boiling house' and then proceeds to name the implements and operatives (paras 139–46). However, there is no mention of the *khandsāri*, the owner of the *bel*, either here or anywhere else in the Glossary. It isn't as though the extant sources do not mention the sugar refiner, it is simply that within the framework of Crooke's Glossary the landlord–moneylender-sugar refiner (the *khandsāri* in short) somehow slips through.

Appadurai, ed., *The Social Life of Things: Commodities in Cultural Perspectives* (Cambridge, 1986), p. 273.

[38] The Index to the present volume contains over half a dozen references to *gur*, but a majority of these are by way of additions to Crooke's *Materials*.

[39] For details see Amin, *Sugarcane and Sugar in Gorakhpur*, pp. 56–61.

II

In his Glossary Crooke is more concerned with things agricultural. Social organization and economic arrangements are noted only in passing. His purpose is to describe the immediate physical world of UP peasants. He sees this world as principally inhabited by implements and gadgets, utensils and appliances.

There are fifteen major divisions in the Glossary. The conspectus opens with details about implements, appliances and utensils used in field, workshop and home, and terminates with lists of business accounts, rates of interest and measures of length, weight and volume. In between, 'general agricultural operations', agricultural products and insects are itemized, the local names for 'wages', 'advances' and 'perquisites' established, and the varieties of land tenure hurriedly gone over. The naming operation is then performed on 'the native house' and 'food and its preparation', with a sequence of domestic and agricultural ceremonies rounding off the sphere of 'Rural Life'. Awkwardly squashed between weights and measures and the rituals of rural life, 'trade and moneylending' are almost pushed out of reckoning.

In the first section, on agricultural implements, the *auzārs* are retailed in temporal sequence—preparation of land, sowing, interculture, protecting the ripening crops, and harvesting. However, this arrangement is not without its difficulties. The discussion of brooms used 'for various agricultural and domestic purposes', for instance, appears rather inexplicably under the broad category 'Implements used in sowing, weeding and irrigation'. The 'ordinary sweeper's broom' (*jhāru*) is distinguished from the house broom, *buharni* (para 35). Neither of these has much to do with the agricultural operations mentioned above.

Such occasional incongruities apart, the overall format of the Glossary—the divisions, the subsections, the flurry of local names and terms—all convey the impression that peasant life is being dissected and its parts laid out and arranged after a legitimate and natural fashion. It is this arrangement which makes the UP countryside knowable to officials in Gorakhpur and elsewhere; it is with the aid of constant fragmentation that 'useful' information gets catalogued and kept handy for reference.

III

Crooke's work scores over all previous glossaries in its preference of a classificatory rather than an alphabetical arrangement.[40] It is therefore instructive to examine the limitations of this mode of presentation. A discussion of north Indian food lends itself fairly well to several classifications according to the indigenous mode. Distinctions could be drawn between wheat and rice-based items, meals and snacks, *namkeen* and *mītha*. Food could be characterized by whether it is boiled, steamed or fried, or considered 'hot' and 'cold' in terms of its essence (*tāsīr*). There is the food of the upper and the lower orders, food of the period of plenty, and surrogate preparations for periodic times of scarcity. And finally, there is the obvious distinction between 'vegetables' and 'meat and fish'. What the Glossary gives us instead is five and a half pages of alphabetically arranged 'preparations of food' (pp. 146–51). Precisely where native systems of classification would have appeared appropriate, Crooke turned to the English alphabet for ordering his material.

It was not as if he was unaware of these distinctions. As a junior officer he had written a detailed note on the 'average amount of food consumed by the labouring and cultivating classes' of Gorakhpur.[41] Crooke discovered that these classes consumed more salt than those better off, adding that 'probably . . . they require more [salt] to make their vegetables palatable'.[42] Mr Speeding, Crooke's superior at Gorakhpur,

[40] See p. xix above.

[41] *Report of the Indian Famine Commission, 1874–75*, Appendix iii, Cmd. 3086 (1881), p. 288

[42] Ibid., p. 288.

made a distinction during the course of the same inquiry between the sweets consumed by the poor and the well-to-do. In the *gatta*, *lai* and *lirna* eaten by the former class, observed the Collector, 'gur is used instead of chini and oil for ghi'. The food available to the poor also changed with the seasons. In hot weather 'they make food out of the bark of *semhal* (*sic*) tree', and during rains the poor of Gorakhpur ate a 'coarse bread made of mango kernels (*am-ki-gutli*) . . . known as *Koeli-ki-roti*'.[43] All this information is left out of Crooke's list. We learn about *Koeli-ki-roti* (p. 149), but minus the social and seasonal information.

As there is very little room for the play of indigenous classifications, native terms, tools and implements are processed through translation. Paradoxically for a glossary of Indian words, hoes and harrows and rakes and pickaxes loom larger than *pharua, kudāri, henga, bilna, gaita* and *dantāoli*. The power of the master language is never brought into doubt. Even north Indian regional dishes get translated as 'a mess of pounded vegetables', 'a thin sweet pastry' or 'a thick cake of bread'.

IV

A glossary that Crooke fashioned and which Grierson developed was not just an ordered stringing together of words and phrases. It also underscored difference and sameness. The mutiplicity of terms in the subsections resulted, in effect, from differences across space, social group and time. In Crooke, as in Grierson, time poses no problems. The identification of items listed is in the ethnographic present, and this present stretches well back in time. Little wonder that Max Müller expected to find in *Bihar Peasant Life* 'the houses and carts and utensils of the people very much as they are described in the Vedas . . .'.[44]

[43] Reply by Mr Speeding, Collector of Gorakhpur to question no. 9, ibid., pp. 280–1.

[44] Max Müller to G.A. Grierson, 5 January 1896, Grierson Papers, MS. Eur. E. 226/xi, no. 77(b), India Office Library, London.

While the spatial spread it encompasses is the underlying cause for the proliferation of terms and gives the Glossary its sense of completeness, regional variations are noticed only in terms of linguistic dissimilarities. On the very first page we read: 'The ordinary country plough is generally known as *hal* in the west and *har* in the east' (para 1). What this dialectal shift from *la* to *ra* does not tell us is that the east UP *har* was quite dissimilar to the west UP plough *in fact*, and not merely phonetically. It was very much lighter, had less iron content, and its ploughing edge was just a short spike and not the long iron bar of the *pacchua-hal* which projected backwards and was thrust forward as its point blunted. The weight of 'the country plough' decreased from west to east as the size and strength of the cattle diminished in the same direction. Consequently, tillage for identical crops required a greater number of ploughings in Gorakhpur than in Meerut.[45] Crooke's opening section on 'the plough' does indeed tell us about several such specimens, including *bākhar*, 'a bullock hoe', but the full range of the difference between these various *hals* never quite comes through. Between the number of terms and the levels of meanings, Crooke opted for the former. The form of the comprehensive Glossary was here dictating its content, in this respect at least to its detriment.

Speech also differs across class and caste within the same village: sociolinguists have identified this as the one-way traffic between *sāf* and *moti boli*. A landlord may have his own 'language' (the high style) and yet stoop to a lowly dialect to communicate with the low castes of the village, such linguistic freedom not being permitted in the reverse direction.[46] Crooke and the linguist Grierson must have been aware of these distinctions, but their implications for naming largely go unnoticed.

[45] Amin, *Sugarcane and Sugar in Gorakhpur*, pp. 46–7.

[46] John Gumperz, *Language in Social Groups* (Stanford, 1971), pp. 170–1, 194. See also Ranajit Guha, *Elementary Aspects of Peasant Insurgency in Colonial India* (Delhi, 1983), pp. 40ff.

In sum, the general system of the Glossary is a positivist one aimed at describing native reality in its detailed, tangible form. In Crooke this description adopts a classificatory procedure whose features are division and fragmentation. And yet the effect is to produce a homogenized representation of native life. The influence of caste, class and sect is largely absent from his compendium of agricultural and rural terms.

V

There is one exception to this homogenized representation. The creation of unidimensional categories goes hand in hand with distinctions attributed to the two faiths of Hinduism and Islam. Thus, metal vessels are itemized in terms of the religion of the persons using them: ch.II.2, section VIII, subdivides pots and pans into 'vessels ordinarily used by Hindus' and in 'general Mohammadan use'. As it turns out, there are quite a few items in common between the two lists, but the initial distinction is still made to stand. I am not suggesting that there were, and are, no Hindu and Muslim signs; to maintain this for a highly semiotized society like ours would be absurd.[47] It is the use of the division Hindu/Muslim for purposes of categorization that appears untenable at times.

Consider the way *lungi* and *angochha* are pigeonholed in Crooke and Grierson. In para 264 of the Glossary we read:

[47] For *badhna* (a special kind of *lota*) as a Muslim sign, see p. 46, note 12, below. It was not just in UP that the *badhna* stood for 'Musalman'. Nazrul Islam, cautiously celebrating the Das Pact of 1923, used the *badhna* and the *gāru* as expressive signs to refer to the Muslims and the Hindus of Bengal. His caustic poem 'Pact' begins with the lines: *Badhna garu te galagali kare, naba pacter ashnai; Musalmaner hathe nai churi, Hindur hather bash nai*. 'Badna and Garu are embracing each other in the romance of the new Pact; the Musalmans have given up the dagger, the Hindus have thrown away the bamboo-sticks.' (Nazrul Islam, *Sanchita* (Calcutta, BS 1364), p. 249.) *Badna* was distinguished from *gāru* by its longer spout; *gāru* was a *lota* of the 'pot-belly' type. For the UP *garua*, see para 211 below. I am grateful to Dipesh Chakrabarty and Gautam Bhadra for the reference and for the translation of Nazrul's poem.

'The cloth tied round the loins while bathing, and used for drying the body afterwards, is *angochha* among Hindus and *lungi* among Muhammadans'. What we have here is the beginnings of 'Hindu' and 'Muslim' loincloths. In Grierson this sectarian classification is carried a step further. Para 733 of *Bihar Peasant Life* announces a new kind of cloth, bathing cloth, in bold italics: a descriptive phrase here becomes a category. 'The *bathing cloth*, worn round the loins while bathing and used for drying the body afterwards, is named differently by Hindus and Musalmans'. The first sentence underlines the sectarian difference in the names given to this special cloth. The next four sentences provide the linguistic proof: *angauchha*, *gamchha, angochha* (Hindus); *lungi, lūngi* (Musalmans), and to press the point further, *hajuriya*, a 'bathing cloth' similar to the *lungi* but 'worn by Hindu mendicants'.[48]

True, the *lungi* is associated with Muslims of the Gangetic plains; in fact it is a sartorial sign of the Muslim weavers of east UP.[49] But we know from Grierson that the word was also used for the cloth which the *hajām/nau/naua* 'spreads in front of the person he is shaving, and on which the hairs fall'.[50] The *lungi*, by Grierson's own account, was a multipurpose piece of cloth; in Patna, Shahabad and Gaya it was the *regional name* for the more general *dhoti*.[51] To expound its meaning in terms of a restrictive category, 'bathing cloth,' is to divest this fabric of its significance. The sectarian nomenclature merely compounds the mistake.[52]

[48] Grierson, *Bihar Peasant Life*, pp. 145–6.

[49] Abdul Bismillah in his recent novel repeatedly uses the *lungi* as an all-purpose dress to emphasize the markedness of the Muslim weavers of Banaras. See Abdul Bismillah, *Jhini Jhini Bini Chadariya* (Rajkamal Paperbacks, Nai Dilli, 1987).

[50] *Bihar Peasant Life*, para 383, p. 81.

[51] Ibid., para 726, p. 143.

[52] Similarly, *angochha*, 'the bathing cloth of the Hindus', is used in east UP for tying in foodstuff like *sattu*, as well as protective headgear. It is also utilized for straining *tari* (if the need arises), and of course for wiping the body and the face.

VI

Crooke's Glossary is a mine of information for the north Indian countryside, but its full import emerges only when we begin to inquire closely into its foundations of faith and practice. Its range is wide but it also splinters rural economic and social relations. In fact that is the price of its success. Its system of classification is elaborate but it still falls short of indicating the complexities of peasant conditions at a glance. More than two hundred and fifty paragraphs intervene between the listing of loans in kind and the identification of the grains and crops in which they were advanced and recouped; the moneylender, who is noticed only briefly in para 679 (eight pages before the end of the main text), is almost marginal to the Glossary's considerations.[53] We are told about 'agricultural operations' but not how peasant proverbs dictate the tasks to be performed in the different lunar asterisms.[54]

VII

A final question may be asked about the usefulness of a draft text such as this. The question must have been answered in the affirmative in 1879 for the *Materials* to have been published at government expense. However, a code, a manual or a glossary derives its sustenance from the knowledge system of which it forms a part and which it furthers in practice. The value of the Glossary, it would appear, lay in a region-wise codification of existing knowledge of rural and agricultural terms within a *given province*. The revised Glossary, with the missing terms for each district marked in red,[55] could then

[53] Cf. pp. xxxiv and xxxv above.

[54] See Appendix D: 'A Calendar of Agricultural Sayings', below. See also V. K. Ohri, 'How Custom-bound is the Indian Farmer', *Indian Economic and Social History Review*, xviii: 3 (1981), for an attempt at statistically testing the effectiveness of some of these sayings.

[55] See Crooke's Preface, and p. xviii, above.

have functioned as a ready reckoner for the UP bureaucrat when transferred from a Bhojpuri to a Braj-speaking area, or in administrative terms from, say, Gorakhpur district to Mathura district. Crooke's *Materials* was meant—if one may borrow the expressive title of another such tract—to be *A Glossary of Terms Rural, Official and General in daily use in the Courts of Law and in illustration of the Tenures, Customs, Arts and Manufacture of Hindustan.*[56]

The choice of the entire province of UP (then NWP and Oudh) suggests that the territorial scope of the work might have reflected the official will to unify the entire region by a single provincial administration. Such an all-UP coverage appears peculiar because linguistic and dialectal areas did not coincide with administrative units. How artificial the provincial boundary was is evident from the ease with which Grierson could incorporate east UP terms into his *Bihar Peasant Life*.

[56] This is the full explanatory subtitle of Patrick Carnegy, *Kachahari Technicalities* (Allahabad, 1877).

Author's Preface

These notes are published merely as an attempt at a Digest of the information immediately accessible regarding words and phrases used in these provinces in connection with agricultural and rural life. It is believed that many officers will be ready to assist in the compilation of a fairly complete Rural and Agricultural Glossary. What is required is—

(1)—To correct the words given in these notes, particularly in spelling and transliteration.

(2)—It will be important to ascertain, as far as possible, the portion of the provinces in which special words are used. This can be done by marking with red ink the words used in each district.

(3)—The lists of local words are particularly incomplete for the Doab and Rohilkhand. It is hoped that the information given in the notes can be greatly increased by local enquiries. Mr Griffith has promised to recommend the work to the Deputy Inspectors of Schools. It is believed that they, Native Deputy Collectors and the Kanungo staff, will be able to give valuable assistance.

It is requested, in order to secure uniformity of transliteration, that new words and corrections may be given in Devanagari and Persian characters, with an English transliteration; and that the copies now circulated be returned, with the corrections, at as early a date as may be possible, to the office of the Director of Agriculture and Commerce, North Western Provinces and Oudh.

List of Illustrations

Notes on the Illustrations

The present work, unlike Grierson's *Bihar Peasant Life*, had no illustrations accompanying it. Crooke's 1888 alphabetically-arranged *Glossary* contains some excellent line drawings, but I have been unable to tear them away from their context. Drawings of agricultural implements in gazetteers and settlement reports, most notably in the Azamgarh report of 1881, posed reproduction problems. I have therefore chosen to include herein a set of twelve illustrations from three quite different sources. All these illustrations are reproduced courtesy the India Office Library, London.

Illustrations I–III are from the Meerut Settlement Book of H. M. Elliot, the author of the *Supplemental Glossary*. These drawings of agricultural implements, Mildred Archer tells us, were most probably made for Elliot by an Indian draftsman while he was Superintendent of Revenue Surveys, and are dated *c.* 1838. No. IV, a detailed drawing of the typical north-Indian wooden cane mill, is taken from Buchanan-Hamilton's Dinajpur Report, *c.* 1808, and is also reproduced in *East India Sugar: Papers respecting Sugar etc.* (1822). The third set of eight drawings (nos. V–XII) is taken from the IOL, Add. Or. 1660–1745, *c.* 1850–60.

The inclusion of this last set from a *Book contain[ing] illustrations of the various traders in Kashmir with their respective implements and the corresponding accounts of the process of manufacture* perhaps requires some justification. In her *Company Drawings* Mildred Archer remarks that these Kashmir paintings are 'very different from those of Patna or Banaras', being more indigenous in 'the type of paper, technique and general style. . .'. (p. 232). I am not competent to comment on how prevalent this mode of detailed representation of craftsmen and agriculturalists was in pre-colonial, Mughal India. It is the employment of what could be called the 'glossary mode' of representation that is particularly noteworthy in these drawings from distant Kashmir. The *tashbīh* (representation) here moves from top to bottom, from the general to the particular, in three distinct steps. The top section names the craftsman; the middle section shows him at work with his implements; the lowest arranges and displays the tools of the trade. The eye thus moves along three layers of description: the textual, the contextual and, finally, the decontextualized. Looking from the bottom up, the basic tools are combined in the operation of the craftsman (and his assistant/housewife), and the work of the craftsman is then described to give meaning to the picture as a whole. Description is here predicated on subdivision, cataloguing and naming—the hallmarks of a glossary such as the present work.

Illustration I: 'Three Agricultural Implements. *Nagpur* with *Surta* behind the share; *Nagur—Surta* behind; *Mogara* with two *Surtas* attached'

Nagar is a 'heavy plough with a perpendicular frame'. In Bundelkhand it is a 'four-ox plough'. Note that the *mogara* has two shares, and ropes rather than pegs are used to tie the various parts of the plough in all the three drawings. The seed tubes are also tied to the ploughs rather than handled separately.

Illustration II: 'Group of Agricultural Implements'

1. *Kirlee* (large rake).
2. *Toplee* (basket).
3. *Jharnee* (broom).

4. *Datar* (small rake).
5. *Phoura* (mattock).
6. *Soop* (winnowing sieve; q.v. *sūp*).

Kirlee—the biggest and the most intriguing of the implements—is not described in any of our standard sources. The drawing approximates most closely to *bīdar*: 'a sort of rake or harrow, worked by oxen to loosen the soil and extricate weeds from a crop of young rice' (para 29; s.v. *khakhorni* and *kanta* in *Bihar Peasant Life*). It is uncertain as to whether there would have been a specialized weeding instrument for rice in a wheat belt like the Upper Doab in the early 1830s. Could the *kirlee* of Meerut be the *pachpariya* of north Bihar, 'a kind of plough with five shares used in indigo factories'? (cf. Grierson, para 37).

The *jharnee* (broom) is called *barhni* in eastern UP. The *datar* (*datara* in Rohilkhand) is 'a rake used for collecting cut grass'.

Illustration III: 'Sugar-cane press, boiling pans and spoons'

This illustration of a triple wooden roller cane-press from the Meerut region, *c.* 1840, is somewhat puzzling. All our sources are agreed that it was the mortar-and-pestle *kolhu*, as detailed in Illustration IV, which was characteristic of the Gangetic plains in the first three-quarters of the nineteenth century (see also Irfan Habib, *Indian Hist. Rev*., v: i-ii, 1979, pp. 156–8). In Punjab geared wooden horizontal rollers were observed in the 1830s. Illustration III, showing three *vertical* rollers, is therefore of considerable interest for an understanding of the geographical distribution of this important agricultural machinery. The puzzle of this illustration still remains, for we have no other description of vertical wooden rollers from western UP for this period. Unlike in the mortar-and-pestle contraption, sugarcane in this press could be crushed without having to be chopped into small bits, a laborious and 'expensive operation', as Buchanan noted in his commentary on Illustration IV.

Illustration IV: The wooden mortar-and-pestle cane mill, and ground plan of the 'boiling apparatus'

Buchanan's text accompanying this drawing needs to be quoted in full:

The mill . . . is on the principle of a mortar and pestle. The pestle however does not beat the cane, but is rubbed against them, as happens in many chemical operations, and the moving force is two oxen. The mortar is generally a tamarind tree, one end of which is sunk deep in the ground to give it firmness. The part projecting (*a a*) may be about two feet high, and a foot and a half in diameter. In the upper end of this is cut a hollow in form of the small segment of a sphere (*b b*). In the centre of this a canal (*c*) descends a little way perpendicularly, and then obliquely to one side of the mortar, so that the juice as squeezed from the cane, runs through the canal, and by means of a spout (*d*) is thrown upon a stainer (*e*), through which it runs into an earthen pot that stands in a hole (*f*) under the spout. The pestle (*g g*) is a tree of about eighteen feet in length, and one foot in diameter, rounded into a foot (*h*) which rubs against the mortar, and which is secured in its place by a button (*i*) that goes into the canal of the mortar.

The moving force is applied to a horizontal beam (*k k*) about sixteen feet in length, which turns round the mortar, and is fastened to it by a bent bamboo (*l l*). It is suspended from the upper end of the pestle by a bamboo (*m*) which has been cut with part of the root, in which is formed a pivot that hangs on the upper point of the pestle. The cattle are yoked to the horizontal beam at about ten feet from the mortar, move round it in a circle, and are driven by a man, who sits on the beam to increase the weight of the rubbing power. Scarcely any machine can be more miserable, and it would be totally ineffectual, were not the cane cut into thin slices. This is an expensive part of the operation. A man sits on the ground, and has before him a bamboo stake (*n*), which is driven into the ground, and has a deep notch formed in its upper end. He passes the cane gradually through this notch, and at the same time cuts off the slices with a kind of rude chopper (*o*).

The boiling apparatus is better contrived. The mill is without shelter, but the boilers are placed under a shed. The fireplace is a considerable cavity dug into the ground, and covered by an iron boiler (*p*). At one side of this is an opening (*q*) for throwing in fuel, and opposite to this is an opening which communicates with a horizontal chimney. This is formed by two parallel mud walls (*rr ss*), about twenty feet long, two feet high, and eighteen inches distant from each other. A row of eleven earthen boilers (*t*) is placed on these walls, and the interstices (*u*) are filled with clay, which completes the chimney, an opening (*v*) being left out at the end for allowing the smoke to escape.

The juice as it comes from the mill, is first put into the earthen boiler that is the most distant from the fire, and is gradually moved from one boiler to another, until it reaches the iron one where the process is completed. Cited in *East India Sugar* (London, 1822), appx. iii, p. 25; and Montgomery Martin, *History, Antiquities, etc. of Eastern India* (London, 1838), ii, pp. 878–80.

'The mill and the boiler used in preparing the extract of sugarcane', Buchanan noted in 1808 for Dinajpur, were 'usually let by the day'. In UP, in the late nineteenth century, the *kolhu* was often jointly owned by three to six peasant households, but the boiling pans, much fewer in number and usually of iron, were hired for the season. Crooke relies heavily on an advanced copy of the *Azamgarh Settlement Report* of 1881 for his account of the 'Cane Mill' and the 'Boiling House' (paras 114–32 below). The report on Azamgarh district contains separate drawings for the mortar, the pestle and the moving gear. These show only minor variations on Buchanan's 1808 *kolhu* from Dinajpur. The one obvious difference is that, unlike in most other parts of northern India, *kolhus* in Azamgarh, and the cis-Ghaghra districts generally, were fabricated from blocks of Chunar stone.

Note that the 'boiling apparatus' described by Buchanan is more elaborate than the one depicted from Meerut in Illustration III. The Meerut drawing, *c.* 1838, also shows the pan and the spoon/mallet (*guranda* and *gurdam* respectively in east UP) used for thickening and kneading the boiled juice into a solid state (*gur*).

Illustration V: 'Representation of the Barber; his tools for cutting and shaving off hair are given below.
The Barber, razor in hand, is shaving [the client's head.]'*

Bottom half, right to left:
Ist row: The turban of the client whose head is being shaved. Tooth—extractor (*jamura* in UP). Scissors. Mirror.
IInd row: Cup for holding water. Nail-cutter (*naharni* in UP). Horn for cupping (?). Tweezers (*mochna* in UP). Comb.
IIIrd row: Implement for shearing sheep. Earthen pot. Tools for performing circumcision (*khatna, sunnat, kanuri* in UP).
IVth row: Razor. Big razor. Small razor (*Ustara* here and in UP).
Vth row: Lancet and cup. A strip of leather for cleaning the barber's kit-bag (*kisbat* in UP).

Note that here, as in the plains, the functions of the *nāi, nau, hajjām* (barber) and the *jarrāh* (the country surgeon) are combined. The inclusion of the shears is of course atypical. Notice that the north Indian terms *qainchi, kanghi* and *naharni* are not mentioned in the illustration. The term used for scissors is the Arabic *miqrāz* rather than the humdrum *qainchi*. The term *miqrāz* was not in common use in north India except in the pithy commercial phrase: '*Qarz miqrāz-ul-muhabbat*', now literally rendered into Hindi as '*Udhār prem ki qainchi hai*'! The *naharni* (nail-cutter) figures in another proverb: '*naya nāi bāns ki naharni*' (an inexperienced barber has a nail-cutter made of bamboo). By an oversight Crooke missed out the barber altogether in his Glossary!

---

* I am most grateful to Muzaffar Alam for his invaluable help in deciphering and translating the text in this and subsequent illustrations.

Illustration VI: 'Representation of the Mutton Butcher, sitting in his shop and selling meat. His tools and implements are described below'

The picture in the top half has the self-evident caption: 'The butcher is holding the knife in his hand, and having cut the meat is putting it into the weighing scales'. Pieces of meat dangling from hanging hooks, the (wooden) board on which cut meat is put (showing those bits of the goat which are sold separately and cheaper than mutton proper), weights, and a stick to chase off dogs are also depicted.

The bottom half, with the beam functioning as a natural divide, shows (from right to left):

Ist row: Hanging meat hooks (attached to ropes). A second weighing balance, with weights and meat.
IInd row: Pitcher of water. Knife. The butcher's block, with the large knife (*bugda* in UP) stuck in a characteristic resting position.
IIIrd row: A pot to wash meat in. Earthen pot (of the *badhana* variety). Stick. Decapitated goat, unskinned.

Notice the spouted earthen pot, like the *badhana* of northern India, in both Illustrations v and vi. The only difference is that the *badhana* of UP and Bihar is without a handle.

Illustration VII: 'Representation of the Cotton-weaver; his tools are described.' The weaver has stretched the warp on a wooden frame between two posts. He is applying starch (*māya*) with a comb of soft twigs and separating the threads. Below the frame are trays for starch

In UP the thread is stretched out on pieces of bamboo (*pai*) and brushed clean with the *kūnch*, a common word for brush. *Māya* and *kalaf* are two common words used for starch.

The bottom half shows, from right to left:
Kāngri, a portable heater, a pitcher and *māya* placed on a board.

Below this, a woman reels cotton, using reels with iron and wooden pins. The wooden reel with iron pins, and the starched thread stretched out on wooden pins, are also shown.

In UP the thread is wound off after leaving the spinning wheel on a *charkhi*; and it is again wound off the *charkhi* on a similar drum called *paretha*. The hank of thread after cleaning is *lundi*, and when arranged for the warp *bhānj*.

Illustration VIII: 'Representation of the Dyer with his tools. The Dyer is taking out a dyed *thān* from the cauldron'

In the bottom half, dyed woollen thread, scales with weights, water containers of various sizes, a reel with woollen thread wrapped on it, and two sticks for mixing up the dyes and taking the dyed cloth out are depicted.

The pot sunk in the ground for dyes is called *māth* in UP; *athra* is a similar half-round pot. The stirring stick (the generic Persian word *chob* is used in the illustration) is called *chalni* in UP. *Thān* is a piece of uncut woven cloth.

Illustration IX: 'Representation of the Carpenter with his tools'

The carpenter is shown fabricating a wooden frame, adze in hand. *Kulhāri* and *basūla* rather than the Persian *tesha* are the common terms for the adze in UP and Bihar.

The bottom half shows the entire range of the carpenter's tools: saws, planes, chisels and measuring and drawing instruments like the yard and the compass.

The pair of pincers for drawing nails (first row) is *jamūra* in UP (the same word is used for the barber-surgeon's tooth-extractor). The other instruments in this row—the different sized planers and the compass—are called *randa* and *parkār* in the picture, and in UP and Bihar as well. The chisels (*torakh*) are of many sorts (Crooke lists at least six different kinds of chisels in para 156). The terms *āri* and *āra* for the small and the big saw are common to the illustration and to the north Indian countryside. What is missing is the *barma*, a revolving awl worked with a bow and string, used for piercing holes for fixing iron screws or wooden pins.

Illustration X: 'Representation of Blacksmiths, with tools'

The blacksmith, aided by his assistant (note the difference in headgear) is working on the anvil. He is holding the hammer in one hand, while with the other he tackles the heated iron in the furnace.

The lower half shows the blacksmith's tools and accessories, along with a sample of the finished products. Some of the tools listed are: the file (*sohān*), hammers, pliers and piercing instruments. The anvil is prominently displayed. Alongside are shown a basketful of charcoal, a small tub with water, and a mud platform for fixing in iron pieces. Among the products (middle of the picture) are a small piece of chain, a horse shoe and two nails.

Illustration XI: 'Representation of the Potter and his tools'

The potter, having thrown the clay on the wheel, turns it and shapes a cup. The string to remove the earthenware (called *cheuni* in UP) is in his left hand. His wife kneads the clay. A water cup and the potter's turning stick are also shown in the top portion.

In the lower half, the potter's kiln (*āwa* in UP) is prominently displayed. Alongside are shown dried leaves, used both by potter and grainparcher for firing the *āwa* and the *bhār*, respectively. Next to it are the potter's wheel and the turning stick (*chāk* and *chakāit*, respectively, in UP). A pitcher of water and the pottery rammer (*kūba-i-chubi* in the drawing, *peta, pīnr* or *thāpi* in common parlance in UP) are placed alongside. Three lumps of freshly-kneaded clay placed on a wooden board, a strainer and a big pot in which the clay is prepared by mixing it with water are the other important items shown in this part of the illustration.

Illustration XII: 'Representation of the Grain merchant and the accessories used in selling grain'

The grain merchant is sitting in his shop. He has kept a variety of grains in different baskets. He weighs the grain, holding the scales in his hand.

Among the grains shown in the top half are: rice and wheat flour, white rice, red rice, peeled *singhāras* (?), *lobia* and *mūng dāl*.

The bottom half shows large earthen jars and pots (with lids) in which grains are stored. An earthen pot, weighing scales and weights, and a ladle and stick (shown stuck in the basket containing red rice in the upper half of the picture) are also depicted separately.

I Implements and Appliances Used In Agriculture and Rural Manufactures

I. I IMPLEMENTS USED IN PREPARING LAND FOR CULTIVATION

Section I—The Plough

1. The ordinary country plough is generally known as *hal* in the west and *har* in the eastern districts.[1] The *bākhar* is a bullock hoe. The *dubehri* is a light plough used in West Oudh and Rohilkhand. There are two kinds of plough in use in Oudh—that with a perpendicular body or frame is called *tariah* or *nayra*; and that which has a horizontal body *lotan* or *dabihar*. A plough with only one pair of bullocks is known as *ādha hal*. A four-ox plough is in Bundelkhand *chaukath, pakka hal, nagar,* or *nagari*. The *khapariya* is a heavy plough for stiff soils.

Its Parts

2. The various parts of the common plough are as follows:

3. The beam—In the eastern districts *haras* or *haris*, to the west *halas*, and in East Oudh *har*.

4. The body—In the Central Doab and Gorakhpur *kūr*, in the Doab and North-Western Provinces, generally, *hal, nāngal* or *nagra*, in Gorakhpur *jāngha*, and in Azamgarh *har*, in East Oudh *agwāsi,* in other parts of Oudh *pato*.

5. The handle or stilt—*Hathali, hathu, chirya, muthia* (East Oudh and Gorakhpur). In Gorakhpur, however, *muthia*

[1] See Introduction, p. xxxviii.

properly means a knob at the end of the body. In Benares *chandauti*, in the Upper Doub *tindi*, in other places *chandava*, in Azamgarh *parihat*, in Cawnpur *kūr* or *kurāi* is the step, and *paretha* is the stilt.

6. The notches on the beam by which the share is raised or lowered—In Gorakhpur *ārband*, and in other places *khura, barnel, narhel* or *banel*.

7. The sole in which the share is fixed—*Panhāri, parautha*, in the Upper Doab *pātha,* in Cawnpur *parhāri*, in the Doab *parihāri* or *parari*, in Bareli *parhai*, in Oudh *khod*, and in Gorakhpur *dabi*.

8. The share—In the east districts *phār*, in Cawnpur *phāra*, in the Central Doab *phāro*; in the Doab, generally, *phal, chāu*, or *kūsa*. In the Upper Doab the circular piece of iron fixed on the share to prevent it going too deep is *katha*, and the *kharua* is a peg to prevent the share slipping off the sole.

9. The pegs used to fasten the different parts together are as follows:

The wedge fixing the beam into the body—*Og, pachār* (Gorakhpur and Azamgarh as well as Cawnpur); in the Upper Doab *banel*, in the Central Doab and in Benares *pāth*; in Oudh *biroli*, or *marāchar*. A second wedge is sometimes added, which is known as *gandheli*, in Central Doab *parel, kilri,* or *killi*, and in East Oudh *ropi*. The wedge of peg connecting the beam and body is in Gorakhpur *dānt*, in Azamgarh *tareili*, in Cawnpur *pachmāsi*.

The wedge which holds the share and sole in the body—In Gorakhpur *agwāsi*, in Azamgarh *pāta*; in other parts of the province *pachela, pachhīla, phanna, agmāsi* (Cawnpur); in Central Doab *pachhmānsa* or *pachhra,* and in Benares *nareli*.

10. The yoke—In the western districts *jua* and to the east *juāth*. The upper bar of the yoke is *jua* in the western districts, and to the east, generally, *juāth*, and in Azamgarh *palla*. The lower bar is a *tarmāchi, tarwānsi* (Gorakhpur); and in the Central Doab *taroncha* or *macheri*. The outer pin which joins the two bars is known throughout the province as *sail*, which, in Gorakhpur, likewise means the inner pin, which in other places is usually called *gāta*. These inner pegs are also known as *galtar, samhal,* or *pachāi*.

11. The leather thongs which attach the yoke to the beam of the plough, are, in Gorakhpur *duāli*, and in other places *nādha, nāri, nāra,* or *jogra, nareili, nurka* (Upper Doab).

12. The ropes which go round the bullocks' necks, are, in Gorakhpur *jenwar*, and in other parts *jota*.

13. The projecting knob in the middle of the upper part of the yoke round which the thongs which fasten it to the beam are fixed are, in Gorakhpur *dilla*, and in Benares *mahādeva*.

14. The notches near each end of the yoke to which the ropes which go round the bullocks' necks are pitched are *khari* in the eastern districts.

15. The mould boards are *roh* if made of one piece of wood, *pākhi* if of two.

16. A drill plough is *haltaddi* or *bānsa*. The bamboo pipe is *bānsa, kūr* (Eta), *samai, orna* (Delhi), *chonga* (Cawnpur), also *nal* or *sain*. The cup at the top into which the grain is poured is *daura* or *nāla* in the east, and *waira* in the west; also in the Upper Doab *wairna*.

17. The sharpening of the ploughshare is *kaskut* (Mathura).

18. When a man wishes to plough deep he harnesses the yoke higher up on the beam. This is called in the Upper Doab *lagu*. Light ploughing is done in the converse way and is known as *askulsiya*. This is called, respectively, *awāi* and *seo* in Gorakhpur.

Section II—Spades and Hoes

19. The *pharwa* or *phāora* is a large hoe or spade. In Azamgarh the *pharusa* is a broad hoe. The *kudār, kudra, kudāri,* or *kudāli* has a narrower blade. The *kasi* is a smaller mattock. The *kilwa* is an implement like the *pharwa*. The *bel* is a kind of spade, and the *belchak, belcha,* or *belak,* is a small mattock.

20. The handle of these implements is called *bent*, which becomes in Rohilkhand *bita* and in Delhi *binta*. The end of the handle is *hūra* in the eastern districts. To the west the ring in the blade in which the handle is fixed is *pāri*, and to the east *pāsa*. The curved part of the blade is in Azamgarh *lābh*.

Section III—Harrows

21. Harrows may be divided as follows:
The flat plank dragged along the ground to break the clods after ploughing, while a man stands on it to give it weight. This implement is known as *henga, sohāga, māi, mainra* (Upper Doab), *sirāwan, patoi, pahtan* (Doab and Bundelkhand), *patela* (Doab and Rohilkhand), *patri* or *dandela*.

22. The part to which the hauling ropes or thongs are attached is *marwah*. The pegs to which the ropes are fastened are in Cawnpur *keora* and in the eastern districts *khūnti*.

23. The hauling ropes are in the east districts *barha* (Gorakhpur), or *barahi* (Azamgarh), in Cawnpur *baghan*, and in the Upper Doab *guriya*.

24. The cylindrical roller is called *rari* (Rohilkhand), *bilna* (Lower Doab and Benares), *belan* (Lower Doab and Benares), *gheri* (Delhi and Upper Doab), *girari* (Delhi and Upper Doab), *kolhu* (Delhi and Upper Doab), *lakar* (Upper Doab), *dhalāphor* or *dhelāphor* (Upper Doab), *ūd* or *or* (Upper Doab), *tor* (Upper Doab).

25. The block itself is called *lakar* (Upper Doab). The pivots on which it works *chūl* (Upper Doab), the traces fastended to the yoke *guriya* (Upper Doab).

26. The harrow made of two parallel planks joined together—In Delhi and the Doab it is called *mainra, sohāga*, and in Rohilkhand *sohal*.

27. The harrow with teeth, for eradicating grass and weeds—In the Upper Doab *gāhan* or *dahan*. The teeth are *khūnti* (Upper Doab).

28. A bundle of thorns dragged over a field for the same purpose is in Delhi and Upper Doab *dhīnkhar* or *phalsa*.

Section IV—Rakes Used in Field Work

29. The *khilwāi* in Rohilkhand is a heavy wooden rake used to collect weeds. It is sometimes also employed to rake and soften the surface of a field which has been baked hard by the sun after rain or irrigation. The *bīdar* is a sort of rake or harrow, worked by oxen to loosen the soil and extricate weeds from a crop of young rice. The *dantāoli* is a harrow or rake with teeth. The teeth are called *dānt*. The *datara* in Rohilkhand is a rake used for collecting cut grass. The *pachguriya* is a small rake used in the Central Doab for scattering indigo seed after sowing.

Section V—Pickaxes and Pitchforks, etc.

30. A pickaxe is *gaita* or *awāi* (eastern districts); *sumbha* in Azamgarh is a pickaxe used for digging the calcareous nodular limestone (*kankar*) employed in metalling roads.

31. The dredger used in well sinking is *jhām* and the pointed iron spear used in tapping the spring in a well is *sāng* (Cawnpur).

32. A pitchfork for removing grass, etc., is *jandra* or *laggi* (Central Doab); *phāori* is a sort of rake for collecting manure. The *ankri* is a forked stick for pulling down fruit from trees.

I.2 IMPLEMENTS USED IN SOWING, WEEDING AND IRRIGATION

Section I—Baskets

33. The *bhogiya* and in Gorakhpur the *oriya* and *binauthi* are used specially by the sower; there are likewise several other kinds of baskets used indiscriminately for this and other domestic and agricultural purposes. The *changel* and the *mauni* are small straw grain baskets. The *dhāka* (Azamgarh) is a large open basket; in the same district the *jhānpa* is a wicker basket for carrying wild fowl or clothes. The *khāncha* or *tokra* is a large coarse basket made of twigs of *Cytisus cajan* (*arhar*) or tamarisk (*jhāu*).[2] A smaller basket of the same kind is known as *khānchi, khachiya, khancholi* or *khacholi*. The *dagra* or *dagri* in Azamgarh is a large shallow basket. The *kurui* (Azamgarh) is a little basket made of the stalks of the *mūnj* grass. The *daliah* is a basket generally made of bamboo used in sowing and winnowing. The *chhitri* is a broken basket. The *jhanpia* is a little basket with a lid. The *jhawwa* is a large open basket made of twigs of tamarisk (*jhāu*); *deli* is a basket in which wild fowl, fish, or young pigs are kept; *chhāj* is a winnowing basket. *Gānja* (Azamgarh) is a basket in which fish are caught. *Bondhi* in the Upper Doab is a basket for carrying molasses. In Azamgarh *bhauka* or *bhauki* is a small basket with a wide mouth. *Tarauna* is a basket made of tamarisk for carrying refuse. The *tāpa* is a basket under which chickens are kept. *Batti* are in Azamgarh twigs of tamarisk for weaving baskets. These are also called *sāl*.

Section II—Brooms

These are used for various agricultural and domestic purposes.

34. The ordinary sweeper's broom is *jhāru*. The broom used by women in sweeping out the house is *barhni*, so called because the family is supposed to prosper (*barhna*). The *buhāri* or *buhārni* are also house brooms. The broom used for

[2] *Jhāu: jhāo* or *jhāukar* (*Tamarix dioca*) is a common shrub which grows on marshy, and inundated ground, and is used in thatching, hedging and as fuel in *desi chini karkhanas*. See John Beames, ed., *Memoirs on the History, Folk-lore and Distribution of the Races of the North Western Provinces of India, being an amplified edition of the original supplemental Glossary of Indian Terms by the late Sir Henry M. Elliot* (London, 1869), II, p. 353. Hereafter Beames, *Supplemental Glossary*. In alluvial tracts near major indigenous sugar-refining centres, peasants often neglected rice and raised *jhāu* on a commercial basis. For details, see, Shahid Amin, *Sugarcane and Sugar in Gorakhpur: An Inquiry into Peasant Production for Capitalist Enterprise in Colonial India* (Delhi, 1984), p. 82.

sweeping up the grain on the threshing floor is in Rohilkhand *surhet*, and in Gorakhpur *kūncha* or *sehithan*.

35. The long twig broom used for sweeping up leaves and rubbish is in the east districts *kharhara* or *kuchara* (Azamgarh). The *palwat* (Azamgarh) is a broom made of palm leaves. In the Central Doab the *khanera* is a broom made of twigs of the cotton plant with which the sower distributes tobacco seed in the beds.

Section III—Implements Used In Weeding, etc.

36. The *khurpa* is a sort of hoe used for loosening the earth round young plants or in weeding. Of this the iron blade is *khurpa*, the handle *bent*, the iron ring fastening in the blade *sām*, the spike of the blade which goes into the handle *nār*, or *dānri*.

37. The *khurpi* is a smaller instrument used for scraping grass or weeding. The *khatpādari* (Central Doab) is a sort of spud used in transplanting tobacco.

Section IV—Implements Used In Connection With Irrigation

38. For making the beds in a field for irrigation (*kiyāri*) an implement with a handle and board fixed at the bottom, like a rake without teeth, is used. One man holds the handle while a second pulls it towards himself with a rope. This implement is known in Cawnpur as *pāchhi, kārha* or *kiyāri*, in the western districts as *jandra* or *mānjho*, in the Central Doab as *pākhi* or *pharāhi,* and in Gorakhpur as *pharuhi*.

39. In the eastern districts a wooden shovel is used in distributing the water in the field, and is called *hatha* or *hātha*.

The other appliances used in connection with irrigation from wells, tanks, or streams will be found in the chapter on irrigation.

I.3 APPLIANCES USED IN FIELD WATCHING

Section I—The Sling

40. This is called in Gorakhpur *dhelwāns*, and in other places *gophana, gophani, gophia*.

Section II—The Scarecrow

41. This is known as *dhokha, ujka* (Rohilkhand). In the Central Doab *ojhak* or *ojpo*, in Delhi *darāwa*; in Azamgarh *taina*, in other places *bijgāh dharalla, dhūha*, in Gorakhpur *gora* and *kūra*; other terms are *darakka* and *bachoka*.

42. A scarecrow pulled by a string and hung on a tree is in Gorakhpur *khatka* or *khatkhata*, and in the Upper Doab *dhai* or *karkara*.

43. Cultivators also usually put an old black earthen pot in a field to keep off the evil eye, which is called in Azamgarh *dithauna*,[3] and in Gorakhpur *karkhai hanria* from *kārakh* (soot).

Section III—The Watchman's Platform

44. This is known as *machān* generally; in the east districts *māncha* or *mācha* or *marhala*; in Delhi as *dāmcha* or *jaunda*, in Delhi and Rohilkhand *tand*; in the Doab as *mattula, menra*, or *mainra*.

45. The shed over the platform is *thaicha* in Azamgarh.

I.4 IMPLEMENTS USED IN HARVESTING

Section I—The Sickle or Reaping Hook

46. This instrument is known as *haswva, hansiya, hasuli* (Azamgarh), *dānti, darānti, dāsa*, or *dānsa*.

[3] Cf. *Dithauna* in *Azamgarh Glossary*, 1881: '(i) A black mark made on

47. The curved part of the blade in the east districts *hasuwa* or *hasuli*—the straight part *nār*, and the handle *bent*.

Section II—The Winnowing Sheet

48. This is in Delhi *jhūli*, in Bundelkhand *sarua*, in Azamgarh *serwa*, in Rohilkhand and the Upper Doab *partwa*, in Benares *parauta*, in the Lower and Central Doab *parti*, in Gorakhpur *bhaunra*, in other places *pāthi*, or *partowa*.

Section III—Rakes Used on the Threshing Floor

49. The *jeli* is a kind of pitchfork or rake. In the eastern districts the *pāncha*, or *panchangura*, has five prongs. The *dhinka*, or *dhīnka*, is smaller than the *jeli*, and has curved prongs, and is used by a man sitting down. The *sikāu*, or *dambāli*, is similar to the *jeli*. The *akain* (Gorakhpur) is a curved stick used for pushing the sheaves under the bullocks' feet, while the grain is being trodden out. In Bareli the *parchāi* is a small wooden five-pronged rake used for raking up the grain and chaff.

Section IV—Granaries

50. These are of three kinds—

Ist—A structure of straw or brushwood in the open air—This is generally known as *bakhār*, or *bakhāri*, in Rohilkhand *chaursi*, and in the Upper Doab *kothi*.

2nd—Underground pits for storing grain are called *chaunra*, or *khād*, in the Doab *khāti* or *khāta*, in Partabgarh *garh* or *khaun*; and in Gorakhpur *bhaunra* or *chahbacha*. In Azamgarh *gār* is a grain pit in the open over which a shed is erected.

3rd—Granaries inside the house—The *dehri* in the eastern districts is a granary made of straw and mud. The *jabra* or *jabri* is of larger size and is generally made of sun-dried bricks.

---

the forehead to keep off the evil eye, (2) An old black pot put out upside down in a field to keep the evil eye off the crops.'

The *koth* (Partabgarh), the *kothwār,* or *kothila,*[4] of Azamgarh and the *kothi* of the Doab, are closets of sun-baked mud for grain. The *dhunki* in Gorakhpur is a wattle receptacle smaller than the *dehri,* in Gorakhpur *gora* is the support of the granary; *pihān* or *dhapna* the cover, *pendi* the bottom, and *ān* the hole through which the grain is removed. *Upta* in Azamgarh is the roof of the granary.

51. An enclosed space for grain is *thek.*

52. In the east districts various vessels are used for grain—the *kūnra, matki,* etc. The mouths of these are covered with earth called *mator.*

I.5 IMPLEMENTS AND APPLIANCES USED IN CONNECTION WITH FEEDING AND WATCHING CATTLE

Section I—The Fodder Cutter

53. This is called *gandāsi, gandāsa, ganrāsi, garāo* (Central and Lower Doab) or *gadāsi* (Rohilkhand).

54. In Azamgarh the broad wooden part over the blade is called *jāli,* the blade *ganrās,* the handle *muthia,* the knob at the end of the handle *gānth,* and the spiked part of the blade which goes into the handle *khura.*

Section II—The Block On Which The Fodder Is Cut

55. This is in the eastern districts *nisuha.*

Section III—The Feeding Trough

56. This is known as *nānd* or *nādh* or *kūrh* (Upper Doab); *charni* is an earthen feeding trough.

[4] The *Azamgarh Glossary* defines *kothwār* as '(i) A large closet made of sun-baked mud for storing grain. (2) The earth of the same—said to be good for prickly heat when ground and plastered on the body'.

Section IV—The Muzzle and Blinkers

57. The cattle muzzle is known as *chhīnka* (Upper Doab), *mukha, mushka, jāli* (Rohilkhand and Doab), *khonta* (Benares), *muska* (Bundelkhand), *jāb* or *jābi* (Gorakhpur), *munhchhīnka* or *mūncha*.

58. Blinkers for cattle or horses are *andhiya* or *andhwat* (Azamgarh). Those used for cattle in an oil-press or sugar mill are *dhoka* in the eastern districts. In Azamgarh *parchha* is a piece of cloth tied over the blinkers.

59. In Azamgarh *dhātha* or *dhāthi* is a piece of wood tied round a bullock's mouth to prevent it from eating.[5]

Section V—The Whip and Goad

60. The whip used in driving bullocks is *paina* or *pain* (Gorakhpur) The lash is *sānta* or *patūki* (Gorakhpur). *Phundna* in Gorakhpur is the thong at the end of the lash. The spike at the end of the handle is *ār* or *arāi*.

61. An elephant goad is *ankus*, and the stick used for beating an elephant is *gajbāk*. In Azamgarh *dhokana, sataha* or *jhantaha* is a short stick for driving cattle.

62. A horsewhip is *kora* or *chābuk* and a spur *kānta*.

Section VI—Hobbles for Cattle

63. These are called *chhān* or *chhand* in the eastern districts. A piece of wood tied to the neck of a vicious or runaway animal is in Azamgarh *tharak, thekur* or *dharak*. A cattle chain is *zanjīr* or *beil* (eastern districts).

Section VII—Ropes

64. A. Those used for cattle—*Pagha* in the eastern districts is a rope used in tethering cattle. *Pandha* is used else-

[5] *Dhātha* more generally is 'a cloth worn over the beard under the chin and tied on top of the head', s.v. *Dhātha* in *Azamgarh Glossary*. E.g. *Dāku san dhāta bandhle rahlān*. See also para 255 below.

where in the same sense. In Azamgarh *khurānw, khurwāns, gurānw* is a tethering rope by which cattle are tied by one foot to a peg; *chhirkhi* in Azamgarh is a double tether for wild cattle held by two men round the animal's neck.

65. B. Ordinary ropes—An ordinary rope is *rassi, rasari* (Gorakhpur) *dor* or *jewara*. In Gorakhpur the string used in drawing water from a well with a brass vessel (*lota,* etc.) is called *dori*; while that used with an earthen pot (*ghara,* etc.) is *ubhan* or *bhareth*. The knot round the neck of the vessel is *ubka* (eastern districts) or *phānsa* to the west, and in Azamgarh *ariwan*. In Azamgarh the rope used in drawing water from a well is *chhor*, and *panchhor* is a small piece of rope attached to the vessel, and then tied on to the regular well-rope. *Lenjur* or *lenjuri* in Azamgarh is a thick well-rope.

66. The rope which is used in working the irrigation lever (*dhenkli,* etc.) is *barāri* (Central Doab), *bart, lao, rassa* (Gorakhpur), *bareri* (Cawnpur), *barha* (Gorakhpur). In Azamgarh *barha* or *nār* is the thick rope, and the short rope joining it and the bucket by a slip-knot is *chhor*.

67. The strings used in working the irrigation swing basket are known as *daur, juta* or *joti*, and in Gorakhpur *daun; gora* is a smaller rope used for the same purpose. The ropes used for dragging a harrow are *barha* or *barahi* in Gorakhpur and eastern districts, *guriya* in the Upper Doab, and in Cawnpur *baghan*.

68. In Azamgarh *gatār* or *gāta* is a rope for tying up bundles of sugarcane; *gūrhi* is an imperfectly twisted hemp rope or one made of straw for tying up bundles of crop; and *mūrha* or *murra* is a rope of stems of the *Cytisus cajan* (*arhar*) for tying up bundles. *Jenua* is a similar rope made of *kusa* grass, *sūt* is thread for sewing or weaving and *sutli* is twine. *Bān* is rope made of the stems of the *mūnj* grass. *Tara* is twisted string. *Bakel* in the eastern districts is twine made of the root of the *dhāk* tree. *Jenta* is a rope put round the roots of young trees to hold up the earth as they are being transplanted. *Barahi* is a thick hemp rope. *Jūna, jūn,* or *jūnar, juina, juin,* is a grass rope for cleaning vessels or tying up bundles.

69. *Agāri* or *galkhor* or *garkhor* is a headrope for horses and *pachhāri* is the heelrope; *bāgdor* is a rope for tying up a horse. *Painkra* is a heelrope for a camel and *nath* is a headrope for cattle, passed through the animal's nose. *Muzamma* is the thin rope tied round a horse's hocks.

Section VIII—Pads for Cattle

70. These are known as *gāchhi, gaddi, gathi, bakhra, palān* (Gorakhpur), *līwa, padād,* or *chhāi.* These words change in use. For instance, where the pad for an ass is *līwa,* that of a bullock is *chhai-bakhra*, and so on. An elephant's pad is *gaddi* or *gadela.*

Section IX—Grain Bags and Panniers for Loaded Cattle

71. These are *gathiya, ākha, khurji* (Upper Doab), *palān* (Upper Doab), *pākhal,* and in Azamgarh *jora*, or *chhānti*. One of the panniers is called in the Upper Doab *mānchi*. If made of hemp fibres such bags are called *bhangela* or *ganjeli; bora* is a rice sack.

Section X—Canvas or Tarpaulin Covers

72. These are *pākhar*, or *tārpāl*; *kandhela,* is a body cloth put over bullocks in the cold weather.

Section XI—The Grain Bag from which Animals are Fed

73. This is *gaun* for cattle and *tobrah* for horses.

Section XII—Dairy Utensils

74. The milk pail—*jhākari, dohni,* or *gorasi,* and in Gorakhpur *goncha* or *gonchi*.

75. Vessels used in the manufacture of clarified butter (*ghi*)—*Kadhauni, Jamauni, biloni bharuka* (Gorakhpur) *kahathori* (Gorakhpur) or *dahenri*. The churn—*Kamori* (Gorakhpur) *chati, kahathari* (Gorakhpur). To churn is *bilona,* or *mahna* (Gorakhpur). The stirrer or stick moved in the churn is *rai, badhāwah,* and in Gorakhpur *mahni, mathana,* or *khailar*. The rope with which it is twisted is *khichna* in Gorakhpur. The vessel for holding the clarified butter is in Gorakhpur *gora,* and the leather vessel in which it is exported is *kuppi*.

I.6 APPLIANCES USED IN THE CONVEYANCE OF GOODS OR PASSENGERS

Section I—The Country Cart

76. The ordinary cart is called *gāri* or *gārhi, larhiya* or *chhakra. Rath* is a lighter cart used by rich people and women. The *bahli* is a similar cart of a smaller kind. The *ekka* is a two-wheeled light trap, generally drawn by a pony. In Bundelkhand the *sadaha* is a light rude cart used for conveying country produce. The *dahmarda* is a large cart calculated to hold ten men. A cart drawn by one pair of bullocks is *dobarda* or *dobalda,* with two pairs *chaubarda* or *chaubalda*. In a team of three bullocks the wheeler bullocks are in Azamgarh *dharia,* and the leader *binriha* or *binraha,* and in a team of four the leading bullocks are called *juār*.

77. The parts of the country cart are as follows:

78. The wheel—*Pahiya* throughout the province, in Cawnpur *pair,* and in Gorakhpur *chakka*. The spokes are in the Upper Doab *āri,* in Cawnpur *āra* and in Gorakhpur *ārā-gaj*. The quadrant of the wheel is *putthi* throughout the province. The spikes which run from one felloe into the other are in Gorakhpur *johani,* and the holes in which they are inserted *chheda*.

79. The iron hoop round the nave is in the Upper Doab *andhi,* and in the Lower Doab and eastern districts *ban*. The iron axle box in the nave is throughout the province *āwan*.

80. When the edge of the wheel is bevelled to prevent

wearing, it is called *nagar* in Cawnpur; and in Gorakhpur *mangar*, or *chāthar*; and in Gorakhpur when it is flat it is said to be *pāthar*.

81. The linch-pin is in the Upper Doab *chaket*, in Cawnpur *chakol*, and in Gorakhpur *dhūrkilli*; and in Gorakhpur the peg inside the wheel is *pharkilli*.

82. In Gorakhpur and Cawnpur the fend or washer of hemp inside the wheel is *khāndan* and that outside *chendi*.

83. The axle—This is usually called *dhura* or *dhuri*.

84. In some carts which are made particularly strong, the outer end of the axle passes through a piece of curved wood, which is fixed to the body of the cart outside the wheel. This piece of wood is called throughout the province *painjani*, and in some of the western districts *bānk*.

85. The bars which run transversely across the cart to which this piece is attached on both sides are known as *tikāni, takāni,* or *sūja*. According to Elliot, the *sūja* are the pegs which fasten these bars to the pieces running outside the wheels. In Gorakhpur they are fastened together with ropes which are called *jant*.

86. The shafts which support the body of the cart—These are known in the Doab as *phār*, in Gorakhpur as *phari*; and in other places as *harsa*. They are sometimes strengthened by a band of iron which is called in Cawnpur *patti*, and in Gorakhpur *jor*.

87. The thinner poles which run along the bottom of the cart parallel to the thick shafts are in Cawnpur *mājhia*, and in Gorakhpur *phari*. They are fastened to the body of the cart by pegs or iron nails which are called in Cawnpur *kathkilli*, and in Gorakhpur *khūnti* or *pharkilli*.

88. The short transverse bars in front of the driver's seat which keep the shafts in their places are in the Upper Doab *patri,* or *patti*, and in Gorakhpur *phari*.

89. The flat board forming the driver's seat is in the Upper Doab *panjāla*, in Cawnpur *pateli*, and in Gorakhpur *mohra*.

90. The cross bars behind the driver's seat in which the posts forming the siding of the cart are fixed are in the Upper Doab *patri,* or *patti,* in Cawnpur *murhia patela,* and in Gorakhpur *makhara.*

91. The bamboos which run along the sides from end to end and form the bottom of the siding are in the Upper Doab *mungi*, and in the Lower Doab and eastern districts *bangur*. These are fastened to the body of the cart by ties known in Cawnpur as *sontha*, and in Gorakhpur *rasara*. The upright posts forming the siding are in the Upper Doab *khalewa*, or *kharua*, and in Gorakhpur *khūntari*. The long pole or bamboo forming the top of the siding is in the Upper Doab *chandoi*, in Cawnpur *bānsa*, and in Gorakhpur *balli*; when a high pole is fixed in to support a lofty load of sheaves or grass it is called in Oudh *panjuri*. The ropes forming the siding are in the Upper Doab *phūrka*, in Cawnpur *gurau*, and in Gorakhpur *hathwāsa*. The posts to strengthen the siding fixed in the curved bars which run outside the wheels are in the Upper Doab *dege*, and in Gorakhpur *khūntari*. In Cawnpur there are extra cross bars which run above the bottom of the cart behind and below it in front. These are called *sāli*. The wooden block or fend which separates these from the cross bars supporting the curved pieces of wood which go outside the wheels is called *mathakha*.

92. The block in which the axle pin is fixed is in Cawnpur and Gorakhpur *nasauri*. The cross bar below which supports this is generally *ānkh*, and in some places *bānkara* or *gaj*. The axle pin is *dhuri*, and this is fastened to the last mentioned cross bars by the *ghinni*.

93. The fastening of the curved beam outside the wheels to the transverse bars is in Cawnpur *jantra* or *kharkharia*.

94. The yoke is *jua* or *juāth*, the latter used in the eastern districts. Its parts are the same as already described in I.1 in connection with the plough.

95. The pointed piece of wood in front which joins the two ends of the shafts is in Cawnpur *shāguni*, and in Gorakhpur *sāguni*. The centre piece of this is in the Upper and Lower Doab *māthāpāra*, and in Gorakhpur *munthapara*. The prop in front is generally *untara*, or *utara*, also in Cawnpur *utharpa*. The pole forming the tail of the cart is in the Upper Doab *udhiyār*, and in Gorakhpur *pachhlakara*. The drag is *dandeli*. In Gorakhpur the pole forming the front of the side is *tich*, and the prop which supports it *khūntari*. The prop which supports the cart behind is in the Upper Doab *dāhi*, and in other places *sidhwāi*.

96. The hooks on the yoke to which the ropes which go round the bullocks' necks are tied are in Cawnpur *chireya*.

97. When three bullocks are yoked, the rope which goes over the leader's neck is in Gorakhpur *bīnr*. The ropes which go round the bullocks' necks are in Cawnpur *khūnth*, and in the eastern districts *binriya* or *gāta*. The rope by which the yoke is fastened to the body of the cart is in the Upper Doab *nār*, in Cawnpur *nāri*, and in Gorakhpur *jhatka*. The rope binding the yoke to the head of the cart is in the Upper Doab *joga*, and in Gorakhpur *pāncha*. This is kept in its place by hooks which are in Cawnpur called *bichhua*.

98. The mat put in the bottom of a cart to prevent grain from falling out is in Gorakhpur *dhāla*.

99. In Gorakhpur the prop to prevent the cart falling back is *ularwa*, and the iron chain for tying up the bullocks at night *sikar* or *beil*.

Section II—The Bullock Carriage

100. This is in the eastern districts *bahal*, and to the west *bahli* or *baili*.

101. In the eastern districts its parts are as follows:

102. The wheel—This is *pahiya*. The thin spokes are *gaj*, and the thick spokes *āra*. The *tulāwa* are strengthening spokes outside the wheel. The *painjani* are curved pieces of wood which run outside the wheel, and in which through a hole the outer end of the axle works. The *ānkh* are cross pieces which run from side to side at the back and to these the *tulāwa* are fixed. The *takāni* are similar cross pieces in front to which the *painjani* are attached. The *patra* are curved pieces of wood outside the wheel fastened to the *ānkh*. The *bān* are chains and ropes fixing the *tulāwa* to the body. The *hāl* is the iron rim of the wheel. The *putthi* is the quadrant of the wheel. These are fixed one to the other by spikes called *johnia* which run into mortice holes in the next quadrant known as *chheda*. The nave is *nāha*. This is surrounded by an iron ring called *bān* to prevent splitting. The axle box is *āwan*. The leather washer of the wheel is *chendi*.

103. The axle is *dhuri*.

104. The body of the vehicle—The frame of the seat is *patti*, of which the supports are *khūnta*. On these there are ornamental brass knobs called *phūliya*. *Danda* are the posts supporting the awning, of which *chhattri* is the top and *gadda* the stuffed cover to keep off the sun. The net forming the bottom of the seat is *sāngi*. The *dhamāka* is the leather guard of the body inside the wheels.

105. The two long shafts which run from end to end are *tānga*. Between them are placed narrow planks, *mānjha*. The *dārua* are supports of the body behind. Similar smaller supports are *bāwali*. The *dāntua* is the back seat used for carrying luggage. The *dori* are the strings forming the side of the awning, and *parda* is the side awning. The *balli* are rails on each side of the driver's seat.

106. The yoke is *jua*.

107. The parts in front—The two lower shafts are *phār*. The yoke is fastened to the body by a rope, *jhatka*. The *mohra* is the rope which fastens the yoke to the end of the shafts. This is tied to iron hooks in the yoke called *kara*. The pointed end of the body under the yoke is *shāguni*, and this is supported by props, *untara*. The iron spikes on the yoke are *samhal*.

Section III—The Pony Carriage

108. This is called *ekka*. The wheel is *pahiya*, of which the spokes are *ārāgaz*. The nave of the wheel is *nāha*, which is surrounded with an iron band (*ban*) to prevent splitting. The axle box is *āwan*, the leather washer *chendi* and the hemp washer inside the axle box *khāngar*. *Dhuri* is the axle, and is supported by ropes, *jant*, which fasten the outer supports, *salāi*. The outer pieces which connect the axle with the body are *tulāwa*. These are fastened to cross pieces which run behind called *ānkh*, by iron bands called *akuri*. The front transverse pieces corresponding to the *ānkh* behind are *takāni*. The quadrants of the wheel are *putthi*, which are fastened one to the other by pegs called *johnia*, which run into mortice holes, *chheda*; *hāl* is the iron rim of the wheel. The leather dashboard over the wheel is *patra*. The four bars forming the body are *patti*. *Sāngi* is the twine net under the seat. The props of the body are *danda*. *Bileya* are small pieces of wood connecting these with the body. The top of the awning is *chhatri*, and the roof of it is *chhat; gadhela* is a cushion at the top to keep off the sun. The awning at the sides is *parda*, which is fastened by iron rings, *kari*. The ropes which support the awning poles are *hathwānsa*.

109. The axle is *dhūra*, which is strengthened inside by a brass ring, *sāma*. The *khūnta* are posts which support the body in front on the axle. *Puchia* are the pointed ends of the lower shafts, and *dārua* are posts which support the body on the axle behind the *khūnta*. *Bāwali* are smaller similar supports behind. *Thān* are iron bars which support the body on the axle. The *mānjha* are similar wooden supports. The *sāngi ki nāri* are straps which keep up the net under the seat. The *guriya* are side ropes which fasten the dashboard to the axle. The *dhamāka* is the leather siding inside the wheels. The four carved bamboo shafts are *tānga*. The *chathi ki nāri* is a strap inside fastening the body to the axle in front of the *sāngi ki nāri*. The *ladāu* are cross pieces of bamboo from shaft to shaft forming the body of the cart. The net at the bottom is *jāla*. The *jhatka* is a strong rope behind and below fastening the cross pieces of the body.

110. The driver's seat is *karthali*. The *lather* are pieces of bamboo which run underneath it from shaft to shaft. The *guriya* are pieces of wood which join the upper and lower shafts. *Pankhi* are pieces of leather joining the upper and lower shafts near the yoke. These shafts are also fastened together by a leather rope, *mohra*.

111. The pointed part of the saddle is *khogīr*. The pad is *gaddi*. The wooden block inside is *kātra*, the rings through which the reins pass *rāskari*. The leather surcingle going over the saddle is *pushttang*. *Tang* is the bellyband, *rās* the reins, *tāwa* the leather cover of the saddle, *jot* the trace rope, *nāgla* the straps which fasten the shafts to the saddle, and *qainchi* the wooden side supports of the saddle.

Section IV—The Country Boat

112. The following are the parts of an ordinary country boat in the eastern districts:

The thwarts *gūrha*; the ribs *bātha*; the outer planking *hār*; the flooring inside the boat *sohar*; the planks at the bottom running athwart the boat *marhia*; the grating in the bottom of the boat *chāli*; the planks at the bottom which run from end to end *lewa*; the platform on which the rower sits *paltha*; the deck planks in the middle *patti*; the rudder is *patwār*, which is properly the lower piece, the rudder post is *gol*, the handle of the rudder *thamua* or *saila*, and the socket in which it works *baura*. *Kunwara* are the posts which support the thwarts. *Jhonka* are iron rings to which the roof of the boat is fastened by ropes. *Raswat* is the calking.

113. *Seota* is the wooden vessel used for baling out the water. An oar is *dānr*, a paddle *karuar*, and the pole used to propel the boat *laggi*; *kachar* is brushwood put in the bottom to stand on. *Ornla* are small transverse ribs at the bottom. The mast is *gonrakh* or *gunarkha*; *darsudha* is a splice on the mast and *morni* is the cross-piece on the mast. *Suthaunia* is the socket for the mast in the bottom of the boat. The mast is also tied to one of the thwarts, *gūrha*. The sternpost is *galahi* or *sikka*. *Daur* are the long side-ribs near the bottom; *gon* is the hauling rope, which is tied to pieces of bamboo called *birua*, which the boatmen press against their shoulders when hauling the boat upstream. *Lahāsi* is the thick rope, and *langer* is the anchor; a large iron anchor is *lohlangar*. The pulleys are *girni*, the sail *pāl*, the bulwarks *māng* or *bār*.

I.7 APPLIANCES USED IN RURAL MANUFACTURES

Section I—Appliances Used in Sugar Manufacture

A—The Cane Mill

114. The cane mill is known as *kolhu* throughout the province. The parts of the mill are as follows:

115. The hollowed wooden block forming the bed of the mill: This is generally called *kolhu*. In this the hollow cavity in which the pieces of cane to be crushed are placed is known in Azamgarh as *kundi*, in Gorakhpur *kothi*; and in the Upper Doab *mohān*. Round the edge at the top of this a rim of mud is placed to prevent the pieces of cane falling off. This is called in the eastern districts *pīnr*. In Cawnpur *bunna* is a frame of acacia wood bound round the top to prevent it from splitting. In the Upper Doab *māndal* is an iron ring fixed round the block for the same purpose.

116. In Gorakhpur an iron ring is in some places fixed under the block to prevent it being worn away by the crushing pestle. This is called *morwār*. The bevelled side of the socket is in Azamgarh *sirwa*, and in that district and Gorakhpur *pāwat*. In Azamgarh the saucer shaped cavity for the cane slips is *chhiti*. In Gorakhpur the upper rim of the block is *pāchar*. In the Upper Doab *rora* are small pieces of wood put into the cavity to help in crushing the cane. These are in Azamgarh *pāchar*.

117. The drain for the juice cut in the bottom of the block is in Gorakhpur *nerua*; in Cawnpur *patokha*; in Azamgarh *naroh*.

118. In Gorakhpur and Azamgarh the wooden spout through which the juice drops is *patnāla* or *patnāri*.

119. In the base of the block a channel is cut in which the shaft of the driving gear works. This is in Gorakhpur and Azamgarh *rah*, and in the latter district *ghagra*.

120. The horizontal beam to which the bullocks are attached: This is in Rohilkhand and the Upper Doab *pāt*; in Benares *katri,* in Cawnpur *kāntar*, and in Gorakhpur and Azamgarh *kātar*.

121. The upright beam or pestle which moves in the hollow of the mill, and crushes the cane—In Rohilkhand and the Upper Doab *lath*, in parts of the Upper Doab *gala, churan,* or *nali*; in Rohilkhand and generally in the eastern districts *jāth*, in Benares *pāt*, and in parts of Gorakhpur *mohan*.

122. In Azamgarh the ball at the end of this beam which fits into the hollow in the block is *mūngar*, and in that district and Gorakhpur *mūnri*. The notch above this is in both districts *kān*, the upper end rounded off is *kauri*, in Azamgarh the upper end cut to a point is *chūr* (Azamgarh), and the twisted piece of wood joined to this is in Azamgarh *tāran*, in Gorakhpur *dhenka*, in the Upper Doab *makri* or *dhabka*, in Rohilkhand *chirya*. This twisted piece of wood connects the pestle with the upright post which is fixed in the horizontal driving beam.

123. The upright post is in the Upper Doab *mānakmal*, in the Upper Doab and Rohilkhand *malkham*, in Cawnpur *sena*, in Benares *khūnta* and in Azamgarh and Gorakhpur *markham*. The piece of wood which keeps the beam of the driving gear in the channel at the base of the block is in Gorakhpur *jiba*, and in Azamgarh *jibeita*; in Gorakhpur a second similar piece of wood is called *kanail* or *kanetha*.

124. A rope of straw supporting the pestle by fastening it to the upright beam is in Azamgarh and Gorakhpur *kanmenra*, and in the Upper Doab *khainchi*.

125. In Azamgarh a bamboo called *kārha* is attached to the horizontal driving beam by a piece of rope which is called *duali pachaudhi*, and the other end is fastened by a rope called *duali agaundi* or *nādha* to the yoke. The part of the horizontal beam on which the driver sits is in Gorakhpur *harsa*. The leather thong by which this horizontal beam is connected with the yoke is *nār* or *nāri*.

126. The circle in which the bullocks move is in the Upper Doab *pair*, in Rohilkhand *paith*, in Benares *ghāgra*, and in Gorakhpur *paudar*.

127. The receptacle for the cane before it is cut is in the Upper Doab *gandrāla, gandrāra, gandwāla, gandra,* in Rohilkhand *gandarwāla*, and in Benares *gareran*.

128. In Gorakhpur a wooden mallet is used for pressing the cane under the crusher. This is called *thāpi*; in the Upper Doab the cane as it is being crushed is stirred with a piece of iron called *khel* or *phāl*, and the man who does this work wears a sort of leather gauntlet called *thapki*.

129. The pot into which the juice drops is called in Gorakhpur *tilia*, in Eta *bojha*; in Oudh *māth* or *mathor*, in the Doab *pahaura*; in Azamgarh *nānd* or *haudi*, and in parts of Gorakhpur *hāndi*. In Gorakhpur and Azamgarh a sieve to strain the juice as it falls into the pot is *chhīta*.

130. From this vessel the juice is removed to the boiler in a pot called in the Upper Doab *sahya*; in Rohilkhand *sāya* and in the eastern districts *saika*.

131. The blocks on which the cane is cut are in the Upper Doab *nih*, in Rohilkhand *ota*, in Benares *nesur* and in Gorakhpur and Azamgarh *nisuha*.

132. The apparatus for lifting out the crusher in order to clean the hollow in the mill is in Gorakhpur *lamesa* and in Azamgarh *dhonka*.[6]

[6] Cf. *Azamgarh Settlement Report*, 1881, para 444: 'As little time as possible should elapse between the pressing and the boiling of the juice, for the latter soon turns sour and ferments, especially in damp weather with east wind. Even in dry clear weather the press is washed out daily to remove the fragments of fibre and coagulated matter that sticks about the crevices of the *kundi, pāchars* and *mūngar*. If not removed, these acidify the juice that passes through the press. To clean the press, the driving gear is removed, and the upper part of the *jāth* being turned between two long bamboos placed so as to form a fork, the lower end is lifted out of the *kundi*. The bamboo apparatus is called *lamesa* or *dhonka*'. In Bihar, however, 'the hollow in the mill is. . . cleared by hand while the crusher is

133. The basket from which the mill is fed is in the Upper Doab *jhāla* or *jhāl,* in Rohilkhand and Benares *ori,* and in Gorakhpur *orīya* or *khachiya.*

134. The pieces of cane cut up ready for the mill are in the Doab *ganderi* or *gareri*, in Eta *gadli*, in Azamgarh *angāri*, and generally in the eastern districts *genri*. As much chopped cane as can go into the press at one time is in Gorakhpur and Azamgarh *ghāni*, and as much juice as can be boiled at one time is *tāo*.

135. The cane after the juice is expressed is in the Doab *khoi*, in Gorakhpur *khoiya*, in Azamgarh *khoiya*, and in Eta *pāta* or *pāti*. In the eastern districts it is sometimes soaked in a trough called *khāta*, and a juice called *kakai* which is used in tobacco making is extracted.

136. To work the mill is *pherna*, and when several cultivators take it in turns it is called in Gorakhpur *pheri-pheri* or *bāri-bāri*.

137. In the Upper Doab the workmen sing a song called the *palāwa gīt*.[7]

138. The men employed in the mill and sugar boiling house are as follows:

turning: hence there is no apparatus in existence for raising the latter, as there is in Gorakhpur and Azamgarh'. See Grierson, *Bihar Peasant Life*, para 287.

[7] On *palāwa gīt* or *malhor*, see 'Malhor: Type of Work Song in Western Uttar Pradesh, India,' in Ved Prakash Vatuk, *Studies in Indian Folk Traditions* (Delhi, 1979), pp. 111–36. Vatuk describes this song of the *kolhu* as follows: 'In order to remain alert through the nights the men sing a particular type of song, called *malhor, palhāva* or *gāha*. This kind of song is a short couplet, complete and independent within itself. Anyone may sing; the songs are sung solo, but generally all present take a turn sometime during the night. . .

Each evening the singing begins with one or more invocational songs. Following these, *malhors* of many other types are sung. While in the background the man prodding the oxen makes a loud "burr-burr", and the man near the *kolhu* shouts for another bundle of sugarcane, while another farmer shouts for a change of bullocks and the Dhivar is urged to empty the full pot, a singer raises his voice strong and high . . .' The *malhor* songs, according to Vatuk, have both philosophic and romantic content.

(1) The man who cuts the standing cane is generally in the province *chhola* and in Gorakhpur *chholwāh*.

(2) The man who cuts it into lengths for the mill is in the Upper Doab *gandkat* or *gankata*, in the Doab and Rohilkhand *mūthia*, and in Gorakhpur *genrwāh*.

(3) The driver of the mill is in the Upper Doab *patiha*, in Oudh *patha*, and in Azamgarh and Gorakhpur *katarwāh*.

(4) The man who feeds the mill is in Rohilkhand *piraha*, in the Upper Doab *periya* of *mūthia*; in Oudh *mutaha*, and in Azamgarh and Gorakhpur *ghaniwāh* or *perwāh*.

(5) The man who removes the crushed cane (*khoi)* is in Oudh and Rohilkhand *khauha*.

(6) The man who stokes the fire in the boiling house is in the Doab *jhonkiya, jhūkwa, jhokya,* or *jhonka*, in Azamgarh *jhunkaiwa*, and in Gorakhpur *jhokwah*.

B—The Boiling House

139. The manufactory including the cane mill and boiling house is in the eastern districts *kolhwār*, or in Azamgarh *kolhāra*. The boiling house is in the western districts *bel*, and to the east *gulaur*. The house in which the cane is cut into slips for the mill is in Azamgarh *garinna*, and in that district and Gorakhpur *genriār*.

140. The fireplace in the boiling house is in the Upper Doab *jhokat*; in Rohilkhand and Benares *jhokand*, in Azamgarh *chūlha*, and in Gorakhpur *bhatta*.

141. The hole through which the fuel is put in is in Azamgarh *mohān* or *jhukwa*, and in Gorakhpur *mukhwa*. The hole through which the fire is raked is in Azamgarh *ponchhia*, and in Gorakhpur *puchhwa*. The outlet for the smoke is in the Upper Doab *dhundla* or *dhundhāla*; in Rohilkhand *dhundra*; and in Benares *dhūndka*. In Azamgarh the stick used as a poker is *jhunkani* or *karera*.

142. In Gorakhpur the vessel in which the juice is collected before boiling is *rasāhwa hānda*.

143. The spoon for taking the juice out of the boiler is in Rohilkhand *dhor*; in Benares *dohra*, and in Gorakhpur *tāmbi*.

The scrape to prevent the sugar resting on the bottom of the boiler is in Rohilkhand *chandwa*, in Benares *gurda*, and in Gorakhpur and Azamgarh *gurdam*. The skimmer is in Bareli *hatta*. In Azamgarh an iron ladle called *pauna* is used for the same purpose. In the eastern districts a flat piece of wood is also used for collecting the scum, and is known in Azamgarh as *patri*, and in Gorakhpur and Azamgarh as *chatani*.

144. In Gorakhpur the *pagaura* is an earthen vessel used for removing the cooked juice from the boiler. In the Upper Doab a cloth called *gujhi* is used for straining this cooked juice.

145. The boiling pans are usually three in number, the *karāh, chāshni,* and the *phūlha*. In Delhi the *bojh* sometimes takes the place of the *karāh*, and the *karāhi* of the *chāshni*. In Rohilkhand there are five pans—the *hauz,* which is the largest; then the *nikār*, the *phūlha*, the *phatka*, and the *chāshni*. In Azamgarh the *agla karāh* and the *pachhla karāh* are respectively the lower and upper pan.

146. The pot in which the boiled syrup is placed is in Bareli *karsi*, and in the Upper Doab *mutki*. In Azamgarh *khapra* are little earthenware reservoirs in which the juice is allowed to settle. The receptacle for the boiled syrup is in Gorakhpur and Azamgarh *gurdanda* or *guranda*, and the large jars in which it is finally coagulated are *kūnra* or *chhonr*.

C—The Sugar Refinery

147. The refinery is known in the eastern districts as *karkhāna chīni*. The house in which the sugar is refined is in Gorakhpur *bhatti*.

148. In Azamgarh, in making coarse sugar or *kacchi chīni*, a vat called *pharia*, with an outlet called *nāli*, a reservoir called *dobha*, and a treading floor called *pāta* are used. In making regular sugar or *shakkar* the drain called *nāli*, and the reservoir called *dobha*, are used as before. The bundles (*motari*) of sugar are tied up in cloth called *lotha*, placed on a bamboo framework called *dhār*, and pressed with weights of sun-dried clay called *bhīra*.

149. In Gorakhpur the following utensils are used in the *bhatti* or boiling house: an iron boiler or *karāh*, an iron ladle for removing the scum or *channa*, an earthen pot with holes in the bottom used as a filter or *nānd*, a filter of a river grass known as *siwār*; a scraper for removing the layer of clean sugar, *situa*; a filtering basket for cleaning the scum, *khāncha*; a wooden ladle for cooling the boiling syrup, *tāmbi*; an iron stirring ladle, *tāmba*; an earthenware jug for pouring the syrup into the boiler which in Azamgarh is called *jumani*; a larger jug of the same kind, *nibara*; wooden supports for the filter, *sirhi*; a shovel for stoking the fire, *parua*; a kind of spoon for stirring the hot syrup in the cooling pan, *gurdami*; a piece of matting on which the sugar is dried in the sun, *pāl*; a skimming spoon, *chanauta* or *chanana*; a scraper for collecting the clean sugar, *sikurna* or *situa*; flat wooden pans for cooling the syrup, *kathwat*; rags put inside the bags to prevent wastage of the sugar, *lotha*.

150. In Oudh the factory is *ganj*; the earthen vessels in which the undrained raw sugar (*rāb*)[8] is brought to the factory is *kulsi*, the refining chamber *bojha, ārah* or *kurīa*; the drain is *kundyer*, the lower vat is *nānd*; the treading floor is *pāta*, the sweating vat is *khānchi*.

Section II—Appliances Used in the Manufacture of Indigo

151. The indigo vat is *māth* or *chahbacha*; the water reservoir *khazāna*, *talāo* or *kund*. The deepest vat, *hauz bojhai*; the rake for agitating the fermented liquor, *pharuhi*; the beams of wood for pressing the plant, *dabauta* or *chapeta*, which are supported on projections in the walls of the vat called *killi*; over these are placed other beams, *kari*. The strainer is *chhanna*; the cakes of indigo, *goti* or *bari*, which are dried in a drying house, *bari khāna*, on shelves of wicker-work, *chāli*.

[8] Crooke discusses the various types of raw and refined sugars as 'agricultural products' (and that too very briefly) in the section under sugarcane. See para 505 below and the accompanying table which has been added to clarify matters.

The furnace room is *bhatta*. The machine for cutting the cakes is *mistar*, and the wires with which they are cut *baria*.

Section III—The Spinning Wheel

152. This is called *charkha* or *charkhi*. Its parts are in the eastern districts—the wheel itself, *charkha*; the strings drawn across between the two rims are *āwal*; *seli* are hair strings on the circumference. The drum of the wheel is *muri*, the axle *belna*, the spokes *khūnti*, the band which turns the wheel *mālh*; the handle is *hatheli* in Gorakhpur, in Azamgarh *bhaunti* or *chalauna*; the pivots in which the axle works, *chamrak*. The second axle is *tekua*, and the pegs on which it works *khūnti*; the lower supports of the machine are *pirāi* and these are joined by a piece of wood called *majethi*.

153. The reel on which the thread is wound off is *ateran*; *āti* is a hank of thread, and *pāni* a circular shaped roll of cotton ready for spinning.

Section IV—The Weaver's Loom

154. This is called *kargah* and in the eastern districts consists of the following parts: The shuttle, *dharki*, inside which the thread is wound on a needle, *nari*. The *hātha* is a wooden frame suspended from the roof; as the shuttle passes, the *hātha* is pulled forward by the weaver and drives the thread home. The *bāi* is a comb of reeds or bamboo which keeps the thread of the warp apart. The *rāchh* are the heddles which alternately raise or depress the threads of the warp. *Sarai* are the reeds which are placed in front of the *rāchh* to keep the two sets of thread of the warp apart. The *panik* is an elastic bow which keeps the woven cloth stretched in front of the weaver. The *tūr* in Azamgarh, and the *lapetan*, are the wooden roller behind which the weaver sits, and on which the cloth is wound up as fast as it is made. This is supported by posts called *khūnta*. The woof is supported at the end opposite the weaver by a piece of wood called *karkaut*, which is held up by *khūnta* or pillars. The *pānwsar*, *belan*, or *gād* is the treadle which the weaver moves with his foot. The *nachani* are upper levers to which the *rāchh* and *bāi* are attached by cords or *dori*. This is fastened to an upper beam called *abera*.

155. When the thread is being prepared for weaving, it is stretched out on pieces of bamboo called *pai* and brushed clean with a brush called *kūnch*. The hank of thread after being cleaned is *lundi*, and when arranged for the warp *bhānj*. The thread of the woof is *bharni*, or in Azamgarh *geba*; *charkhi* is the wooden drum on which the thread is wound off after leaving the spinning wheel; and it is again wound off the *charkhi* on a similar drum called *paretha*.

I. 8 TOOLS AND APPLIANCES USED BY COUNTRY ARTISANS

Section I—The Carpenter

156. The carpenter (*barhai*) uses the following tools: the *basūla* or adze; the *kulhāri*, a larger adze used chiefly by sawyers (*āra kāsh*) in squaring logs, and by carpenters for rough work; the *āra* or large saw; the *āri*, a smaller saw; the *hathaura*, a large and the *hathouri* a small, hammer. The *mārtol* is a hammer like the *hathouri*. The *barma* is a revolving awl worked with bow and string used as a gimlet and centre-bit. The bow used with it is *kamāni*, the handle *dastah*, the awl itself *barma*, and the string *tasmah*. The *baldu* is a tool similar to this, except that the handle is twisted in the English shape. Among chisels there are the *majhola*, which is broad at the base and narrow at the point; the *golak*, which has a curved point for cutting grooves; the *ramma*, a long chisel for making mortice holes; the *chaurāsi*, which is broad and straight; the *rukhāni*, which is like the *majhola* but larger and thicker, and used for coarse work; the *girda*, a small chisel with a rounded edge used for making lines on wood; the common plane is *randa*, of which the blade is *tegh*, the body of the plane *kunda*, the wedge for holding in the blade *tenti*; when the blade has a coarse edge for rough work it is *jharna randa*, and a plane with a fine blade is *sāfi randa*; the *drāz* is a narrow plane for squaring boards and levelling the edges; the *gurich kāb* is a plane for cutting square grooves, and the *galtha* for cutting round grooves; the *jhari ka randa* is a plane for making grooves for panelling. Among files are the *reti*, a common file; the *kanāsi* for sharpening saws; the *sohan* a coarse rasp; the *chosa* a broad file, and the *nīmgird*, a half-round polishing file. He also uses the *guniya*, a square or gnomon; the *parkār*, compasses, the *rangmāl* [or *regmāl*], sandpaper; the *jamūra*, a pair of pincers for drawing nails; the *pathal*, a grind-stone, and the *thīha*, a block.

Section II—The Blacksmith

157. The blacksmith (*lohār*) uses the ordinary anvil, *ahran* or *nihāi*, which is fixed in a block, *thīha*.[9] The *bīri* is a perforated anvil over which the piece of iron is placed when being pierced with holes. The *chaprauna* is an anvil on which the heads of nails are made. The *ghan* or *rāchh* is a large hammer for welding; smaller than this is the *hathaura*, and smaller still the *hathauri*. The *jamūra* is a pair of pincers round at the tips, and *sangsi* is a pincer used for taking a hot piece of iron out of the fire, tightening nuts, etc. The *akuri* is an iron poker for stirring the fire. The *chheni* is a cold chisel, and the *sumbhi* a chisel used for making holes in iron. The fixed bellows is a *bhāthi* and the hand bellows *sipāwa bhāthi*. The end of the bellows pipe which goes into the fire is *mūri*, the pipe itself is *phūnkh*, the wooden sides of the bellows *takhta*, the leather sides *cham-*

[9] The *lohar's* anvil called *nihāi* in eastern U.P. was referred to as *lihāi* in south-east Tirhut (see Grierson, *Bihar Peasant Life*, para 408). This is one indication among many of the common switching around of '*la*' and '*na*'. Haven't we all heard Lucknow pronounced as 'Nukhlau'. *Pace* Grierson, *Bihar Peasant Life*, para 1038: 'Indigo . . . is *līl*. The word *nīl* used by Europeans is a Westernism borrowed from Urdu-knowing subordinates.' This is a surprising confusion in the great linguist of Bhojpuri between language and dialect.

ra, the valve *pankhi*, the pivots on which it works *dhuri*, the pillars which support it *khūnta*, the upper iron bar *barera*, and the lever which works the bellow *chhīp*. The *barma* is an awl worked by a bow, *kamāni*, with a leather string, *tasmah*. The iron spike of the awl is *dānri*; when sockets are cut for screws an octangular blade called *parakha* is used. The fixed vice is *bānk*, and the hand vice *hathkal*. The two sides of the vice which grasp the iron are *kalla*, the screw is *musara*, the socket for the screw to work in is *chuchhi*, the handle for turning the screw *bothi*, and the spring *kamāni*.

158. The *bādhiya* is an instrument for making screws, of which the female screw is *kutka*, the tightening screw *chutki*, and the nut-maker *pechkas*. *Dhebri* is the nut of a screw. The common files are *reti*, the *golak* is a round file, the *nīmgird*, a half-round file, the *tīnpahal*, a triangular file. He also uses the *parkār* or compasses, the *sāncha,* a mould, and the *jilairi,* or *jalahri* a vessel for cooling hot iron.

Section III—The Tinman

159. The tinman (*qalaigar*) uses a bellows called in the eastern districts *bhāthi* and to the west *dhaunki*. The two sticks used as handles are *danda*, and the bamboo pipe *chonga*. The solder (*rānga*) is spread with an iron instrument called *kaiyya*. The tincutter is *qainchi* to the east and *sohāni* to the west. He also uses the small hammer, *hathauri*, and the compasses, *parkār*.

Section IV—The Mason or Bricklayer

160. The mason (*rāj*) uses the *basūla*, a pointed hammer for cutting bricks; the *karni*, a large trowel for mixing the mortar (*masāla*); the *manjhola*, a small flat hammer; the *nahla*, a small trowel for polishing the surface of the mortar; the *thāpi*, a wooden beater for consolidating and smoothing the plaster. The plumb is *sahawāl* or *sahul*, of which the string is *dori*, and *patti* are small pieces of wood fixed on the string; *guniya* is the square and *mistar* a maul-stick; *zerband* is a long stick for smoothing the plaster; *qalam* is a sort of knife for smoothing the mortar between the bricks; *dalah* is a scoop for making moulding; *kūnchi* or *pota* is a whitewashing brush; the ladder is *sīrhi*; *chāli* or *par* is the scaffolding; *taghār* is the pit in which the mortar is mixed; the bricks are ground into a powder (*surkhi*), used as sand by a crusher, *dhenka*, of which the pestle is *mūsal*, and the piece of wood on which the bricks are crushed *okhli*; it is supported by pillars, *khambha*, and works on an axle, *qainchi*; the mortar pot is *nānd*; the mortar trough made of clay *athra*, and a similar wooden pan is *kathra*. He uses a large earthen pot for water, the *ghara*; and a smaller pot, *hānria*. The *badhani* is a pot with a spout used for pouring water on the plaster; *mugari* is a mallet for consolidating the plaster.

Section V—The Grain Parcher

161. The grain parcher's (*bharbūnja*) parching house is *ghonsār* or *ghonsāri* in the eastern districts. The fireplace is *bhār* and the pit in front of the stove into which the grain falls is *parui*. The earthen pot in which the grain is parched is in the eastern districts *khapra*, and to the west *karial*; the spoon for taking out the hot sand is in the eastern districts *karchhula*, and *dabīla* is a sort of ladle or stirrer. The sieve is *jharna*. The poker is *chalauni*; *mauni* is a basket for grain, and *kathra* a wooden pan. The grindstone is *jānta*, which works on an axle, *kilni*, and is made to revolve by a handle, *khūnti* or *hathenda*.

Section VI—The Fireworks-Maker

162. The fireworks–maker or *ātishbāz* uses a grindstone, *chakki* or *jānta*; an iron rod, *sāncha*, for ramming the powder; a saw, *āri*; a knife, *bānki*; an awl, *barma*; files, *reti*; a wooden platter, *kathra*; and various earthen pots, *kurua*, *nānd*, etc. Among the fireworks he makes are the Catherine wheel, *charkhi* or *chakkar*; the pipes of this, in which the powder is placed, are *nal*; the pipe in which the axle works *dhebri*, and the spokes and rim of the wheel *dhāncha*. The *bhunchampa anār*, *parākha*, *chakaiya*, *nāshpāl* and *bamgola* are various kinds of bombs. The *gubāra* is a balloon, the *hawāi* a rocket, the *dasti* a Roman candle; besides these there are the *mahtāb*, the *khajūr*, the *qila* (a miniature fort of which the bastions are *burji*), the *ganj sitāra*, *gadamgāchh*, *chādar parākha*, *tisi-ka-chādar*, *chādar sansani*, *chānd charkhi*, *pāte bāz*, *kirm bāz*, *ghanchakhar*, *murāila*, *putli*, *pancharkha* and *dāntua*.

Section VII—The Tobacco Manufacturer

163. The tobacco manufacturer (*tambāku-gar*) uses a crushing lever, *dhenki*, with a peg, *mūsar*, fixed in it; it is supported on pillars, *khūnta*, and falls on a hollow bed, *kauri*, on which the tobacco is placed. When the crushed tobacco is being removed, the beam is supported by a forked stick called *tekni*. The fragments of tobacco are collected by a broom, *kuchara*, and the tobacco is sprinkled from a water pot, *hānria*. The balls of manufactured tobacco are *pinda*.

164. In a tobacco shop the broad, flat metal plates are *seni*, the tobacco pots *degchi*, the cloth covered stand for the vessels *thaila*, and the board on which the tobacco is mixed *patri*.

Section VIII—The Pipe-Maker

165. The pipe-maker (*gargara-sāz*) uses a kind of lathe, of which *adda* is a plank forming the bed of the lathe, *batta* a spike fixed in this plank which holds the pipe stem as it is being turned; *khūnta* is the spike which holds the other end of the stem: in this *khūnta* is fixed an iron spike called *kīli*; *addi* is a piece of iron which keeps the stem in its place as it is being turned, *bagle* is a piece of wood through a hole in which the stem is passed during the operation. The workman uses the revolving awl, *barma*, moved by a bow, *kamāni*, of which the string is *tasmah*; a broad chisel, *chaurasa*; a narrow gouge, *nākhuna*; an adze, *basūla*; a small saw, *āri*; a knife, *chhuri*; a saw file, *chaprās*; and various files, *reti*.

166. In the *huqqah*, or pipe, the coconut bowl is *nārial*; the pipe stem with horizontal grooves for holding the water to cool the smoke *gargara*; the metal pipe outside *kali*; the plain stem used with the common coconut bowl *datta*; the smoking stem *nigāli*; and the pipe-stand *farshi*. In the eastern districts *gauria* or *gauraia*, and *parihath*, is the stem of a Muhammadan pipe.

Section IX—The Baker

167. The baker or *nānbāi* uses an oven, *tanūr*, a roasting spit, *sīkh*, which is fixed on supports, *kānta*, a cushion by which he places the cake on the side of the oven, *rafida*; an iron implement for taking out the cake when it is baked, *jori*; a boiling pot, *degchi*; saucers, *rakābi* or *katora*; a cup, *piyāla*; a wooden spoon, *doi*; a large wooden stirrer, *kafcha*; and an instrument for making ornamental marks on pastry, *kochna*.

Section X—The Pipestem-Maker

168. The pipestem-maker, *naichāband*, uses a revolving awl, *barma*, a polishing knife, *chhuri*, a pair of scissors, *qainchi*, and a pair of tweezers, *muchna*.

Section XI—The Fancy-Silk or Fringe-Maker

169. The *patehra* uses the *kathra*, a piece of leather with four holes in which four threads are fixed for winding; the *batani*, a wooden reel with a handle; the *anti*, a small wooden reel; the *tīli*, a winding stick; the *qainchi*, scissors; the *salāi*, a coarse needle for smoothing roughnesses in thread; *sua*, a large darning needle; *sui*, a small needle; *ankura*, an iron hook with a ring which goes round the toe; and *parthi*, a bamboo frame or drum off which the thread is wound.

Section XII—The Dyer

170. The dyer or *rangrez* uses the *māth*, a pot sunk in the ground for dyes; the *athra*, a similar half-round pot; the *ghera*, a wooden frame on which the cloth is hung like a bag with the dye inside; and the *chalni* or *chhalni*, a stick for mixing up the dyes.

Section XIII—The Confectioner

171. The confectioner or *halwāi* has a fireplace, *bhatti*, of which the stoke hole is *bhatti ka munh*; an open cauldron, *karāhi*, of which the handles are *kara*; skimmers, *jharna, pona* or *chhanna*; a large stirrer, *koncha*; and a small stirrer, *chhalni*; a wooden roller for making dough, *belan* or *belna*; which is worked on a board, *chauka*; a pestle for mixing the dough, *dāba*; a spoon, *karchhul*; a brass ladle with a wooden handle for removing the sugar from one vessel to another, *dabbu*; a wooden platter for sweetmeats, *girda*; a brass salver, *thāli*, and a deep brass pan, *parāt*. The sweetmeats are exposed on stands made of the *sarkanda* reed called in Gorakhpur *tarauni*, and in Azamgarh *tanni*, *tarna* or *tarni*. He also has a wooden basin, *kathra*; a large ladle, *dori*, and a pair of scales, *tarāzu*.

Section XIV—The Cotton Carder

172. The cotton carder, *dhunia*, uses a bow, *dhanus*, *dhanuha* or *dhanuhi*, of which the flexible piece is *dānri*, the bridge over which the string is passed *māng*, the string *tānt*, the broad piece of wood at the end *parha*, the pegs for tightening the string *kīl*, the piece of cloth which the carder holds in his hand as he twangs the bow *hathkara*, the mallet for twanging the bow *dastah*, the leather sounding-board on which the string rebounds *puchet*. The *phatka* is an instrument for teasing cotton; *kathni* is a box for keeping carded cotton. The carded cotton is made up in spindle-shaped lumps or balls called *pūni*, and is then ready for the spinning-wheel or *charkha*.

Section XV—The Felt-Maker

173. The felt–maker, *nāmāsāz*, uses a housewife, *tilādāni*, a sewing awl, *suthāli*, a pair of scissors, *qainchi*, a fine sewing awl, *mahīn suthāli*, and a bow for carding and arranging the wool, *kamtha*.

Section XVI—The Shoe-Maker

174. The shoe-maker, *mochi*, uses the *koba*, a thick iron pounder for joining the edges of two pieces of leather which have been previously smeared with a paste called *leī*; *rāmpi*, a knife for scraping the surface of the leather; the *suthāli*, a large awl; the *katarni*, an awl with a hook at the end for sewing; the *majhola*, a medium-sized awl; the *singauti*, a horn for grease; the *kalbūt* or *pharma*, lasts; the *khurpi*, a sort of chisel for paring the edges of the sole; the *beungi*, like a wooden chisel for smoothing the surface of the leather; the *partaha*, wedges of wood or leather fastened to the last to make it fit; a hammer, *martol*; and a cutter for making lace holes, *gulshan* or '*hole*' *kani*.

Section XVII—The Jeweller

175. The jeweller, *sonār,* uses the *sanrsa* or fire tongs; the *baknāl*, a blow pipe; the *pargahni*, an iron ingot mould; the *sāmdān*, a small pointed anvil; the *gharia*, a small clay crucible; the *chimta* and *chimti*, pincers; the *tikuri*, an iron needle-shaped tool for making the links of chains; the *katni*, a chisel with a round knob for embossing circular ornamentation; the *kansala*, a bell-metal anvil sunk with several depressions for making repoussé work; *chheni*, a cold chisel; *hathaura*, a large hammer, *maria*, a medium sized hammer, and *golmunha*, a round-headed hammer; *qainchi*, cutters; *gahwa*, large pincers; and *gahwi*, nippers; the *kāgmunhi* are nippers twisted at the head for holding the crucible in the fire; the *gahwi jamuri*, wire-drawing pincers; *jandri*, the perforated wire plate; *nihāi,* a square-headed anvil; *kitkira*, moulds of various sizes into which the metal is beaten; *parkār*, compasses; *phunki*, a hollow cane for blowing up the fire; *bursi* or *angethi*, the fire place; *chhah*, blocks sunk in the ground in which the anvils are sunk; *pankhi*, a fan for blowing up the fire; *katāli*, a vessel for holding scraps of silver, the *chhinunki*, a polishing brush.

176. *Kāmi* is an ingot not beaten out, and *chaurasa* a block of silver beaten out flat.

Section XVIII—The Embroiderer

177. The embroiderer, *kārchob*, uses the *chob* or wooden frame on which the work is stretched; the *sui*, a small needle, and the *suthāli*, a sewing awl.

Section XIX—The Brazier

178. The brazier, *thathera*, uses the *nihāi*, a square anvil; *sāmdān*, a pointed anvil; the *sabra*, an anvil round at the top; *qainchi*, cutters; *salāi*, a solder stirrer; *sangsi*, pincers; *reti*, files; *hathaura*, a hammer; *katori*, a vessel for holding the flux (*pain*, or *sohāga*); *bhāthi*, bellows; *gharia*, an earthen crucible; *dast-panāh*, tongs; *ohār*, a perforated cover for the crucible; *kharua*, a circular anvil for shaping the mouth of a vessel; *nītha*, a sort of wooden anvil or block; *mungari*, a wooden mallet; *painkare*, a wooden stirrer for mixing up the flux; and *tarāzu*, scales.

Section XX—The Brass-Founder

179. The brass-founder (*kasera*) uses *sāncha*, moulds of various kinds; *kharāt*, a kind of lathe; *sanrsa*, large pincers; *gharia*, a clay crucible, of which the mouth is *tonti*; and *chaurasa*, a broad chisel.

Section XXI—The Blanket Weaver

180. The blanket weaver or *gararia* uses a simple loom; the *lapetan* is the stick on which the blanket is wound as it is woven; *khūnta*, supports for this beam; *ahāri*, a beam to which the web is fastened at the opposite end from the weaver; *beun* is a wooden implement which is passed between the thread of the web to drive tight each thread of the woof; *bāi*, movable sticks placed at intervals to separate the threads of the web; *chapni* or *sāsath*, an implement for alternately raising and depressing the threads of the web; *khilurna*, a wooden scraper for removing knots or excrescences from the thread; *sua*, a thick iron needle; and *siringa*, a shuttle.

Section XXII—The Gold-Washer

181. The gold-washer or *niyāria* uses the *kathara*, a wooden pan for washing the ashes (*rāk*) or sweepings of jewellers' shops; the *chaithan*, a sifting pan; *bhāthi*, bellows; *suswa*, the earthen pipe of the vessel which remains in the fire; *dastpanāh*, pincers; *salāi*, an iron stirrer; and *gharia*, an earthen crucible.

Section XXIII—The Book-Binder

182. The book-binder (*jildsāz*), uses the *shikanja* or screw press; *katni*, a paper cutter; *qainchi*, scissors; *koba*, an iron mallet; *suthāli*, an awl; *sui*, a needle; *phirki*, an instrument with a small revolving wheel for embossing the binding; *phūl*, dyes for embossing; *saipha*, a cutter for paring edges; *gulli*, a wooden tool for smoothing the binding; *rāmpi*, a leather scrape; and *takhti* or *patra*, wooden boards for putting between the books in the screw press.

Section XXIV—The Lapidary

183. The lapidary (*hakkāk*) uses the *sān* or *sāpal*, the revolving grindstone made of corundum powder and lac; *kamāna*, the bow for turning it; *janthar*, the props of the grindstone; *sāka*, the wooden axle of the grindstone; *ghonta*, agate burnishers; *chimti*, pincers; *qalam*, iron engraver; *qainchi*, cutters; *sohan*, iron chisel; *hathauri*, small hammer, *nihāi*, anvil; *sanrsi*, pincers; *patia*, round agate burnishers; *barma*, a revolving awl with a bow called *kamāni*.

Section XXV—The Rope-Twister

184. The rope-twister (*rassibat*) uses a *bhaunrkali*, a flat stone with a hook to which the rope is fastened as it is being twisted; *pench*, a board perforated with holes by which the strands (*lār*) are twisted with rough pieces of wood (*lakrī*); *kalbūt*, a grooved block in the grooves of which the strands are fixed to secure uniformity in the twisting; *dhera* is an implement formed of two cross sticks with which twine is made.

Section XXVI—The Potter

185. The potter (*kumhār* or *kohār*) uses the wheel, *chāk*, which is turned by a stick called *chakāit*, on a peg or *killa*. The *lehsur* is an implement for mixing up the clay. The *peta* or *pīnr* is a pottery rammer for consolidating the clay, which is smoothed with a tool called *chapra*. The *athari* are moulds for shaping vessels; the pots when ready are severed with a string called *cheuni*. The kiln is *āwa* and the claypit *khadāna*.

Section XXVII—The Glass-Bangle Maker

186. The glass-bangle maker, the *chūrihār* or *manihār*, uses a fireplace, *bhatti* (of which the opening through which the melted glass is removed is *niāra*). The opening is closed by an earthenware cover, *dhapna* or *dhapari*. The earthen crucible is *koha*; the stone on which the ring is shaped *patthari*; the spoon for putting the glass into the crucible *karchhul*; the iron hook for taking out the glass *akuri*; the instrument for turning the glass in the crucible *badarwāri*; the mould with a handle for shaping the bangle *kalbūt*; the long iron poker on the top of which the glass is melted *salāg*; the flat iron instrument for shaping the ring *pāta*; the instrument for widening the ring to the required size *badhana*; and the stamp for making embossed ornaments on the bangle *thappa*.

II Domestic Appliances and Utensils

II. I APPLIANCES USED IN THE PREPARATION OF FOOD

Section I—Sieves

187. The *hāngi* (Upper Doab) and *sūp* are winnowing sieves. The *chhalni* is used for sifting the bran from the flour. The *chilwan* is a bamboo or reed sieve for straining sugarcane juice or catching fish. The *jharna* or *jharni* is a sieve for cleaning grain. The *anghia* or *angia* is a cloth sieve for sifting fine flour, and the *anghi* is a leather sieve with fine holes.

Section II—The Pedal for Husking Grain

188. This is known as *dhenka, dhenki*, or *dhenkul*. In the eastern districts the moveable beam is *dhenki*, the pillars on which it rests are in Azamgarh *khambha*, and in Gorakhpur *khūnta*. In the eastern districts the peg in the beam which crushes the rice is *mūsar*, and the axle *gulli*. In Gorakhpur the hollow wooden bed in which the rice is crushed is *kānri*, and the hand-rail which the workman grasps *otgani*. The place where the grinder rests his feet is *paudar*.

Section III—The Pestle and Mortar Used For Husking Grain

189. The mortar is to the west *okhli*, and to the east *okhari*. The pestle used with it is in the east districts *mūsar* or *paharua*, and to the west *mūsal*. The iron ring at the bottom to prevent splitting is *sām*.

Section IV—The Hand-Grind Mill

190. This is known to the west as *chakki*, and to the east as *jānt* or *jānta*. The *chakki* is smaller and generally turned by one woman. The *jānt* requires two women to work it. The upper stone is in Gorakhpur *uparauta*, and in Azamgarh *ūparka-pāt*; the lower stone is in Gorakhpur *tarauta* and in Azamgarh *nīche-ka-pāt*. The handle is in the east districts *jua*, the axle *killa*, and the feeding channel *gāli*; *jhīnk* in the east districts is a handful of grain poured into the mill. In Gorakhpur the mud seat on which the woman sits is *baithani*. To roughen the stone with a chisel is *rāhna* or *chhīnna*.

Section V—The Grindstone for Spices

191. This is to the east *sil*, and to the west *silwat*. The stone roller used with it is in Gorakhpur *lohra*, in Cawnpur *lurhwa*, and in other places *batta*.[10]

Section VI—The Roller Used in Making Paste

192. This is called *belan* or *belna*. The flat board on which the paste in rolled is *chauki*. *Parthan* in the east districts, and to the west *paletha* is the dry flour sprinkled on the board to prevent the paste sticking to it.

II. 2 DOMESTIC FURNITURE

Section I—Stools

193. The Ordinary stool is *morha* or *machia*. When it has

[10] The word *lohra* figures in an interesting Bhojpuri proverb:
Mūs motaihen lohra hoinhen Ghora na na hoinhen.
(If a mouse fattens, he'll become *lohra* he'll never become a horse.)
It may not be too ingenious to suggest that this proverb of eastern UP suggests both the differences in individual endowments as well as the limits to upward mobility in a hierarchical society.

three legs it is *tipāi*, a small stool is *pīrha* or *pirhai*. The wooden platform for sitting, sleeping or bathing is, when large, *takht* or *takhta*, and when small *chauki*.

Section II—The Bed and Cot

194. An ordinary bed is *chārpāi*, and a cot *khatola* or *khatiya*. The pillow is *takia*, and the bed-clothes *toshak* or *bichona*. The legs are *gora* or *pāya*. The side pieces are *bāi*, and in the east districts *patti* or *pāti*. The end pieces are *sirai*. The head of the bed is *sirhāne*, or to the east *munrwāri*. In Gorakhpur *gorwāri* is the foot of the bed. The network at the bottom is *sānka*, or in Gorakhpur *bināwat*; when this netting is made of one string the bed is said in Gorakhpur to be *ekbaddhi*, if of two *dobaddhi*, and so on. The strings at the bottom by which the netting can be tightened at pleasure are *adwān*, in Gorakhpur *ordāwan*, and in Azamgarh *onchan*. The thick rope at the foot to which the netting is tied is in Gorakhpur *main* or *kardhan*. *Barua* in Gorakhpur are strings tied on to the side as the netting is being made.

Section III—The Weighing Scales

195. The large fixed scales are *rātul*, and to the east *thak* or *dhak*. The small scales are *kānta* or *tarāzu*. *Tūra* or *tora* to the east is a weaver's scale for weighing cotton or thread. The plates of the scale are *palra* or *palla*. The strings of the scale are *das*, or in Gorakhpur *joti*, and in Azamgarh *tanni*. *Pasang, pasangha, dhāra* is a weight put into one scale to balance it. *Jhukna* is a false balance, and in Azamgarh *bankauri* is a small pair of scales. The top bar of the scales is *dandi*.

Section IV—Nets

196. *Jāl* is the fisherman's small net, *mahājāl* is one of a larger size. The *jholi* in the east districts is a net used by cartmen for feeding bullocks. *Jāli* in the Upper Doab is a net for carrying grass. *Gānja* means the same in the east districts.

The *chhīka* (east districts) or *chhīnka* is a net for hanging up pots, etc. in a house. *Sikhar* in the east districts, and *sinko* in Farukhabad is used for the same purpose. The *argani* of the east districts or the *algani* to the west is a stick or rope for hanging up clothes, *chhatri* is a frame used for the same purpose. *Jhora* (Gorakhpur) is a cord net for carrying goods on the head, and *jhonk* is the net used by bearers with the sling pole *bahangi*.

Section V—The Pad used for Supporting Waterpots etc. on a Woman's Head

197. This is in the east districts *binra* or *genruli*, in the Upper Doab *judhua*, and in other places *indhua*, or *indua jūna, jūra, chakwa, gurari, genruri, gorari* or *induri*. A pile of waterpots one above the other is *jehar* or *jeghar*.

Section VI—The Stick

198. The ordinary long stick is *lāthi*, in Gorakhpur *laur* or *lauria*. The butt end is *hūra* in the east districts. *Sonta* is a thick club, and *chhari*, or in Gorakhpur *labdi*, is a thin stick. *Deng* in Azamgarh is a thick walking stick; *pahāri* a thick club; *theghuni* a small walking stick; *patkan* is a walking stick, and *phattha* or *phalta* a piece of split bamboo used as a stick; *subarani* is a light walking stick, and *bajar bong* a heavy stick.

Section VII—Boxes

199. *Sandūq* is an ordinary box of which the diminutive is *sanduqcha*. *Sendūra* or *sindhaura* is a box used by women for carrying red lead. The *pitāra* is a travelling box for clothes, etc., carried by a man on a slung bamboo, *bahangi*. The *dibi*, *dabbi* or *dibia* are small boxes for jewellery or other valuables. The *chunauta* is a box for carrying the lime (*chūna*) used with betel. The *doki* in the eastern districts is a box in which the *ubtan* or *uptan*, a condiment composed of turmeric and other ingredients, which is rubbed on the bride at a wedding, is kept. The *ingrauti* is a box in which women carry the vermilion which they put on the parting of the hair. The *gelha* or *gelhi* in the eastern districts is a little box made of bamboo chips in two parts for holding betel, etc. *Chapuri* in the east districts is a little straw box.

Section VIII—Metal Vessels Used in Cooking and for Ordinary Domestic Purposes

200. The vessels ordinarily used by Hindus are as follows:[11]

201. *Tasla* made of brass (*pītal*) is a round vessel used for boiling rice. About two seers of rice can be cooked in it.

202. *Tasli* is a similar vessel of a smaller size.

203. *Batula* is vessel made of alloy (*phūl* or *kaskut*). This is used for cooking rice, and about a seer of rice can be cooked in it. It is comparatively higher and narrower than the *tasla*.

204. *Batuli* is a smaller similar vessel used for cooking pulse or meat.

205. *Patīli* is made of alloy (*phūl*). It has a narrow flat mouth, and is used for boiling meat.

206. *Handa* is a very large copper vessel with handles for boiling rice.

207. *Tāmlet* is a large brass vessel, broad at the bottom, used for cooking pulse at marriages, etc.

208. *Katora* is used for eating from, with a projection at the bottom on which it rests.

209. *Tashtari* is like the *katora*, only it has no stand, but is flat bottomed.

210. *Lota* is used for drawing water and drinking.

[11] The separate catalogue of Hindu and Mohammadan cooking and domestic vessels appears a bit spurious. *Tashtari, ābkhora, chilamchi, ugāldān, pāndān* figure in both the lists. Clearly, the list of 'Hindu vessels' includes many dishes with supposedly 'Muslim' names! Following Grierson, who has copied all the utensils mentioned in para 245 (see *Bihar Peasant Life* para 711), I have provided separate paragraphs to the 'Hindu vessels' and clubbed the 'minority vessels' together in one single paragraph.

211. *Gerua* or *garua* is made of alloy (*phūl*) with a spout (*tonti*).

212. *Tamha* is similar to the last except that it is made of *kaskut*, not *phūl*. Both are used for drinking.

213. *Ābkhora* is a drinking vessel, the sides of which broaden towards the mouth, and it is provided with a stand (*gora*) at the bottom.

214. *Glass* or *gilās* is similar to the last, except that the sides are straight or only slightly curved. It has no stand, and is flat bottomed.

215. *Surāhi* is used for keeping drinking water.

216. *Chilamchi* is used for washing.

217. *Āftāba, āftāwa* is a water ewer used for washing.

218. *Kalchhi, karchhi* is a brass spoon.

219. *Kalchhul, karchhul* is an iron spoon.

220. *Jharna, jharni* is an iron sieve with a handle.

221. *Dabbū* is a brass spoon of which the cup is deep and broad, principally used in marriages.

222. *Thāli* is a flat pan from which food is eaten. The *desi thāli* is made of brass (*pītal*). The *Nepāli thāli* made of alloy (*phūl*), and has the edges curved to the outside, while the *desi thāli* has straight sides.

223. *Parāt* is a large flat pan like the *thāli*, except that its sides curve gradually up to the top.

224. *Bhagauna* is an iron cooking pot with a handle.

225. *Chimta, chimcha, dastpanāh* is a pair of small tongs used for arranging the fire, or turning over cakes on the griddle.

226. *Sanrsi* are tongs used for removing the pot (*batuli*) from the fire.

227. *Karāhi* is an iron or brass broad pot with handles (*kara*), generally used for cooking vegetables.

228. *Tāwa* is an iron griddle plate.

229. *Ugāldān* is a spittoon.

230. *Pāndān* is for keeping betel and other ingredients of *pān*.

231. *Gagara* is a copper or brass vessel used for drawing water from a well.

232. *Dol* is an iron vessel for drawing water from a well.

233. *Kūnra* is a copper or brass vessel used for storing water in the house.

234. *Sarposh* is a cover for other vessels.

235. *Chirāgdān* is a stand for a lamp.

236. *Khuredāni* is an iron poker.

237. *Kotwāl, jhokana, jhokani* is a wooden poker.

238. *Pauna* is an iron collander or straining ladle.

239. *Hawandasta* is a pestle and mortar for grinding spices, etc.

240. *Lonhra* is a small iron pan.

241. *Tāthi* or *tathia* or *tāthi* is the same as the *thāli*.

242. *Tamchara, tamchari* is a round copper vessel.

243. *Khora, khori* is a corruption of *ābkhora*.

244. *Lewa* in Gorakhpur or *anwan* in Azamgarh is ashes plastered on a cooking pot to save it from the fire. In the east districts *ubsan* is a handful of straw, etc., used for cleaning metal vessels.

245. Mohammadans generally use the following vessels:

(1) *Patīla* is a large copper vessel for cooking rice.
(2) *Patīli, degchi* is a similar vessel smaller in size.
(3) *Deg, degcha* is a somewhat larger pot for boiling.
(4) *Lota, badhana* differs from the vessel used by Hindus in having a spout.[12]
(5) *Lutia, badhani* is a similar vessel of smaller size.
(6) *Katora* is similar to the Hindu vessel, but made of copper.
(7) *Piyāli* is a cup.

[12] Crooke at another place derives *badhana* from the Sanskrit *vardhanika*, the Buddhist sacred water vessel, and defines it as 'a water-pot usually made of copper or earthenware, with a spout'. Whatever its etymology, it is the spout of the 'Muslim' *badhana* which distinguishes it from the unmarked 'Hindu' *lota*. One would invariably find the spouted *badhana* in rural mosques for *wazu*, the ritual washing-up before prayers. However the utensil has its quotidian and more humble usage as well. What is significant is that the cultural difference between *badhana* and *lota* prefigures, in eastern UP, even today, as a marker of religious difference. In the countryside and the smaller towns it is an unmistakable 'Muslim' sign.

(8) *Piyāla* is similar to the last but larger.
(9) *Rikābi* is a saucer.
(10) *Tabāq* is a broad flat washing vessel.
(11) *Chimta, chimti, chimchi* is the same as used by Hindus.
(12) *Sarposh* is a cover for other vessels.
(13) *Chilamchi* is a washing basin.
(14) *Āftāba, āftāwa* is a water ewer.
(15) *Tasht* is a broad flat dish.
(16) *Sīni* or *seni* is a broad shallow tray.
(17) *Gagara* is used for drawing water.
(18) *Lagan* is a large vessel for storing water.
(19) *Karāhi* is an iron cooking pot.
(20) *Chhanna, jharna* is an iron strainer with a handle.
(21) *Pāndān* is for holding betel.
(22) *Khāsdān* is for keeping *pān* or betel, with a cover.
(23) *Ugāldān* or *pīkdān* is a spittoon.
(24) *Surāhi* is for keeping water.
(25) *Fatīlsoz, chirāgdān* or *dīwat* is a lamp-stand.
(26) *Tāwa* is an iron griddle plate.
(27) *Karchhula, karchhuli* are spoons.
(28) *Chimta, dastpanāh* are tongs.
(29) *Sikhcha* is a spit.
(30) *Panchhanna* is a metal strainer for water.
(31) *Dabbu* is a large deep spoon.

Section IX—Utensils Used in Worship

246. The appliances of a Hindu temple are as follows: The *āsini* is a sort of mat made of *kus* grass, wool, etc. for sitting on. The *jhāri* is a sort of spoon for throwing water on the *lingam; achmani*[13] is a much smaller spoon used for the same purpose. *Panchpātr* is a small vessel for keeping water. The *jalpātr* is larger. The *argha, jalehri* or *jalthari* is the saucer made of stone or metal in which the stone representing the *lingam* is placed. *Pinri* is the platform on which the *lingam* is placed.

[13] In Saran this is called *anchauni*.

The *ghari* or *ghanta* is the large, and the *ghariya* the small, bell. *Jhānjh* are the cymbals, *sankh* the conch-sell, *singhāsan* the idol's throne, *mūrat* the idol, *horsa* the implement for grinding the sandal wood (*chandan*), *dhūpdañ* the censer, *dīpdān* or *dipakdān* the lamp-stand, *katori* the vessel in which the ground sandalwood is placed, *sumirni* the string of beads held in the hand; the *japmāli* is a sort of bag in which the worshipper keeps the beads, and puts his hand inside and turns them. The *tūnba, tūma* or *tomri* is the hollow gourd carried by religious mendicants (*faqīrs*). The *kamandal* is a brass vessel of the same kind used for drawing water in a temple.

Section X—Leaf Platters

247. The *dona* is a small round leaf platter. The *pattal* of the west districts or *pathari* to the east is broader and flatter. The *gadaura* is a small leaf basket with high sides used for holding cooked provisions, the *pataura* is similar to this, the *panwār* is a large leaf basket used in Hindu marriages when a number of guests have to be fed.

Section XI—Earthen Vessels

248. The number of these is very large and varies in each district. The following list does not profess to be exhaustive:

249. *Ābkhora* is a drinking vessel; *achāri* a pickle jar; *arhia* a little platter; *athra* a pan for making dough.

250. *Bhabka* is a vessel used in distilling; *badhana* a water vessel with a spout; *bharuka* a drinking vessel; *chapta* a large flat jar; *cherui* an earthen cooking dish; *chhāgal* an earthen water-pot with a spout; *chhonr* a large earthen jar; *chukkar* a drinking cup; *chirāg* a lamp-saucer; *dahar* a vessel for storing grain; *diari* very small lamp-saucer; *dubkena* a drinking vessel; *dudhaur* or *dudhaura* an earthen vessel in which milk is boiled; *gagari* is used for drawing water; *gamla* a flower pot; *ghaila* or *ghaili* a vessel for holding water; *ghara* a vessel for drawing water; *ghilahri* an earthen dish in which clarified butter (*ghi*) is cooked; *ghuchchi* a little dish with a narrow neck; *ghuliya* a little earthen dish; *ghuncha* or *ghunchi* a small vessel for milk; *ghurli* a little dish; *hāndi* a vessel for cooking or holding milk curds, etc; *jāla*, a large water-jar; *jhajhar* a water-jar with a long narrow neck; *jhāri* a pitcher with a long neck; *jikara* an earthen saucer; *kachhui* an oblong vessel for drinking spirits; *kamora* or *kamori* a vessel used in making clarified butter (*ghi*); *kamsena* a dish used for the same purpose; *karāhi* a vessel for boiling vegetables; *karua* vessel with a spout for drinking and votive offerings; *kanhatari* a vessel for milk and curds; *khondha* a vessel used in boiling and distilling; *koha* a small vessel for cooking pulse and vegetables; *kosa* a lamp-saucer; *koncha* an earthen dish; *kullhar* a little earthen cup for serving out spirits in; *kulsi* a water jar; *kūnra* a flat platter for kneading flour in: it also means in the east districts a large vessel for grain, holding three or four maunds. The *kūnri* or *kunli* is a smaller grain vessel holding about two maunds; *labani* the oblong vessel in which palm juice (*tāri*) is collected on the trees; *malaria* a small earthen pan; *malsi* a cooking dish used by Mohammadans; *martbān* an earthen vessel with an open mouth; *matka* a vessel for holding water or pickles.

251. *Mitia* is a vessel for water; *mitka* a large vessel for storing grain; *nānd* or *nādh* a vessel used as a feeding trough; *pana* an earthen vessel used as a milk measure; *parai* a saucer generally used to cover other vessels; *patuki* a small vessel used for cooking pulse; *piyāla* an earthen cup; *purwa* a small earthen pot; *rikābi* a saucer; *sanahki* a broad flat dish out of which boiled rice is eaten; *surāhi* water vessel with a long narrow neck; *taula* a large earthen dish for cooking; *tāwa* an earthen plate used as a griddle; *tathua* a flat earthen dish; *tathahra* a vessel for heating water for bathing; *telahanri, telauns, telwans,* or *talaunchhi* a vessel for holding oil; *tuthahi* a small platter; *tomri* a vessel used for holding blood by barber physicians.

Section XII—Wooden Vessels

252. The *kathoti* of the Doab and the *kathwat* of the eastern districts is a large deep wooden dish for kneading flour.

The *katheli* in the Doab is a small wooden dish for scraps. In Azamgarh the *arhia* is a little wooden platter; and the *doki* a small wooden dish. The *kajkol* is a wooden cup carried by mendicants, and the *tomri* is the mendicant's gourd. The *tāmi* is a wooden ladle; and the *doi* a wooden ladle used by Mohammadans in cooking pulse (*dāl*).[14]

Section XIII—Leather Vessels

253. The *jhāba* or *jhabra* is used for holding all kinds of liquids. The *dabba, kūpa, kuppa,* or *gora* is used for holding clarified butter (*ghi*) or oil (*tel*). The *gelha* or *gelhi* is a smaller vessel used for the same purposes. The *jori* is a leather pack-bag for molasses.

Section XIV—Stands for Vessels

254. These are known as *painda* or *palainda, gharaunchi* or *gharthari*. The *latkan* is a stand on which one pot is hung over another to act as a filter.

Section XV—Clothes

255. The general terms are *kapra, parcha, libās, poshāk*; in the east districts *pahrāwa*, and in Gorakhpur *lūga* or *lugga* or *bastar*.

Clothes worn by men are as follows:

The turban, *pagri*, is a piece of cloth woven for the purpose; *muretha* a piece of ordinary cloth wound round the head.

[14] That *doi*, a common, deep wooden ladle for stirring *arhar dāl*—an implement which in the pair *doi-hāndi* signifies the entire range of cooking utensils in Bhojpuri nursery rhymes—was a 'Muslim ladle' seems odd to someone of my generation. Enquiries made in eastern Gorakhpur suggest that the use of the *doi* may well have been confined to the kitchens of the Muslims. As to why this should have been so I have no answer. Another common wooden implement, *mathni,* used for churning and thinning the *dāls*, especially *arhar*, is not mentioned by Crooke. All *dāls* were cooked well into the twentieth century in earthen vessels; q.v. *patuki*.

Chīra is a checked turban; *dhātha* is a piece of cloth wound under the chin and over the head.

256. The cap, *topi*, if shaped so as to cover the ears is *kantop* or *kandhapni; kanchhahi* is a piece of cloth worn loose over the head.

257. The loincloth, *dhoti, mardāni* or *pardani; langota* or *langoti* is a small loincloth. *Bhagwa* or *bishti* is a small scrap of cloth worn by boys, *kāchh* or *kachhār* is the small tight cloth worn by wrestlers. *Phalāng* or *pachhauta* is the tag end tucked in behind, and *phanna* is the loose end which hangs down in front. *Parkhara* is a small loincloth. The knots in the loincloth used for holding money or valuables is in the east districts *anchal, tent* or *phānr.*[15]

258. The drawers, *paejāma*. Those made tight are *chūridār*, if loose at the ankles *mohridār*, and if loose with pieces let in along the thigh *kalidār*.

259. The jacket is *mirzai*.

260. The coat is *anga* or *angarkha* and *chapkan*. Those worn by Hindus open on the right breast and by Muhammadans on the left. It is tied at the neck by a string, *ghundi*, which moves in a hem, *tukma*. The *qaba* is an outer coat open at the chest and sleeves. The *nīmāstīn* is a jacket, the sleeves of which reach only to the elbows; while the *shaluka* and *sadari* leave the arms bare.

261. The sheet—This is *dohar, galef, dopatta* or *khol*. The *pichhaura* is a sheet worn over other clothes.

262. The stuffed quilt is *lihāf, razāi, saub,* or in the east districts *dulāi*. A similar quilt made of rags patched together is *gudara* or *gudari* or *kathri*. The stuffing of the quilt is *bharti*. *Anga* are bits of old cotton padding in a quilt.

263. The long coat worn by well-to-do people is *āba*.

264. The cloth tied round the loins while bathing, and

[15] *Tent*: In keeping with the Hindu/Muslim divide, J. R. Reid in his *Azamgarh Glossary* defines *tent* as 'the upper margin of the dhoti that is tucked in at the waist in which Hindus carry money'. On *phānr*, see Appendix F, para 798.

used for drying the body afterwards, is *angochha* among Hindus and *lūngi* among Mohammadans.

265. The purse is *thaili, batua, tora,* or *potli; tilādāni* or *khalīti* is a tailor's housewife. *Kisbat* is the case in which a barber carries his razors, etc.

266. The shoes are *jūta* or *jūti*; in the east districts *pana paina,* or *panahi*; the wooden bathing shoe is *paula, kharaun paira* (Farrukhabad), or in Azamgarh *kothauhi*.

267. The Brahmanical cord is *janeo*. The knots in the cord are *parwar*. Its length is measured by hand-breadths (*chaua*). A Brahman's cord is 96 hand-breadths long, while a Rajput's is 80.

268. The blanket is *kammal,* and to the east *kamara*. *Tūs* is a kind of thick blanket made in Gorakhpur. *Rāl* is a large kind of blanket. Herdsmen tie the blanket over their heads in a peculiar way to save themselves from rain. This is known as *ghonghi, ghoghi, ghogha* or *chot*.

269. A patch on clothes is *pewand* or *paiwand*. When the cloth is doubled the outer piece is *abra*, and the lining *astar*.

270. Washing of clothes—The washerman's plank is *patra,* and in the east districts *pāt* or *pāta*; the smoothing iron *istiri*; the ironing cloth *bethan*; the mallet with which he beats the clothes *katka* or *mungar*, the clothes line or drying frame *tanāo*. *Pachhārab* is to beat clothes on a plank or stone.

271. Among women's clothes are —The sheet, *sāri, chādar, dopatta, khol, lugra,* and in Azamgarh *khilua*. *Pharia* is a small sheet worn by little girls. The hem of the sheet is *achra*. The wrapper tied tight is *gānthi; phupti,* is the end of the sheet gathered and tucked in front. *Khoinchha* is the pocket in front formed by loosening the part tied round the waist; and *gojhnaut* or *gojnāwal* is the loose fold on the left side. The single sheet worn by women is sometimes called in the east districts *dhoti zanāni*.

272. The petticoat is *lahanga;* if loose it is *dhable; kachhāur* is a mode of tying it under the leg. The waistband through which the string is run is *toi*.

273. The bodice is *kurta zanāna, angia, jhūla* or *sīnāband*.

274. The veil or cloth worn over the head is *orhna* or *orhni*.

275. The drawers are *paejāma*.

276. *Surma* is the antimony put on the edges of the eyelids; *sendur* the red lead put in the parting of the hair; *kangi* the comb, and *thakri* the hair brush.

Section XVI—Carpets and Mats

277. A carpet is *dari*, a floor-cloth *qālīn* or *farsh*. *Shatranji* and *galaicha* are thread mats. *Jamkūra* is a mat worn round the shoulders in wet weather. *Chatāi* is made of the stems of the *narkat* (*Arundo tibialis*, Roxb); *gondari* is made of the *gond* reed; *saj* a long *gond* mat used when a number of people are assembled at a marriage, etc., *sītalpāti* is a fine mat for sleeping on; *tarāi* is a reed mat.

Section XVII—Jewelry

278. The following are some of the varieties of jewelry commonly worn:

A—Worn by Men and Boys

279. On the ears. The *bāli* is a plain ring. The *lurki* is a stone set in wire.

280. On the arms. The *bijāyath* is an ornament fastened round the upper arm. The *jaushan* is a similar ornament. The *ta'awīz* is a sort of amulet. The *tainti* is a similar amulet.

281. The neck. The *māla* is a bead necklace. The *jugauli* is a neck amulet in the eastern districts. The *kanthi gop* and *jauhār* are kinds of necklaces.

282. The fingers. The *angūthi* and *chhalla* are finger-rings.

283. Ornaments for the wrist. *Kharua* and *gunjahra* or *gunjha*. These are chiefly worn by boys.

284. The waist. *Kardhan* is a chain hung round the waist.

285. The ankles. *Gorahra* is a boy's anklet.

B—Worn by Women

286. Ornaments for the forehead. The *bandi* is a sort of spangle or wafer. The *bendi* is an ornament of the same kind. The *tīka, bunna,* or *bunda* are similar to this. The *ār, chānd, satia, patia, chāndla, dhanuh, choti, chandwa, dank* and *chandarbijwa* are other ornaments worn on the head or forehead.

287. Nose ornaments. *Nath, nathia, nathuni, kīl, jhulani, bulāq, besar, chuchhi* and *phuruhuri.*

288. Ear ornaments. *Karanphūl, jhumka* (a pendant), *bāli, pāt* or *patta bijli, bāla, sabza, daria, tarki* and *dhār.*

289. Neck ornaments. *Kāntha, pachlari, tilari, chandarhār, champākali, ta'awiz, jugnu, hasuli, motimāla, kāntha, zanjīr, baddhi, sitala, humel* and *nādali.* The *konchhi* or *ganthi* is worn on the fold in the sari or sheet and the *tikuri* or *torwa* on the veil.

290. Arm ornaments. *Bahunta, bāzu, taria, jaushan, bijāyath, chūhādanti, salunia, naugraha, pachhela, chania, kangana, hathsīkhar, kathari, kara, birua, bahūn, barekhi, tora, barthāna, anant, naunaga, jahāngīri, tosha, darkwa, bera, mathia* or *māthi* (a pewter bracelet worn by Ahir women), *rākhi* (an amulet) and *chūri.*

291. On the fingers. *Chhalla, puria, batāsha, angūthi, pherua.*

292. On the waist. *Kardhani, kamarkash, kānchi, thagri.*

293. On the feet. *Pāezeb, anwat, angūtha, bichhua* or *bichhiya, chhalla, palāni, kara, chhara, gorahra, ghungru, pairi, newara* or *newari, churla, chhalla, ghungrudār* and *phulua.*

III Soils

Section I—Classification of Soils

294. Soils may be classified—
According to their distance from the village site.
According to their constituent elements.
According to the crops for which they are prepared, or which they usually produce.

Section II—Soils Classified According to Their Distance from the Village Site

295. The concentric circles (*hār*) are generally three in number.

(a) The belt near the homestead (*ābādi, dih, basgit,* etc.), which is better manured, more carefully cultivated, and adapted for the superior kinds of crops. This belt is known as *banjin, dahiya, goenr* (eastern districts), *gorha, jamai* (Eastern Oudh), *gauhāni* (West Oudh and Central Doab), *khirwa* (Bundelkhand), *bāra* (Central and Upper Doab), *per* (Azamgarh).

(b) The next furthest belt from the village site is *kauli* (East Oudh), *majhār* (East Oudh), *mūnda* (Upper Doab), *majhola* (Upper Doab), *agla* (Upper Doab), *miāna* (Gorakhpur), *manjha* (Farukhabad).

(c) The belt furthest from the village site is called *barha* (Central and Upper Doab), *barheta* (Farukhabad), *jangal* (Upper Doab), *hār* or *ūparhār* (Central Doab and Rohilkhand), *pālo* or *palāi* (Benares Division).

296. In parts of Oudh there are only two divisions; in Unao and Rai Bareli *goenr* and *hār* and in West Oudh *gauhani* and *ujur*.

Section III—Soils Classified according to Their Constituent Elements

A—Sandy Soils

297. Classifying soils according to their constituent elements we have first, *sandy soils.* Among these may be mentioned the *bhūr* or *bhud* or *bhuda* of Rohilkhand, which in Bareli is applied to soil containing more than 75 per cent of sand over clay. There are sub-divisions of the soil such as *bhūr khāki, bhūr parāni, bhūr milāuni,* and *bhūr ūrāni.* A similar soil is known to the east of the province as *balua, barua* or *balui*; and as *belh* (Rohilkhand), *bhatia* or *bhatti* or *bhatua* (Bundelkhand), *retla, retili barda* or *bardi.* In Gorakhpur *dhūsi* is an arid and sterile soil consisting of an admixture of reddish sand with loose clay. A loose sandy subsoil in which a clay well will not work is known as *dohur,* and in Bareli as *lelwa. Kabsa* in Mainpuri is a red sand underlying the watershed.

B—Clayey Soils

298. Secondly, *clayey soils.* Among these the chief is the *matiār* or *matiāra* or *matera,* a bluish or blackish clay soil, well adapted for rice; the *chikkan* or *chiknot* of Rohilkhand, because it feels greasy when rubbed in the hand. A whitish heavy clay with traces of iron is called *khapat* in Bareli. *Katmāti* is a clay soil which soon dries on the surface. *Dākra* in the Upper Doab is a stiff dark clay prevailing in natural dips and hollows where water collects and lies during the rains. The *mār* of Bundelkhand is the black cotton soil peculiar for its power of retaining moisture, and the rifts and cracks which its contraction through drought causes. The *kābar* of Bundelkhand is very similar to the *mār,* but lighter both in character and colour. In Mainpuri this soil is also known as *maiyar* or *mahiar,* and is described as the worst kind of clay or *matiār* soil found in low-lying situations. The *gapsa* is hard whitish clay; the *geru* is red and ochreous; the *ghār* is found in low-lying situations where water remains for a long time; the *narmat* is a soft clay. The *jhābar* of Etawa is an inferior clay soil found in low ground. The *khalār* or *kapsa matiār* of West Oudh is a clay soil in the bed of tanks.

299. The *bijar* is a clay soil as hard as *matiār*, and intermixed with very fine gravel. In Azamgarh the *karail* is a black soil which contains more organic matter than the *matiār*, and the *kabsa* is a whitish or yellowish grey soil.

C—Loamy Soils

300. Thirdly, *loamy soils*. The *chahal, rausti* and *dakara* are three classes of loams in the direction of Delhi, of which the *chahal* is the strongest. The *domat* or *dumat* is a sandy loam, and the *doras* clayey loam. This soil prevails in Gorakhpur on the highlands, and is hence sometimes known as *bāngar*. The *kapsa doras* of West Oudh has an excess of sticky clay. In the *piliya* of the Central Doab the sand is somewhat in excess of the clay. In the Central Doab and Rohilkhand a mixture of *domat* and sand is known as *miluna*. The *setwāri* of Banda is a greenish sandy loam, and the *garauti* is a light loam easily pulverized.

301. The *bālsundar* or *bālsundara* of Azamgarh, like the *barua* of Banda, is a sandy loam. The *bamhni* of East Oudh is a light red soil; and the *doansa* a light clay mixed with sand.

Section IV—Soils and Water Action

302. Lands thrown up by fluvial action are *gangbarār*, and those cut away in the same way *gangshikast; chhāran* is land left by the retrocession of a river. *Patpar* is newly-formed land so situated as to receive an annual accretion of alluvial deposit. The high alluvial lands in the Jamuna valley are called *bhāgnar*. In Gorakhpur the *bhāt* or *bhānt* lands are a chalky alluvium in the valley of the Gandak. They require little or no irrigation. In Rohilkhand *būk* is applied to lands recovered by the recession of a river. *Nihal* is alluvial land recovered from water courses. *Dīra* [*diāra*] is fresh land thrown up by the shifting of the course of a river. *Baran* is alluvial soil or fresh earth thrown into hollows by water. *Katri* is land recovered from large rivers. In Oudh such alluvial soils are called in the first year they become available for cultivation *bijar*, in the second *dosāl*, and in the third *peh*. In Azamgarh *nikharab* means, in the case of such lands, to become dry and fit for cultivation.

303. The alluvial deposit left by rivers is called *naulewa* in Bundelkhand, *khādar* in Rohilkhand, and in the Doab *pāng;* and *kāmp* in Rohilkhand.

304. Land rendered useless by deposits of sand is called in Rohilkhand *būkāra*.

Section V—Muddy and Water-Logged Soils

305. Land in the bed of a tank is in Jhansi *tari* or *kachhār*, and in the eastern districts *karoh*. *Bās* (east districts), *chīk, labdar, lahli, pachpach, chihel, chabhār, chilbil, dahal, daldal, dhasān, dhasāo* and *hīla* are terms for marshy or muddy soils and quagmires. The *choil* is a kind of swampy soil in Muzaffarnagar. In Gorakhpur the low marshy lands in the Nepal Tarai are called the *dhāb*. Lands usually saturated with water are *pangācha, panmār, lia, jhāda, dahar, dhada* (Rohilkhand), *dehri, jhāwar, kachhwa, hālgara, johar* (Central Doab), *ugāla* or *āla*. In Rohilkhand *akorhai* is land with retentive subsoil, liable to flooding from canals, and which has to be continually watered to produce a crop. *Banga* in the Central Doab is land saturated with oily or brackish well water. In the Upper Doab *gārak* are lowlands on which water does not lie long. *Dubsi* means land liable to be submerged. *Dahr* in the Upper Doab means low marsh lands, the same as *bajha* or *gajjar*. The lowlands in a river valley are *khādar* or *diwāra*. *Lāna* in Mathura are lands which have a chance of being left dry by the subsidence of the waters in time to be sown with hot weather crops. An old dry bed of a river is *dohar, johar* or *jhor*.

Section VI—Highlands and Lowlands

306. Highlands, as contrasted with the river valleys, are *bāngar, ūparwār* or *ūparhār*. In Etawa the highlands on the right bank of the Jamuna are known as *barroh*. *Bulandi* generally is highland. In Bundelkhand *pātha* are the uplands of the

Vindhya plateau. In Azamgarh *ūsar khābhar* is uneven barren ground; *tikur* or *tikura* is high dry ground or hard ground in the shallows of a river; *dibba* is a high spot of ground. The lowlands in the river valleys are *khādar, diwāra*, and in the eastern districts *kachhār* or *khelār* or *khalār*.

Section VII—Ravines, Mounds, etc.

307. Land cut up by ravines and broken ground is *bīhar* or *bihand*. In Bundelkhand the soil found near ravines is called *dandi*. *Parua* is similar to this and of a light colour. *Dhuh* in the Central Doab is elevated soil in the midst of ravines. The *segon* of Bundelkhand is a variety of *parua* of a dirty red colour. A belt of fertile, alluvial soil which winds through the ravines in Mainpuri is known as *bhagna*. In Azamgarh *kharhi* is a ravine, *kharoh* is a ravine or land near ravines, and *khābhar khūbhar* uneven ground. A high river bluff is *dānd* or *karāra*.

308. Sand hills are *dhūs* in the eastern districts and *pūth* in the Upper Doab. The soil near them is *dhūsi* in the eastern districts and *pūlaj* to the west. *Dhīha, diha* or *tīla* are mounds generally. *Damka* in East Oudh is a hillock. *Deola* (East Oudh) means the same. The sites of ruined villages are *dīh* or *khera*. *Thikraur* in the eastern districts is the site of an old village covered with potsherds (*thikra*). An ant-hill is *bambha, bambhi* (west districts), *bamitha* (Lower Doab), *bithak* (East Oudh and Benares), and *bimaut* (Gorakhpur).

Section VIII—Stony Soils

309. The *rākar* of Bundelkhand is a gravelly soil. There are two kinds, *moti*, coarse, and *patli*, fine. The *pathari patharo*, or *patharila* of Lalitpur is a poor red gravel. The *chatān* or *chāpar* is a hard rocky soil. Soil mixed with nodular calcareous limestone (*kankar*) is known as *kankarila*.

Section IX—Cultivated and Waste

310. Classifying soils according to cultivation, we have cultivated land known as *ābād, harghasu* (Lower Doab), *bāsat* or *basat, chain, jatar* (Upper Doab), *chalti* (Delhi), and *chaltu.* An inhabited village is *chhapparband*; a deserted village *ujār, bechirāg* or *bila chapparband.* Waste land is *banjar, parti* (eastern districts), *uftādah, ujār, atarpāl, antarpāl* (Central and Lower Doab), *bejot, patpar* (Eta). In Azamgarh *khīl* is waste land broken up for the first time, and *khilpah* land the second year after it was broken up.

Section X—Fallow

311. *Pandūr* in Azamgarh is land left fallow for sugarcane from the previous spring harvest (*rabi*) till the season for sowing the cane. *Palihar* in the eastern districts is land left uncropped in the autumn harvest and ploughed during the rains for the cereals of the spring harvest following; *choumās* is another term for the same. *Ābga ukhāo* in Azamgarh is land kept fallow for sugarcane to the exclusion of the early autumn crops. *Ukhāo* (Azamgarh) is land kept fallow for sugarcane after the early autumn crops. The *jari* or *juthahand* lands in Azamgarh and the eastern districts are those on which a spring crop is sown without any interval after the autumn crop is cut. In Gorakhpur the *kurhil* are waste lands which are ploughed up during the rains and cold weather, and sown in rice at the commencement of the next rainy season. In Eta the *narua* are lands left fallow after the spring crop is cut, and the *karel* are lands left fallow after the cutting of the autumn crops. In Oudh *parauti* are lands left waste for a time to recover their strength. In the *pural* or *parua* lands of Bareli, a spring crop is sown after a previous autumn fallow. *Chanchar* are lands left untilled for a year or more. The *jaunāl* of the Doab and Rohilkhand are cultivated alternatively in the spring and autumn harvests. In the Upper Doab *polach* or *polcha* is fallow land which was cultivated in the preceding autumn. In other places it means land constantly in cultivation which never requires rest. *Boyar* is land which never lies fallow; *rulla* or *rull* requires to be left fallow for a year or two; *phanph* is similar to this and *khankh* means the same. *Nimar* is land which has lost its fertility, and *āokhal* or *ūkhal* is land reclaimed from waste and brought under the plough.

Section XI—Richness and Poorness of Soil

312. *Moti* and *poras* or *gambhīr* are terms for rich soils. Poorness of soil is *patri* or *patli*.

Section XII—Irrigated and Dry Lands

313. Land artificially irrigated is *bhariya*, if irrigated from tanks or ponds *ābi*, and from wells *chāhi*. Land which depends only on the rain is *barāni,* unirrigated land is *asīcha*; if watered after ploughing it is *pareha* or *panola*. Spring crops, if unirrigated, are in the Central Doab *sahiriya*, and if irrigated *bharai*. In the Upper Doab the term *muhita chāhi* is applied to land usually irrigated, but thrown out of cultivation during the year. Lands sown only on the chance of rain are *tukhm sokht*.

Section XIII—Lands Bearing A Single and A Double Crop

314. Lands which produce only one crop in the year are *ekfarda, ekfasli, fard* or *fardāi*. Lands bearing two crops in the year are *dosāhi* (Rohilkhand), *jutiān* (Benares), *juthāli, jhunthar, jhūthan, juthiyāīl, dosāre* (Central Doab), *dohar* (Central Doab).

Section XIV—Terms Used In Connection With Different Crops

The following are some of the terms used in connection with different crops:

315. Sugarcane—Land prepared for this crop is *bhadwār*. In North Bareli the land is left fallow in the spring harvest, rice and the millets being sown in the previous autumn. Cane grown in this way is called *kharik*. Lands constantly ploughed for cane from Asārh to Māgh are *athmās*. Land under cane is in Rohilkhand *ikhbāri żamīn*, and in the eastern districts *ūkhwār* or *ūkhwāri*. Land sown with sugarcane after a rice crop is in Rohilkhand *bartush*. Land cropped in the previous year with cane is in Rohilkhand *mūnda*, and in the east districts *peri*.

316. Cereals—Lands prepared for cereals are in the Lower Doab *bījar*. In the eastern districts *harjinsa* lands are those which grow all crops except poppy, cane and transplanted rice. *Del* (Bundelkhand) is land ploughed and ready for the spring cereals. *Jaunāl* (Delhi and Oudh), *jaunār* (Azamgarh), *binār* (Upper Doab) and *narua* are lands which have been cropped in the past season with wheat and barley.

317. Garden crops—Land growing garden crops is in Rohilkhand *birhāna*, in the eastern districts *koirār*, and in the western parts of the province *kāchhiāna* or *kachhwāra*.

318. Cotton—Land on which cotton has grown in the previous season is *bankhara, baraundha* (Rohilkhand and Upper Doab), *mūdi* (Delhi).

319. Pulses—Land under gram is in Rohilkhand *chaniyāda*, in Delhi *chanial* or *umri*, in the Lower Doab *onr*, and in other places *chanara*. In Azamgarh *kirwat* is land after a crop of peas and *khutahan* after *arhar* (*Cytisus cajan*). Land lately under maize or millets is *datoi* in the Upper Doab.

320. Rice—*Biās* in Rohilkhand and *kiār* in the eastern districts is land under cultivation for rice. *Kurhil* is land ploughed up for rice after being waste or fallow (Gorakhpur). *Kira* is the term in Bundelkhand. Lands after the early autumn crop or early rice are in Azamgarh *juthahand*. *Dhanthiya* in Rohilkhand means land from which rice has been cut.

321. Land under trees, brushwood, etc.—Forests are *ban* or *jangal*; groves *bāg*, *bāri* or *birwāhi*. A *kauch bāg* is an orchard enclosed, irrigated and stocked with fruit trees. Buildings are not usually attached to such a grove. A *sehan bāg* (East Oudh) is one attached to a shrine or other building, and growing flowers as well as fruit. A mango grove is *ām ka bāg* or *amwāri*. A clump of bamboos is *basūr, baswāri*, or in the eastern districts *kot bāns* or *ghāri*. A young grove of fruit trees is *naurangu* in the eastern districts. A belt of trees round a village is *khandi, ghāna, jhari, rakhiya* or *ban*. Brushwood is *jhūnsi* or *jhamra* (Azamgarh), *jhāngi* (East Oudh), *jhār, jhāri, jhalār,* *khandar* (Central Doab), *kūnriya* (east districts), *jhūr, jarīta.* In Azamgarh *chhinla* is small stunted brushwood. *Jhād* in the Upper Doab is land on which brushwood grows. Lands producing reeds are *katri* in Eta.

Section XV—Land Impregnated with Salts, etc.

322. *Rehar* or *ūsar* is land impregnated with *reh* or impure carbonate of soda; *khāri* with sulphate of soda, *noncha* or *kallar* with common salt. *Chand bījar* in Azamgarh is *ūsar* land in which spots of good ground are scattered.

IV General Agricultural Operations

IV. I PLOUGHING

Section I—Ploughing

323. To plough is *hal jotna* or *hal chalāna* to the west; to the east the phrase *hal nādhna* is used.[16] Other expressions are *harauri par jana*, and *bāhna*. One ploughing is in Azamgarh *bānh*, and in other eastern districts *chās*.

324. The first ploughing is in Rohilkhand *eksiri jot lena*, and in the eastern districts *ek chās karna*. Lands sown after a single ploughing are called in Delhi *chhānta* and in the Upper Doab *pār*. In Gorakhpur *maghārna* is applied to the ploughing in the month of Magh (January–February) of lands intended to be sown with rice at the next rainy season.

325. The second ploughing is in Rohilkhand *dobār*; in the Upper Doab *dūsar,* or *ara, dosāri* or *dor*; in the eastern districts *somara*. Land twice ploughed is *jāīl* in western Rohilkhand, or *chail* in Rohilkhand.

326. The third ploughing is in Rohilkhand *tibār*, in the eastern districts *tikhar* or *tikhara*. Land ploughed thrice is *tāse*.

327. The fourth ploughing is in Rohilkhand *chauhār* or *chonwar*, and in the eastern districts *chaukara*. Land ploughed four times is *chaus*.

328. The fifth ploughing is in Rohilkhand *pachwār*, in the eastern districts *pachāwar*. Land ploughed five times is *pachbāsi*. In Gorakhpur the phrase used for successive ploughings is *ek chās, do chās,* etc. After the fifth ploughing they say *chha bāri, sāt bāri*, etc.

[16] *Nādhna*, from *nādha*, the rope by which the beam of the plough is fastened to the yoke, s.v. in *Azamgarh Glossary*.

329. The ploughing of the millets (*joār, bājra*, etc.) when they are about a foot high is in the Upper Doab and Rohilkhand *gurab,* and in the eastern districts *dhūr dahani*. To the east of the province it is the custom to flood a rice field and then plough it to kill weeds. This is known as *pandahani*. The process of weeding the millets in this way is also known in Delhi and the Central Doab as *bidāhna*, and *chhanta dena*, and in the Lower Doab *dadahrna*.

In Azamgarh ploughing with a plough of which the block is new and full-sized (*nauhara*) is known as *awāi*, ploughing with a small worn block (*khunta hara*) is *seo*.

330. In rice cultivation after sowing, the field is lightly reploughed to clear the weeds and cover the seed. This is known as *uthāwan* or *bidahni* in the eastern districts, and in Rohilkhand *dohrāna*. In Azamgarh *chauki* means the small pieces of the field which the plough has not touched.

331. Cross ploughing is *ārah* or *āra*, ploughing from corner to corner is *nok nāka*, and in Gorakhpur *kona koni*. The straight furrow is *khara*. When a rectangular field is ploughed along its length it is in Gorakhpur *chās*, and in the Upper Doab *antara*; ploughing breadthways is in Gorakhpur *somara* and in the Upper Doab *pānsa*. Ploughing from a corner is *kon*.

Section II—Fields

332. A field is *khet*. The beds made in a field to facilitate irrigation are *kiyāri*, and in Azamgarh *barahi*. The similar divisions in a sugarcane field are *koha* in Azamgarh. In Gorakhpur *bāndhi* are the raised banks between the irrigation beds which in the Upper Doab are *mendi,* or *menri*. In the Upper Doab small fields in the decreasing order of size are *gāta*, *dabra* and *kirayiya*. *Genra* is a plot marked off by a boundary. In Gorakhpur *kola* or *kolwa* is a small patch of ground generally adjoining a house. When the fields of one proprietor's share are scattered over the village it is *khetbat*. When they are divided like the squares in a chequered cloth it is *chundaribat*.

Section III—Boundaries

333. The boundary of a field is *mend* or *merh*. A dyke used as a boundary is *khāi, khandaq, khānwān* or *khāwa. Dunruha* or *dunruhi* in Azamgarh is a line or mound separating fields. *Genra* is a low field-boundary mark. An ordinary boundary mark is *damcha, daul* or *daula, dhūha* or *dhūhi, dokhi* (Delhi), *dānd, gad* (Delhi). A place where three boundaries meet is *sihadda*, and where four meet it is *chaugadda, chaukha, chaurāha, chompta* or *chaumukha*.

Section IV—Furrows

334. A furrow is *gund* or *kunr; khūd* or *khūr* is a furrow in stiff soil. *Mūṛh* in Azamgarh is a furrow in which sugarcane or betel is grown.[17] *Harai* in Gorakhpur are the deep furrows in a field at distances of 25 or 30 feet in which extra crops are grown. The deep furrow used as an irrigation channel is *baraha*.

Section V—Miscellaneous Terms used in Connection with Ploughing

335. *Ghumāo* in Delhi, *jawāra* or *jawāri* in the Central Doab, and *sānjlo*, mean as much land as can be ploughed in a day; *jawāra* in Delhi means the area ploughed in half a day which is in the Doab *chhakwār*. The portion of land included in the circle of one plough is *harāi*. To commence another circuit is *harāi phāndna*. The place where ploughing is going on is *harātar* or *harauri*.

336. The first ploughing of the season is *halāita, harīta* (Rohilkhand), *harsotea* (Delhi), *haraini, harait, harauta, harwat* or *hari*. The first ploughing of a fallow field after the first fall

[17] It is symptomatic of the specialized cultivation of sugarcane and betel that there are separate terms for the same operations when applied to either of these high-valued crops. Thus divisions made in the field to facilitate irrigation with the wooden shovel (*hātha*) is *barahi* generally, and *koha* when applied to cane fields (para 332). The same holds for *mūrh*.

of rain is *chirwai*. Bringing home the plough across the back of a bullock or with the share inverted is *harsot*, and in Gorakhpur *har chhutān*. The worship of the plough when the ploughing and sowing work are ended is *harpūja*. This day is called *nibauni*.

Section VI—Ploughmen

337. A ploughman is *halwāha* to the west, *harwāha* to the east, *hāli* (Rohilkhand) or *hariya* (Rohilkhand). In Gorakhpur ploughmen are distinguished as (a) *darmahādār*, who work half the day for one master and half for another; (b) *tihāra*, one who works two days for his master and receives in return the loan of a plough and cattle for one day to till his own field; (c) *sānwakdār* or *chhatiyan*, who works on advances. He receives as his pay one-sixth of the produce and a blanket.[18] When a ploughman receives the use of a plough instead of wages in cash or kind he is called *angauriya* in Benares, and in Gorakhpur *angwār*. This practice is known as *jitra* in Bundelkhand and Rohilkhand. An agricultural labourer paid in kind is called *bajīdār*, in contradistinction to *mihdār*, one who receives money. A man paid solely in cash is in the eastern districts *koranja*. In Benares *baninhār* is a labourer paid in kind. A hired labourer attached to an estate but free to remove is *kamera*. Payments in kind to agricultural labourers are *bhanta* (Rohilkhand), *bhatta* (Delhi and Doab), *banni* (Benares), *bhalia, haliyāk* (Delhi and Doab), *harwāhi* (Gorakhpur), *manni, mend ka anāj* or *lāi* (Upper Doab). Advances to a ploughman when first employed are *harauri* (Benares), or *harwal* (East Oudh and Benares).

Section VII—Reciprocal Assistance in Cultivation

338. In Azamgarh *paith* or *painch* is exchange of labour for labour by agriculturists. A man who cultivates with a

[18] The Gorakhpur terms have been picked up by Crooke from present-day Basti district. See Report on Pergunnah Basti and Mahul, c. 1860, in *Goruckpore-Bustee Settlement Report* (1871), II, p. 161.

borrowed plough is *bhūndia* in the Central Doab, and in Gorakhpur *bhānja haria*. A cultivator who for the loan of a plough for eight days works the rest of the month for the lender is *athwāra*, and when he works for two days and gets the use of a plough on the third it is *tijaria* (eastern districts).[19] *Angwāra* (eastern districts), *jitera* (Rohilkhand and Bundelkhand), *jitta, dangwāra* (Delhi and Upper Doab), *hari, harsot, harsajja, bhānja* and *hundh* are terms used for reciprocal assistance in tilling.

IV.2 MANURING

Section I—Kinds of Manure

339. Manure is *khāt, khād, khāo, pāns* or *sār*. *Kūra* is rubbish or road sweepings. Cowdung is *gobar*. *Līd* is the dung of horses, elephants, etc. Other filth of various kinds is *maila*. The refuse of indigo after maceration used as manure is *sīth* or *jutthi*. A manure pit near a house is in Gorakhpur *ghūr*, and in Azamgarh *ghūrkatwār* or *ghūrkatwāri*; ashes are *rākh*.

Section II—Modes of Manuring

340. In Azamgarh *khadgor* is heavily manured land. It is the custom to allow cattle to stand in a field for the purpose

[19] The context of *tijaria* is spelt out thus by J. R. Reid: 'In parganas in which there is little rice land, from four to five acres can be cultivated with a fair pair of bullocks. Rice land requires little ploughing, and the average is greater in those parts where it prevails. The size of many tenants' holdings is considerably less than the area just named. Some of those tenants who have not land enough to employ two bullocks keep only one, and club with other cultivators on the plan known as *harsaj*. Many of those who have only an acre or less of land keep no bullocks at all. They cultivate on the plan known as *tijaria*. Working two days for another cultivator, they get the use of his bullocks in exchange on the third'. *Azamgarh Settlement Report*, para 350.

of manuring it. This is known in East Oudh and Gorakhpur as *hirāna*; in Rohilkhand *khatāna*, in Oudh *pānsa*, in Azamgarh *bhenrwāns, hirāwal* or *hirāwar*.

Section III—Manure used as Fuel

341. Manure is collected in the forests and grazing grounds and dried for fuel. This is known as *bankanda, bangauntha*, or *bangointha* or *arnikanda*, in Delhi *rāna gosa*, and in the eastern districts *binua gointha.*[20] When made up into blocks like bricks mixed with chaff and other refuse it is called *chāpre, gobar, upra* or *upla*, *gosa, doja, thepri* and *chhot*. The very large cakes are *goha* or *kande* and in the eastern districts *gohara*, or *danda*. In Gorakhpur *gointha* or *goitha* are the rough pieces dried and stored. The *chipari* of Gorakhpur and the *upli* of the Upper Doab are the small pieces stuck on a wall to dry. The *dohothi* are larger than the *chipari*. The *kankatiya* of Azamgarh and the *madhukari* are small pieces of cowdung fuel.

342. The pile of cowdung fuel is known as *bhitaura*; in Rohilkhand this is called *battaiya* or *bathiya*, in East Oudh *gurhaur*, in Gorakhpur *gohraul* or *gohraura*, and in Azamgarh *goharwāra*. The house in which the fuel is stored is in the Upper Doab *gohāri*, and in the eastern districts *gothaila* or *goithaula*. The operation of making the cakes is *pāthna*, and the place where they are made *pathwāri* or *pathaura*.

IV.3 SOWING

Section I—Sowing

343. Sowing is *boāi, boara, boani, boni*; and in the Upper Doab *bora*. To sow is *boṇa*. To scatter the seed is *chhīntna*, and

[20] It seems that *kanda* is the usual form in the west and *gointha* to the east of the province.

in Rohilkhand *bakherna*. Seed is *bīj* to the west, and in the eastern districts *bīa*; a grain of seed is *dāna*.

Section II—Modes of Sowing

The following are the modes of sowing:

344. (a) Furrow sowing—*Sī, burri, gurri,* or *gulli*. In this case a plough goes in advance of the sower who carries the seed in a basket. He drops it into the furrow as soon as it becomes visible. By this method the seed is sown deep, the stalk is stronger, and not so liable to be laid by high winds. This mode of sowing is known in Azamgarh as *khutahar boab*. *Bhathiārab* is to fill up with soil the furrow in which the seed has been sown, by ploughing a second furrow beside it. This is chiefly done in the case of sugarcane. When the seed is sown in long lines in the field it is known in Gorakhpur as *pānt* or *pānti*, and when it is sown along the sides of the field it is in the Upper Doab *kunr*, and in Gorakhpur *munr*.

345. (b) Sowing by drill—This is known in Bundelkhand as *bob* or *nārū*; in Delhi *jaīya*, and in the Doab and Rohilkhand *wair* or *wairna*.

346. (c) Broadcast sowing—This is in Rohilkhand *pabera bona*; in Benares *chhitua*; in the Doab, Rohilkhand and Delhi *paberi, pabar phenkdena* or *jelkarna*; in Bundelkhand *parbeda* or *chhirka*, or *chhīntab*; and in the eastern districts *pair* or *paira*.

347. If the seed is sown on lands which have not been ploughed, the phrase in Rohilkhand is *baithe per bona*, or *chhintua*. The same word *chhīnta* is used in the eastern districts to signify lands in which the seed has been scattered after a single ploughing, more particularly at the extremities of villages with a view to secure possession. This word is also specially used for sowing the spring (*rabi*) crop on the *jari* lands, or those from which the autumn crop has just been cut as contrasted with the *palihar* or carefully prepared fallow fields. In the eastern districts the *dhuria bāwag* or *boan* is the sowing of the early rice in dry lands. Throwing more seed among a growing crop of rice is in Delhi *chhānta*, sowing wide apart is in Rohilkhand *chhīda*, and in the eastern districts *bhīra*. Sowing thick is *ghan, ghana* or *ghinka*. Grain that fails to germinate is *abīj, nirbīj* or *bījmār*. When from excess of rain followed by heat a crust is formed on the surface which prevents the young plant from coming up, it is called in Gorakhpur *seota*, and in the western districts *rapara*.

Section III—Seed-Beds and Nurseries

348. A nursery generally for rice is *biār*, in the eastern districts *behnaur* or *behan*; in the western districts *panīr*, in Bundelkhand *jāyi*; in Delhi *pīad*. The young plants which are transplanted from the nursery are *paudh, behan* or *bichra*. *Hāpar* is a sugarcane nursery.

Section IV—Sowing Time

349. The sowing season is *boni, bora, bera, boāi* or *boāra* in the western districts, and to the east *baug* or *bāwag*. The end of the sowing season is *daliya jhār* (literally the brushing out of the sowing basket), *kunr mundla, hariar, baibhari, kunr bojhi*, and in the eastern districts *kurmundan*.

IV.4 DIGGING, HOEING AND WEEDING

Section I—Digging

350. To dig is *gorna, korna* or *khodna*. Digging is *gorāi, korāi* or *khodāi*; *ārmārab* is digging or hoeing the edges of fields in Azamgarh.

Section II—Hoeing

351. Hoeing is *korāi* or *khurpiāi*. In Rohilkhand the *asārh kor* is a special hoeing of sugarcane in the month of Asārh (June-July). Hoeing in Azamgarh is *patānr* or *baithāwan*, and *dhuriāwan* or *dhurāwan* is the first hoeing of the sugarcane.

Section III—Weeding

352. Deep weeding is *gorab*, superficial weeding is *nikāi, nirāi*, or *nirwāi*. The weeding of the rice crop is in Gorakhpur *sohani*. In Gorakhpur and other eastern districts *tāmna* is to clean a field of weeds before ploughing. The operation is *tamāi; kirkhi nirāb* is weeding in Azamgarh. Weeds and grasses collected out of a ploughed field by the weed harrow (*dhīnkhar*) are called *godhar* in Delhi; and in the eastern districts *khedhi, gurhal, akan* or *ghūr*. Weeding by hand is *chutki se* in the Lower Doab. Weeds collected and burnt as manure are *alāo*, or *kaura* in the eastern districts.

353. Wages for weeding are *chikarwāi* (Eastern Oudh), *nirāi, naulāi, nikāi, nirwāna*, and in Gorakhpur *sohani*.

IV.5 WATCHING OF CROPS

354. Watching of crops is in the western districts *rakhwāli*; in the eastern districts the terms *rakhwāi* and *khetwāi* are used. It is also known as *bālrakhi* or *shahnagi*. *Karkarāb* in Azamgarh is driving crows off a field. A field watchman is to the west *rakhwāla* or *shahna*, and to the east *rakhwār, agor* or *agoraiya*. *Ahīta* is a man appointed to watch on behalf of the landlord to see that none of the crop is carried away before the demand is paid. When cultivators club together to watch their crop in turn it is called *bāri bāri* or *pāri pāri*. Fields cut by stealth are *burīda* (Rohilkhand).

IV.6 REAPING AND GLEANING

Section I—Reaping

355. Reaping is in the west districts *lāi* or *launi*, in the east *katia*. To reap is *kātna*. To cut cane is *chholna*. The man who cuts the cane is *chhola*. A reaper is *lahāra* (Rohilkhand), or in East Oudh *launhār*.[21]

Section II—Cutting of Unripe Crops

356. Unripe crops are sometimes cut for food. This is known as *dadri, alo, arwan, awāsi, kawal, kawari, bhadahar* (Rohilkhand), *bhadbhadāna* (Doab), *hureha* (Doab), *gādar, dhesar, gaddar, gādra, harkat* (Rohilkhand). In Gorakhpur *anwala* is a little grain cut first, and *umbi, unbi* or *ūmi* is unripe wheat or barley cut for parching. *Holha* or *horha* is unripe gram cut and parched. To shake the fruit off a tree is *bhadbhadāna*. Harvest time is *katni, katāi* or *katia*. *Launi* are wages for harvesting. To cut the ears without the stalks is *bajhwat* (eastern districts), *balkat* (Lower Doab, Bundelkhand), and *katāi* (Benares).

Section III—Gleaning

357. A gleaner is *silāhār*; gleanings left on the field for the lower orders are *bīsar* (eastern districts), *sila* or *salla* (generally

[21] The regional variation *launi* (west) and *katia* (east), was not as rigid as made out by Crooke. We read in *Azamgarh Settlement Report*, para 389 (note): 'Reapers are called *launahar*, the reaping being called *katia* or *launi*. The reapers carry the crop to the threshing place, as well as cut it. The custom of paying them varies in different parts of the district. In some places each reaper receives four sers of barley or rice or two and a half sers of wheat, besides a handful of the cut crop. In some the reapers make a bundle of crop for themselves, which, after inspection by the employer, they are allowed to take away. In others, one load (*pūri*) out of every twenty-five cut by the labourer is his wage. If labour is employed in threshing, two sers a day per man is given out of the grain'.

In the case of sugarcane, the cutters stripped the cane of dry leaves on its side with a *hansia* (an unserrated sickle) and also cut off the green tops which, when chopped with a *gandāsi*, served as fodder during January–March. Throughout the province in the nineteenth century the cane cutters received their remuneration at a given rate of five canes per head together with all the green tops which had been chopped off. These latter were seldom sold and their value as fodder must have been considerable, for on the face of it this remuneration seems to have been less than that received by the Azamgarh *launahars*.

throughout the province), *medh* or *maindh*; in Gorakhpur *binna*, and in Azamgarh *pachhua* or *phūta*.

IV.7 THRESHING AND WINNOWING

Section I—The Threshing Floor

358. The threshing floor is *khalihān* (which is also used in the forms *khaliyān, khariyān* and *kharihān*), *pair* (Upper Doab and Rohilkhand), *khirmangāh, pharwār* (eastern districts), *āphar* (Oudh). The shed erected on the threshing floor is in the eastern districts *marai* or *palāni*.

Section II—Sheaves and Bundles

359. *Lāk* or *lānk* in the western districts is the cut grain. *Pūla, gaddi, puria* (Gorakhpur), *gaira* and *gara* are sheaves. In Gorakhpur *muttha* is a handful of cut crop. A *dabbiya* is about ten handfuls of the autumn (*kharif*) crop. *Lehna* is used in the same sense for the winter (*rabi*) crop.

About 4 *muttha* = 1 *lehna*
4 *lehna* = 1 *dabbiya*
5 *dabbiya* = 1 *bojh*
100 *bojh* = 1 *pahi*

360. Five *dabbiya* of the autumn crop make one *dhoka*, about ten *dhoka* make one *bojh* or load, and an aggregation of several *bojh* make a *kūndar*. These terms are generally taken from the eastern districts. In Gorakhpur *lehni* is a small sheaf and *bojha* a large sheaf, sixteen *bojha* make one *sorahi*, which is a common unit for measuring produce. A Gorakhpur cultivator says his field gives so many *sorahi* to the *bigha*. In Gorakhpur *atia* or *aunsa* are large bundles of rice and *tema* is a smaller-sized bundle, and *akwār* is as much as can be carried under the arm.

361. In Azamgarh *kera* is a small bundle of grass or cut grain; *gointh* a head load of straw; *jaukta* a bundle of cut pulse; *bhīri* or *bhīr* a bundle of the stalks of the *arhar* (*Cytisus cajan*) or similar brushwood. In the Doab *bharota* is a bundle of fodder.

Section III—Treading Out Grain

362. The treading out of grain is *dāen, daona, dāwan, danwāna* (Azamgarh), *gahāi* or *gohāi* (Rohilkhand); *dhīnkhar* is a bundle of thorns dragged over the corn to beat out the grain; *khamsāh* (Azamgarh) is to thresh corn thoroughly. The beating out of the heads against the ground or a bed to disengage any grains that remain is *satkanu* (Azamgarh), or *satakna*. The second treading out of the grain is in Rohilkhand and the Doab *khurd dāen* or *khūr dāen*. The stake to which the bullocks are tied in treading out the grain is *menh* or *menhia*. The inner bullock, which is the slowest and weakest, is *menhia* or *menihān*. The outer bullock, which is the smartest of the team, is called in Benares *pāt*, in Gorakhpur *pāti* or *dahinwār*, in Rohilkhand *paghariya* and in Delhi *pankarari*. The yoking of the bullocks is *gāta* in Delhi, and the rope which ties them is *dauri* or *dānwari* in the east districts; and in other places *gandāwar, dāmri, garāwar, pakkar, jor* or *ber*.

Section IV—Crops on the Threshing Floor

363. The piles of sheaves—When the crop is roughly piled for threshing on the threshing floor it is known as *gānj* or *pahi* in the eastern districts. When the cut crop is piled like a stack in England with the grain heads inside to save it from rain it is called to the east *tilganj*; *arhar* (*Cytisus cajan*), when piled on end to ripen before threshing, is in Gorakhpur *bhīri* or *bhīr*. The platform on which a stack is raised is *ghai; chulli* are the supports on which the stack is raised. *Garri* in Delhi and the Upper Doab is a large stack of wheat or barley containing two or more *senka*, which generally comprises several thraves of corn, the produce of one field. In Rohilkhand it means a large stack of the produce of the autumn harvest.

364. When the crop is spread out flat on the threshing

floor ready to be trodden out by the bullocks it is in Gorakhpur *pair*.

365. After the crop is trodden out the pile of chaff and grain ready for winnowing is in Delhi *silli* or *dhar*; in Rohilkhand *gurhāo* or *silli*; in the Upper Doab *silli, neora, dhar* or *siliya*; in the Central Doab *dehi* or *marni*; in the Lower Doab *kalha* or *gurānw*; in East Oudh and Gorakhpur *kunāo* or *ukānw*; in Bundelkhand *thūa*; in Benares and Azamgarh *gurānw* and *ukānw*; and in Cawnpur *sairh* or *kunāi*.

366. The heaped grain is in Delhi *rās* or *tār*, and in other parts of the province *rās*; over this a cake of cowdung is placed to avert the evil eye. This is called in the eastern districts *barhāwan*, to the west *chānk* and *chhattūr* or *chhāpa*, and in Gorakhpur *gobardana*. A piece of moist earth stamped is sometimes used in the same way, and is called *barkat ki mitti*.

367. The heaped straw and chaff—Straw is *pūla* when in a bundle; when loose *puār, puāl, payāl, pora* or *poara*. *Bhūsa* or *bhus* is husks of cereals. The husk of the pulses are known in the eastern districts as *chhimaur*. Bran is *bhūsi* or *chokar*. The heaped straw on the threshing floor is *bhūs* in Delhi; *osa* in Rohilkhand; *osa* or *bhus* in the Upper Doab; *silli* in the Central Doab; *silli* or *bhusour* in the Lower Doab, East Oudh and Gorakhpur; *silli* in Benares; and *bhusaul* in Bundelkhand. A stack of hay or straw is *garri*, *bunga* or *bonga*. A heap of straw is in the eastern districts *porwat, porauta* or *porauti*. An enclosure for stacking straw or fuel is in Mathura *got; syi* or *sua* in the Upper Doab is a small stack of the fodder of the millets *joār* and *bājra*, and *chhaur* is a larger stack. A house for holding chaff is in the eastern districts *bhusauri* or *bhusaura* or *bhusehra*, and in Delhi *obra*; *khonpi* in the eastern districts is a small shed for chaff. A stack of chaff covered with a thatch to save it from weather is in Gorakhpur *mandil*, and in the Upper Doab *kūp* or *bonga*. A bundle of chaff is *khāra* or *pānsi*. *Pānk* or *pānki* in the eastern districts is the fine chaff which is blown away by the wind in winnowing.

368. The refuse straw or fodder—This is in Delhi *dondli, gantha* or *bhulari*; in Rohilkhand *gānth, gānta* or *sānta*; in the

Upper Doab *gāntha* or *gānteh*; in the Central Doab *gathuri* or *sathuri*; in the Lower Doab *gānta, guthri* or *jangra*; in East Oudh and Gorakhpur *khūnti* or *gethara*; in Benares *gānth* or *ganteh*; and in Bundelkhand *guthri* or *suthri*. The refuse of harvest floors especially applied to the autumn crop is *dānth, jhora, datua, danthla, khūnthi, khūntla, dūnd, danthal, thūnth, khutel* and *khobari*. The knots in the stalks are *katri* or *katli*. The dry stalks of mustard (*sarson*) are in the eastern districts *tiskhut* or *tiskhur* and *tiltha*, or to the west *turi*. The dry *moth* plant cut and given as fodder to cattle is *gharar* or *kurar*. The stalks of cereals without the ear are in East Oudh and Gorakhpur *bajhwat*, and *jangra* in the Lower Doab is the haulm of the autumn crop.

Section V—Winnowing

369. To winnow grain is *sailāna* (Rohilkhand); *dhariyāna* (eastern districts); *dhārdharna* (Delhi); *surhetna* (Rohilkhand); *osāna* (Bundelkhand), *osauna* or *barsāna* (eastern districts); in Azamgrah *dāli dena, phatkārab*, or *phatkorab*. The grain which is only winnowed once is in Rohilkhand *khajūra*, in the Upper Doab *gajaura*, and in the Central Doab *sili*.

Section VI—Miscellaneous

370. The gathering or the collecting of grain at one place in the time of harvest is *batoran* or *batolan*. When the grain is being weighed an extra handful is thrown in to make up for dust, etc. This is called *khakīna, bharti* or *mutthia*. The grain left on the threshing floor after removing the bulk of the crop is *mer* or *thāpa*, and in the east districts *pachhua*. The gleanings and refuse grain on the threshing floor are known as *gharwa, ghūndar* or *gatharwa*; in the eastern districts *agwār, agela, buhāran, jhāran*, or *batoran*. The small heaps put aside for the god and penates (*bhūmi ganesh*) are *ujari* or *syāwarh*.[22].

[22] Cf. Beames, *Supplemental Glossary*, II, p. 311: 'Kali Rai says; "The small heaps put aside for *bhūmi ganesh* (as the offerings to god and penates)

IV. 8 DIVISION OF CROPS

Section I—Division and Valuation

371. The division of crops between landlord and tenant is *batāi, pair batāi* (Rohilkhand); *agor batāi, bhaoli, kan* (Upper Doab). The valuation of the crop for the purposes of division is *kūt* or *kankūt.* The valuation of the crop, as fixed by the appraiser, is *bakār*; a rough estimate of the produce is *bāk* in the west districts, and in Bundelkhand *dekha bhāli.* When the produce of a *bigha* is estimated from that of a *biswah*, the process is *āoli* in East Oudh, or *dāna bandi.*

Section II—The Shares into which the Crop is Divided

The shares are as follows:

372. Half to landlord and half to tenant. *Ādhi, nisfi, ādh batāi, adh-i-ādha* in the west and to the east *adhia.*

373. Seven-sixteenths to landlord and nine-sixteenths to tenants. This is *nauāna* (Rohilkhand), *batāi nawāsiya* (Benares), *hariyānw* and *nausāt.*

374. Nine-sixteenths to the landlord and seven-sixteenths to the tenants. This is *nausatti* in Azamgarh.

375. When the landlord gets 16 *sers* 5 *chhataks* to the maund. This is *tihāra siwaia* in Bareli. When the landlord receives 14 *sers* 15 *chhataks* to the maund = $^{239}/_{640}$. This is *tihāra panseri* (Bareli).

376. Two-fifths to the landlord and three-fifths to the tenants. This is *pachdo* in Bareli; also *bakand* and *pachdoli.*

377. When the landlord receives one-third and the tenant two-thirds, it is *tihāra* (Bareli) or *tihāi*, and to the east *tikur* or *tikura.*

---

are called *ujari* and *syāwarh*; grain left on the threshing floor after removing the bulk of the crop is called *menr* and *thāpa*, and the grain which falls to the ground with the chaff in winnowing is called *ghūndar* and is the perquisite of the Chamars. It is also called *gatharwa.* Gleanings of field which any one may carry off are called *sila*" '. See *Khet Karm* (1870 edn), p. 29.

378. When the cultivator gets two-fifths and the landlord three-fifths, it is in the Upper Doab *tihāra* or *siwāna*.

379. When the landlord gets five-sixteenths and the tenant eleven-sixteenths it is *sārhe chauhāra* (Bareli).

380. When the landlord gets one-fourth and the tenant three-fourths this is *chauhāra* (Bareli and Upper Doab) or *chahārum*.

381. When the landlord receives one-fifth and the tenant four-fifths it is *pachāra* (Bareli).

Section III—Deductions and Remissions

382. A deduction of one-sixth on the amount received by the tenant is in Gorakhpur *batta harwāhi*. The allowance to the tenant on account of deficient produce is in Rohilkhand *nābūd*; when a fixed deduction of 10 per cent is made it is known as *nawādasi*; a remission to a high-class tenant is in Fyzabad *charwa* or *kūr*;[23] *khakīna* in Bareli is an allowance

[23] The phrase 'remission to a high-class tenant' is slightly confusing, for in actual fact *kūr* was 'a remission in rent in favour of *high-caste cultivators to enable them to employ a ploughman*'. P. Karnegy, *Kachahri Technicalities* (Allahabad, 1871), p. 178. 'Kūr, usually consists of an allowance of one and a half *kaccha panserīs*; i.e. of seven and a half *kaccha sers* in the *kaccha man* of forty *sers*; as a rule it entitles the recipient to pay as rent, the equivalent of two-fifths instead of half the gross produce. It is granted in the first place to a large class known under the general terms *amnek*. These are generally high-caste men such as Brahmans or Rajputs, etc., and it is a point of honour with them to cultivate on these terms or none. Large numbers of them were at no distant period actual liege-men or retainers. All had a *talwār* ready at their landlord's call . . . The privilege was [not] generally granted as a mere acknowledgement to the claims of caste. It seems to have been granted rather as an equivalent for advantages, real or expected, in return. The *amnek* was not only master of a stout sword and a ready arm. His oxen were more, and stronger; his supply of manure larger, and his means of cultivation better, than those of the ordinary *raiyat*. He was too, a better payer. The real origin of the privilege is this:—It is properly the allowance, if not the only wages, of the *halwāha* or ploughman, with whom every amnek is supplied. To plough with his own hands would be to the *amnek* an indelible disgrace. All menial work must be performed by the *halwāha*. The latter is a predial slave, if not an actual slave.

made by the tenant for dust in the landlord's share of the grain. In Kheri the *agāwar* is an allowance of 1¼ *sers* to the maund; *biswi* is when the cultivator gets the whole produce of one *biswah* in his holding; *anjuri* is from 2 to 10 *sers* per plough, *khaliyāni* or *khatri* is an allowance occasionally taken by the tenant. In Azamgarh there are certain cesses which come out of the tenant's share and vary from 1/20th to 4/5ths—these are known as *serahi, pachhua* or *neg*.

Section IV—Mode of Division

383. When the crop is divided by sheaves before the grain is trodden out it is known as *bārbatāi, bojhbatāi* (Rohilkhand), *garābatāi* (Rohilkhand). When it is divided at the threshing floor it is *batia khaliyāni*. The man who weighs the grain is *taula, baya* (Lower Doab and Rohilkhand), *kayāl, dharwāi, kaniah, jokhai,* or *dandia*; the weighman's fees are *taulāi, bayāi,* or *jokh*.

There exists in full force in these parts [i.e. in Dariyabad] the wretched system known as *sanwak* by which, on a petty loan of Rs 10 or Rs 20, the *halwāha* will bind himself and his heirs as serfs to his security (*māl-zāmin*) until principal and interest at 24 to 37½ per cent per annum have, to the last farthing, been repaid.

Again: *kūr* is often the inducement held out to Kurmis, and [other] skilful cultivators, whom it is an object to settle in a deserted spot. It is the usual perquisite of the *mukaddam*: of the man who undertakes estimation of the crops (*kankūt*) or who, in any other way, does extra work (*kār o bār*) for the landlord. It is not given to an *asāmi*, merely because he is *kadīm*: and is not necessarily an hereditary privilege. The above principles are not confined to payments in kind. To a great extent they regulate money payments also'. *Kachahri Technicalities*, pp. 178–9. See also para 595 below.

V Cattle and Other Domestic Animals

Section I—Cattle Generally

384. Cattle generally are known as *maweshi, poha, chaupa, chaupāya,* and in the east districts *goru* or *chawwa chāngar.* A head of cattle is *rās* or *hanja.* In the Upper Doab horned cattle exclusive of buffaloes are called *dāngar,* which also means cattle worn out from old age; this is also expressed by the terms *baisak* or *khāngar. Thānth* in the east districts is a worn out or useless cow or buffalo.

Section II—Bulls

385. The usual terms are *bijār* or *sānr*; and in Etawah *nālkol.*

Section III—Bullocks

386. These are called *bail* generally; also *bald* or *baladh*; and in the east districts *bard* or *baradh.* A pair of plough oxen is *goin, goi*[24] or *dogāwa*, and in the Upper Doab *gora* or *jot.* In the east districts in a team of three bullocks the wheelers are *dhuria* and the leader *binriha*; in a team of four bullocks the leading bullocks are *juār.* A yoke of well-bullocks is *jawāra.* Bullocks are distinguished by various peculiarities, such as the following:

387. A bullock with only one horn is *dūnda*, in the Upper Doab *tūnda*, in Gorakhpur *būnda*; and in other places *sīng tūta.*

388. A bullock whose horns project in front is *jhunga, jhungi, jhingaur, jhingli, jhindi, ghoncha* or *ghonchāh* in Azamgarh; and in Gorakhpur *kothia.*

[24] Readers of Premchand's *Godān* will recall that it was Hori's desire to purchase a '*goi*' that led to his hopeless indebtedness.

389. A bullock unbroken to work is *adahāri, harha*, and in Azamgarh *ochhar kāndhi*. One that sits down at work is *galiya*, or in Gorakhpur *parua*. A vicious bullock is *markaha* or *chotār*. A bullock that shies is *bharkan* or *pharkan*. To butt is *jhaukna*. To break-in cattle is generally *nikālna*, and in Azamgarh *karhāb*.

390. A bullock one of whose horns is erect and the other hangs down is *kaincha* or *sarg patāli* (that is, one pointing to heaven, and the other to hell).

391. A bullock whose horns join in the centre is *maina* and in Gorakhpur *chaur*.

392. A bullock whose horns grow backwards is *mora*.

393. A stunted bullock is *natwa*, and in Azamgarh *nānta*.

394. When the horns are stunted a bullock is called *mundra*, and when it has no horns it is *bhūnra* or *bhunda* in Gorakhpur. When one of the horns is broken it is *munda*, and when one horn turns to the right and the other to the left, it is *phulsapel* (literally one who shoves against a doorway), and in Gorakhpur *chātar*.

395. When a bullock has no hair on its tail, or a small tail, it is called in the east districts *bānri*, the opposite of which is *ponchhigar* or *punchhgar*. And when the ears are covered with long hair it is known as *jhabra* or *jhabbua*.

396. A bullock not used for agriculture because it has excrescences on its body, but purchased by religious mendicants, is known in the eastern districts as *jatāh* or *anandi; chharua* is a best [let loose in the name of a deity]. The trident mark of Shiva branded on it is *tirsūl, trisūl* or *tirsūla*.

Section IV—Cows and Breeding

397. A cow is *gāe* or *gau*. A cow or buffalo within six months after calving is *dhen*. After this she is called *baken*. *Purebha* or *kurebha* is a çow that gives two calves within a year. A barren cow or other animal is *bahla*, corresponding to *bānjh* in women. In Azamgarh, to be covered by a bull is *bardāb*; the copulation of animals is *bāhab*; used in regard to buffaloes it is *būna* or *būjāna*; and in Azamgarh of a goat, *chhagarāb*.

398. The act of calving is *bed, bent* or *bet* or *byān* or *byant*. In Azamgarh *chherab* is to give birth to a number of young.

399. A cow that gives little milk is *chochar*.

400. A cow or buffalo gone five months in calf or that which has given milk for five months is *bākhri*.

Section V—Calves

401. These are known in the Upper Doab as *labāra*, in Azamgarh *lairu*. In the east districts *bāchha* or *bachhru* is a male calf, and *bāchhi* or *bachhiya* a female calf. *Dohān* in Gorakhpur is a calf when it has two teeth; *jaingra, jingra* or *jingar* is a calf in the Doab. *Udānt* in Azamgarh are cattle which have not yet got their true teeth. *Kalor* in Gorakhpur is a young heifer. In Azamgarh the phrase *birkan kāni* is applied to oxen nearly full grown, while full-grown cattle are *sojhhob*; *chhadar* in Azamgarh is a full-grown bullock which has only six teeth. This is considered unlucky. Coaxing a cow that has lost its calf to eat grain is in the western districts *akor*, in Benares *toria*, in Gorakhpur *bhāra*. Sometimes the skin of the calf stuffed with hay is put before the cow. This is called in Azamgarh *laini*. To reconcile a cow or buffalo to its newly-born calf by smearing the latter with sugar is in Azamgarh *sangharāb*. *Pakheo* in Azamgarh is a kind of food given to cows when they calve. *Chaneth* are drugs for cattle. *Mutīela* is a mash of the *moth* grain, sugar and clarified butter given to sick cattle.

Section VI—Buffaloes

402. A male buffalo is *bhainsa*, and in the western districts *sunda*; a female buffalo is *bhains* or *bhainsi*, and in the western districts *majjh*. *Bākri* or *jhoti* is a small buffalo. A male calf is in the eastern districts *pāra*, which in other places becomes *parva, padda, paro*, or *parba*. The word *katra* is also sometimes used. A female calf is in the eastern districts *parya*, and to the west *katya*.

Section VII—Goats

403. A he-goat is *bakra, bok,* and in the eastern districts *chher.* A she-goat is *bakri* or *chheri.* A castrated goat is *khasi.* A young goat is *pāth* or *pathya.*

Section VIII—Sheep

404. A ram is *bhera* or *mendha*; a sheep is *bheri* or *gādar*, a lamb *bher ka bachha*, or in Azamgarh *ghenta. Revar* is a flock of sheep or goats.

Section IX—Pigs

405. The general term is *sūar.* In Gorakhpur Muhammadan villagers call them euphemistically *bad qaum* (the 'low caste'). A young pig is called in the eastern districts *chhauna*; in Azamgarh *laina.* To the east *ghenta* is also used for the male and *ghenti* for the female. A pig-sty is *khobār.* In parts of Azamgarh there is by custom a kind of licensed robbery of pigs. The people of one village turn out and drive off by force the pigs of another. The owners resist as well as they can, but never prosecute the offenders. This is locally known as *sūar khedwa.*

Section X—Horses, Mules and Asses

406. A horse is *ghora*, a mare *ghori*, a pony *tattu*, a pony mare *tatuāni*, *tāeri*, and in Farukhabad *tatunya*; a foal is *bachhera* and a filly *bachheri*; an ass is *gadha*, and an ass foal *rengta* or *renta.*

Section XI—Camels

407. A camel is *ūnt* or *shutur.* A young camel is *bota.*

Section XII—Straying of Cattle

408. The usual phrase is *āwārah*, in Azamgarh *baunriāb*, in Gorakhpur *aniria* or *haraha.* They also use the phrase *hira* *jāna.*[25] *Thariāib* in Azamgarh is to fold cattle in an enclosure, and *hai* is injury done to a field by stray cattle.

Section XIII—Colours of Cattle

409. White is *dhaul* or *dhaur*. *Sokhan, kair* and *chanwar* are in the east districts various shades of grey. *Loha* and *lohwa* in Gorakhpur and *gora* to the west are red. *Pīara* to the east is red and white, and *kankandha* is an animal black on the shoulders.

Section XIV—Hides

410. These are generally *chamra*. In Azamgarh *goita* is raw cow's leather, and *bhainsauta* that of buffaloes. In the Doab and eastern districts *chām* is tanned cow hide. In the Upper Doab a buffalo hide is *adhaura*, a bullock hide *charsa*, and goat and sheep skins *nari*; a bull's hide cut into two pieces is *dhauri*. The hides of cattle which have died a natural death are *murdāri*,[26] and those of killed cattle *halāli*. *Sābar* is tanned deer skins; a depot for hides is in Gorakhpur *chāoni*.[27]

Section XV—Cattle Slaughter

411. A slaughter-house is *zabah khāna*, and a place where cattle are flayed *bhagār*. A butcher is *qassāb* or *qasāi*; a goat butcher is *bakarqassāb*. The large knife used by them is *bugda*.

Section XVI—Feeding of Cattle

412. To chew the cud is *jugālna, pāgur karna* or *pagurāna*. Cattle fodder consisting of the stems of the *juār* (*Holcus sorghum*) is cut up with a chopper (see para 53 above), and is known in Gorakhpur as *chhānti*, in the Upper Doab as *niyār*,

[25] *Hira-jāna*: from *hirāna*: to get lost; to lose.

[26] Kolhapuri *chappals* available at the Maharashtra emporium in New Delhi bear the equivalent though somewhat intriguing legend: '*ahinsak chāmya*'.

[27] *Chāoni* of course refers to any built out-structure and not just a depot for hides.

and in other parts as *chāra* or *sāni*. In Azamgarh the fodder for stall-fed cattle is called *lehna*, *kānta* or *koir*; in Gorakhpur *koer* or *koyar*. *Gajraute* are stalks and leaves of the carrot (*gājar*) given to cattle; *angāri* or *genri* are the chopped-up tops (*angori*) of the sugarcane; and the stalks of millets given in the same way are *dantha*. *Kurrāchāra* is dry fodder, and *bālab* is to chop up fodder. In Gorakhpur the phrase *chhānti pāni karab* means to feed cattle; a load of fodder is in the Doab *bharota* or *gola*, and in Gorakhpur *bojha*. A net full of chaff (*bhūsa*) is to the west *phānsi*, and to the east *khāra*. *Akhor* is the refuse grass, etc. which cattle leave behind; *nikhurāh* in Azamgarh is a beast that eats little.

Section XVII—Pasturage

413. Lands set apart for pasture are called in Gorakhpur *rakhāt*, in Banda *rakhel*, in Jalaun *rūkh*, *rukhiya* or *rand*, and in other places *gauchar* or *gauchara*. Pasture ground is *charagāh*, *charai*, *charan*, or *chugāi*; towards Delhi *bīr*; in Rohilkhand *bakha*; in eastern Oudh *bathān*; and in Bundelkhand *bagār*. A field in which cows are fed is *barha*; and towards Delhi a place in the forest to which cattle are sent out to graze is *baisak*.

Section XVIII—Fences

414. A fence to keep cattle out of fields is *bār*, *berha*, *gher*, *ghera*, *rīndhna* (Benares); *langa* is a hedge of brambles not fixed in the ground.

Section XIX—Grazing Fees

415. These are of two kinds:

(1) Those paid to the owner of the land.

(2) Those paid to the cowherd (who is known when he herds cattle as *gwāl*, *gwāla*, *gop*, *gorahh*, in the east districts as *charwāh*, and in Rohilkhand as *narha*). When he tends sheep he is called *gareriya*, and when he tends goats in the east districts *chherwāh*.

416. The fees paid to the owner of the land are known as *āng* towards Delhi; in Rohilkhand *baldihai*; and in the east districts *bardaihi*.

417. Those paid to the herdsman are to the east *charwāhi*; in Rohilkhand *narhai*, and in the Upper Doab *pūnchhi*, or tail money.

Section XX—Cowhouses and Enclosures for Cattle

418. A cowhouse is in the eastern districts *ghāri*, towards Delhi *gauwāri*, in the Doab *sār*, in the Upper Doab *bākhar*, in other places *gausāla*. In Azamgarh *bardaur* are stalls for cattle. In Oudh *ghaura* is a shed for breeding cattle. This in West Oudh is called *langhar*. A place where buffaloes are collected is in Gorakhpur *ghottha*, and in Azamgarh *ghotil*.

419. An enclosure for cattle is *nohra* in the Central Doab, and in Benares *darkhāl*. An enclosure for cattle in the forest is in east districts *arār*; in East Oudh *ghurat*; in North Oudh *ghauri*; in other places *aiwāra* and *bathān*; and in Gorakhpur *gaser*.

Section XXI—Cattle Dealers

420. These are called in the eastern districts *bardaha* and in other places *paikār* or *belki*; in Gorakhpur *daharia* is a wandering cattle seller.

Section XXII—Milk and its Preparations

421. Milk is *dūdh* or *goras*. To milk an animal is in the east districts *lagāna*. When the milk of a cow or buffalo dries up the phrase used in Azamgarh is *bisukab*. The milk of a cow for six months after calving is *dhen ka dūdh*; after that it is *bakena dūdh*.

422. Clarified butter is *ghi*. Fresh clarified butter is known in the eastern districts as *ahīrāna ghi*; that stored for a time in leather vessels is *kuppi ka ghi*. The sediment which settles in making clarified butter is *matiār* in the eastern districts, and *phāran* is the refuse left in boiling it down.

423. Curds are *dahi*. The old curds put in to curdle the milk are *jāwan* or *joran*.

424. *Chakka dahi* is thick curds. When the milk is curdled it is called *sajjāo dahi*. When the cream which is known as *sārhi* is taken off it is called *chhinui dahi*, and this mixed with water for sale is *dagari dahi*. *Katui dahi* is the curdled milk with the cream taken off. The thick milk given by a cow just after calving is *peusi* in the east and in the upper districts *kīs*. When a cow drops her milk the phrase in Azamgarh is *peunhāb*. Skim milk in Azamgarh is *pasāwan* or *pasaua*. The butter before clarification is *makhan* or *nainu*, and the buttermilk is *chhāch* or *chhāchh* or *matha*.

Section XXIII—Cattle Diseases

425. Farcy. This is *agiya*.

426. Gripes in the stomach are *aincha* or *ankur*. *Jonki* is inflammation of the stomach caused by leeches (*jonk*). *Petchalna* is diarrhoea, and *pokna* purging.

427. Foot and mouth disease. *Aishu, bātān, bekra* (Bundelkhand). In the Upper Doab *khūr pakka aur munh pakka, rora, akrāo, tephora, khāng* in the eastern districts; in Sultanpur *khangwa;* in Benares, Banda and Fatehpur *khora*; in Saharanpur *sīr*; in Hamirpur *khūr phata*; in Farukhabad *pakka*; in Cawnpur *ganthon sītala*; in Azamgarh cattle with diseased hoofs are called *khāngab*.

428. Diseases of the mouth. These are called *chabla* or *lāl*. *Ghantiyār* is a disease of the throat when the animal is unable to swallow; *kurka* are tumours forming in the throat; *palia* is throat inflammation with cough. In Azamgarh *jībha* or *beruki* is a disease in the tongue.

429. Footrot. This is in Jalaun *khūrsīta*, in Jhansi *gushela, khurent*. *Tausāh* in Azamgarh is a bullock lame from contraction of the sinews. *Naharua* in Azamgarh is a guinea worm which attacks the feet and legs of cattle.

430. Rinderpest. This is known as *andar ka māta, chechak, badah, bhaunra,* (Bundelkhand), *barādukh* (Dehra Dun), *bhawāni* (generally through the province), *basanta, bedan, mahāmi* or *chera* (Muzaffarnagar), *debi* (generally through the province), *debi ka rora, debi ka niksār* (Gorakhpur), *māta, rogi, sitala, mān* (Kumaun), *chapraha* (Oudh), *gabauna, mari*.

431. Windy colic or surfeit—*Aphara* (Upper Doab) or *bairukh*.

432. Hoven—*bādi, bhagi, pet bhagi, bāo band* (Jaunpur). Hoven attended with purging is *bareli*.

433. Pleuro-pneumonia—*Garara* (Jalaun), *ponka* (Jalaun), *gurkhai* (Jalaun), *gurkha* (Mathura). *Bhakla* is tracheal inflammation attended with difficult deglutition.

434. Staggers—*Tapka* (Mathura), *chakki, mirgi, jhapāh* (Azamgarh).

435. Tumours on the eyelid supposed to be unlucky—*Ama* (Azamgarh).

Section XXIV—Grasses and Plants used for Cattle Fodder

436. The following grasses and other plants are used for cattle fodder; the *akra* (*Vicia sativa*), the *anjan,* the *bekas*, a grass like the *dūb*, the *bhada*, a grass which grows on poor soil, the *bhadal,* the *binauriya*, which grows in fields sown with the autumn crop, the *bandri*, which grows in rice, and *kodon* (*Paspalum frumentaceum*); the *bansa* grows in rice and pulse fields, the *bhor* or *bhura* (*Rizophora mangle*), the *bathui* (*Chenopodium album*) grows in wheat fields, the *bondi,* the *chaupatta*, a plant like clover which grows in wheat fields, the *dūb* (*Agrestis linearis* or *Cynodon dactylon*) of which there are three kinds—the *paunda* with a creeper-like stem, the *khutya,* which is smaller and grows on hard ground, and thirdly the white *dūb*, which is called in Delhi *dhauri*. Where the division into three kinds is not known there are two classes, the *ghor dūb* and the *ban dubie*.[28] The *dubiyara* or upright panic grass, the *dal* or the *Panicum stagninium*, the *gadichat*, which is the *dūb* but larger, the *gargawa,* which grows in the rains and is eaten by buffaloes, the *ghundi*, which is eaten by camels and grows

[28] *Ghor-dūb* and *ban-dubiya*: the first is derived from *ghora*: horse, as it is excellent pasture grass; the second from *ban*: forest, as it is of a coarser kind.

in the rice fields after the crop is cut, the *gobi* (Hieraceum?); the *gandel*, a grass which is cut in groves, the *gaurer*, the *jhojhuru*, also called the *jangali nīl* or wild indigo—it is eaten by camels, and cattle are partial to it; the *jharua*, which is also called the *sāwan* or *sawain* because it ripens in the month of Sāwan—the stalks are given to cattle to improve the milk; the *jarga*, which grows on high ground and is given to cattle and especially to horses.

437. The *jaukari* is preserved and cut twice a year for fodder. The *jauka* is a common grass in Shahjahanpur. The *matmur* is a common fodder grass in Shahjahanpur. The *musel*, cut for hay, the *sarwāla*, a common fodder grass in Shahjahanpur (*saccharum sara*). The *Tigra* (*Boerhavia diffusa*) is a fodder grass in Hamirpur.

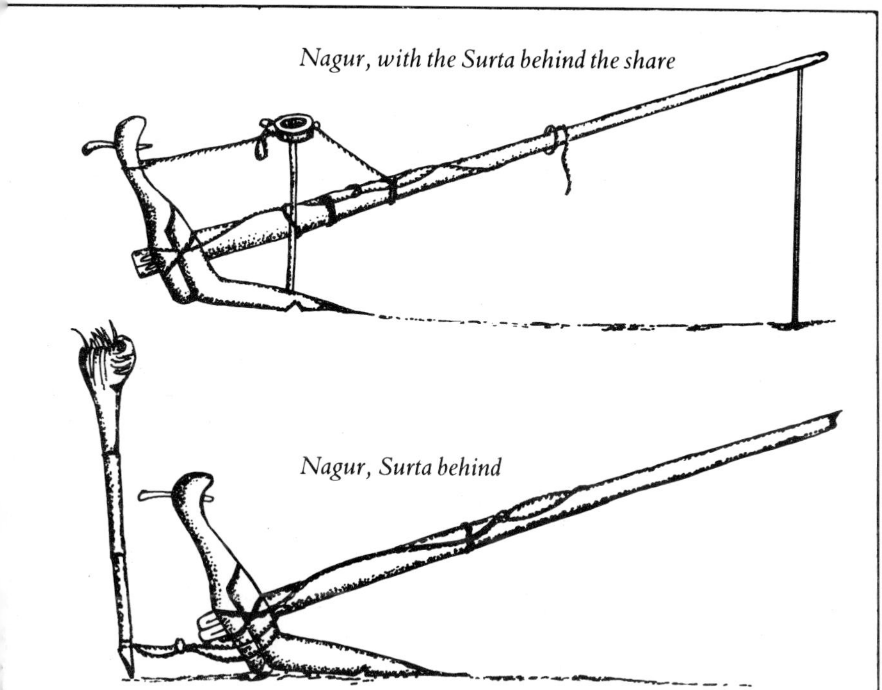

I Ploughs and seed drills

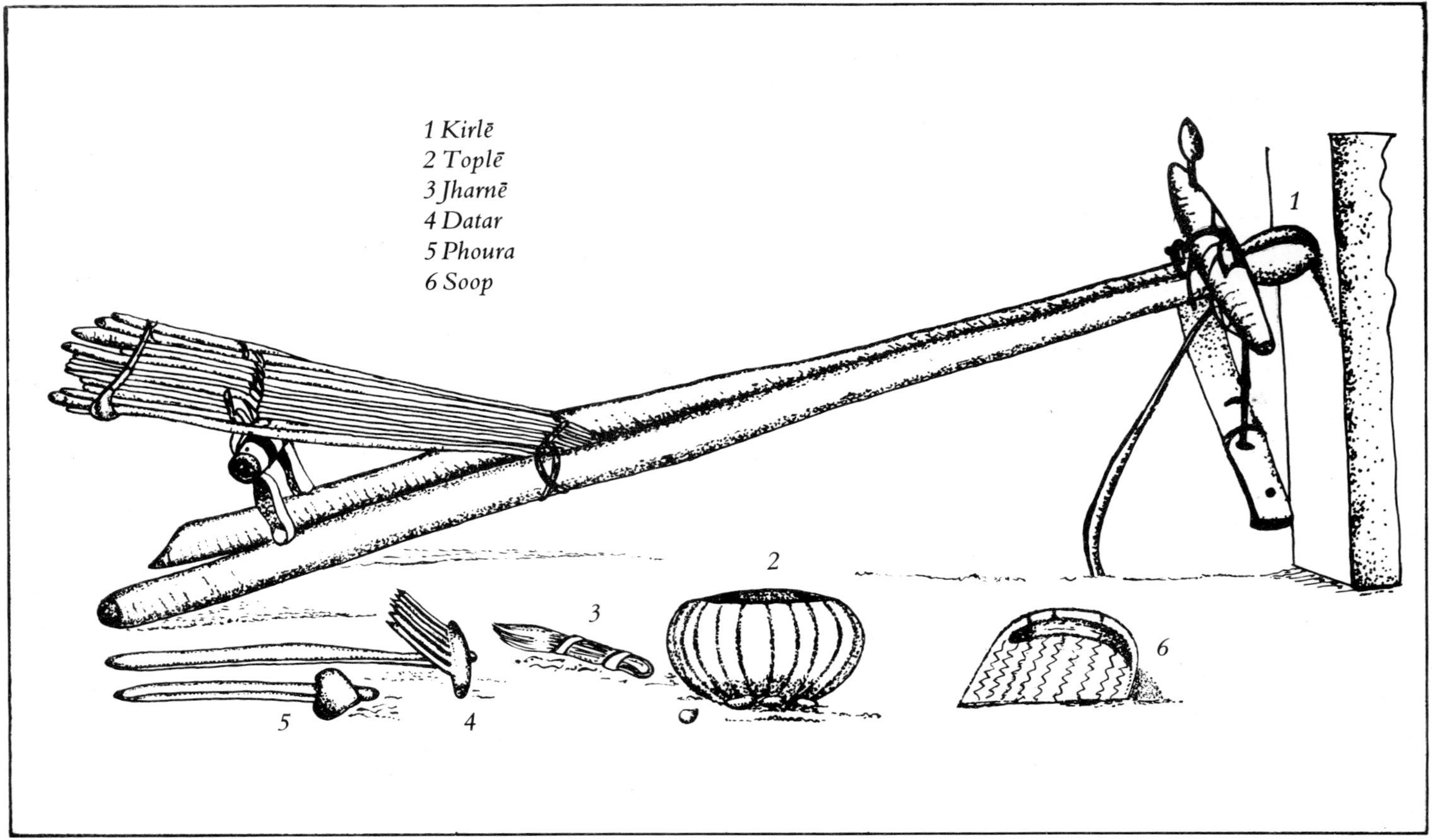

II A group of agricultural implements

III A wooden roller *kolhu*

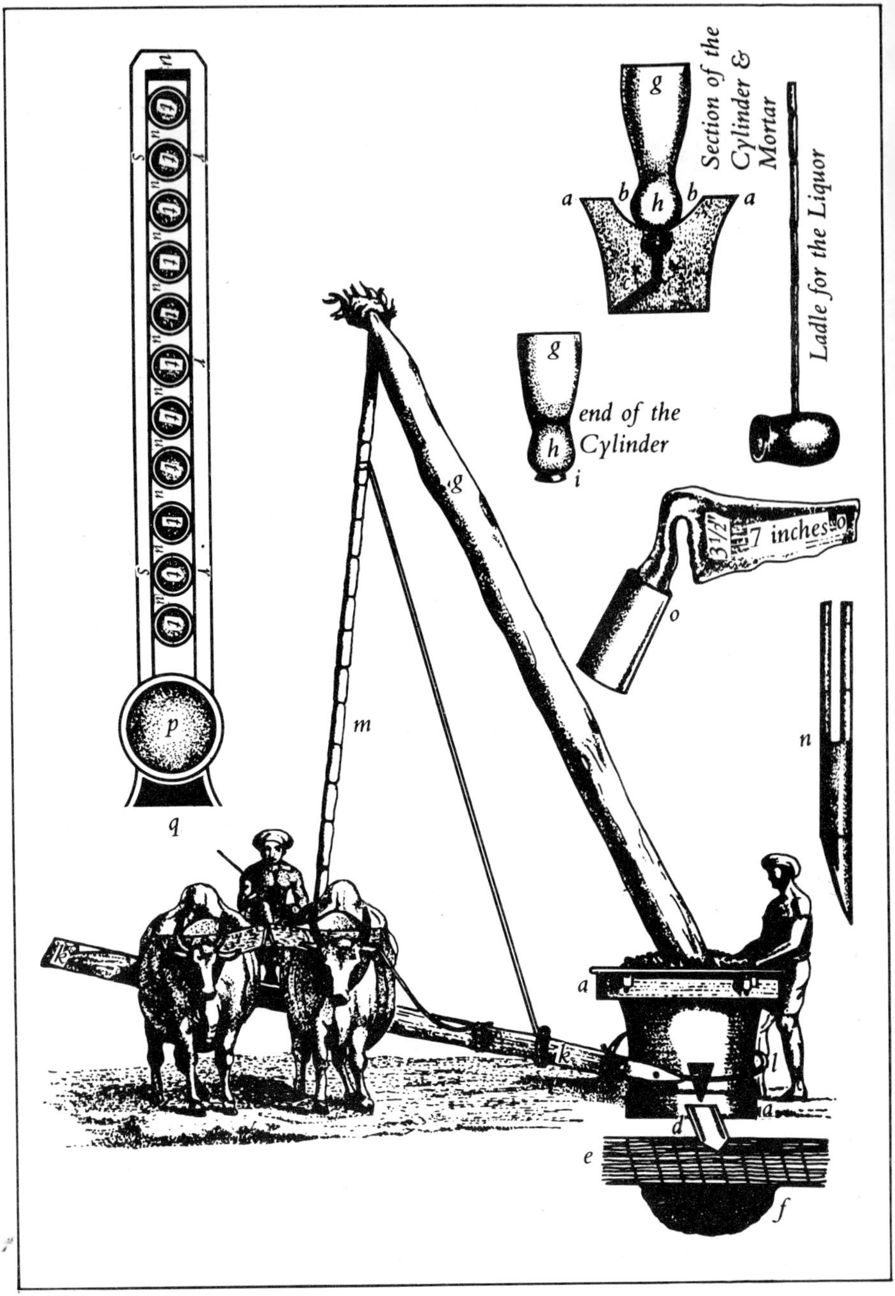

IV A wooden mortar-and-pestle *kolhu*

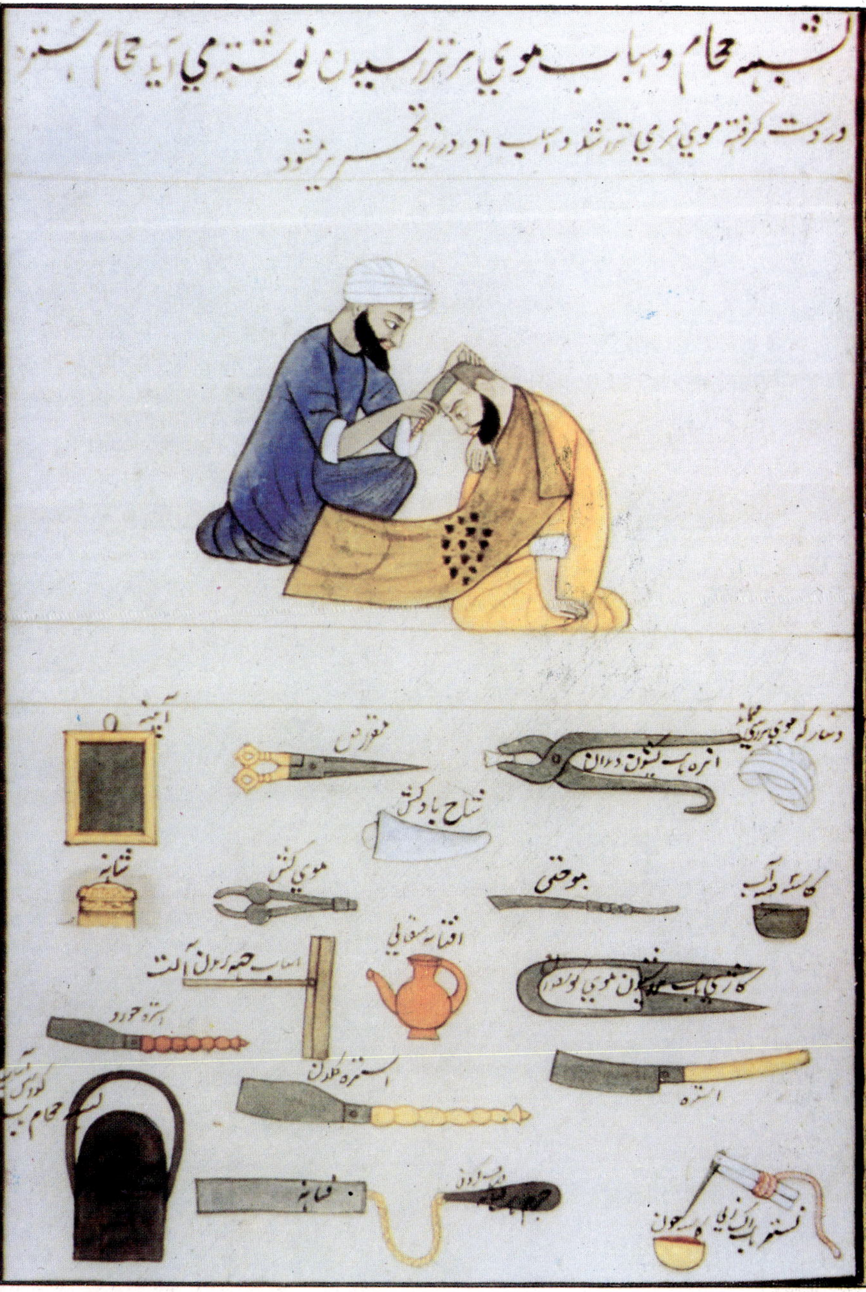

V A barber

VI A mutton butcher

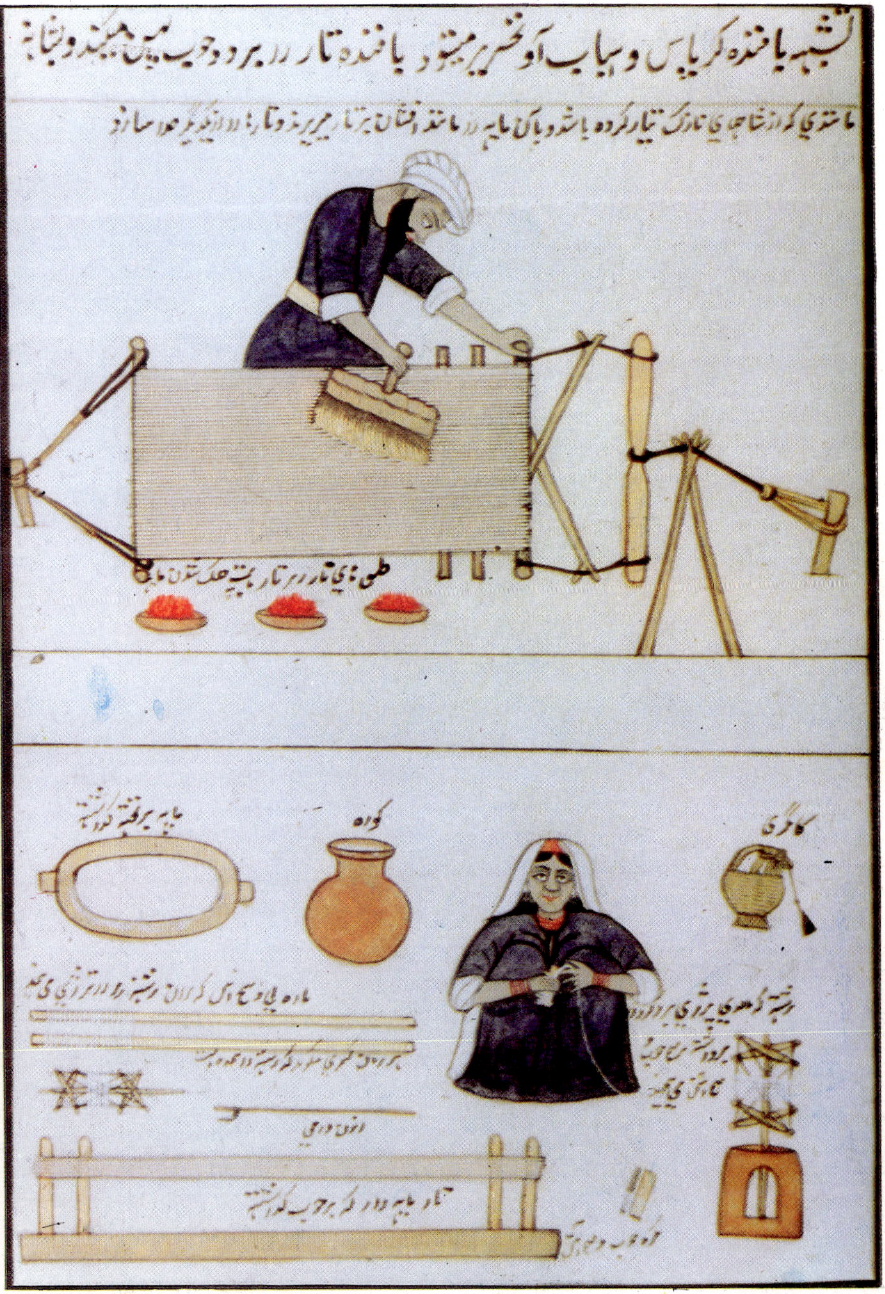

VII A cotton weaver combing a warp

VIII A dyer

IX A carpenter

X Blacksmiths

XI Potters

XII Grain merchant

VI Irrigation

Section I—Irrigation Generally

438. To irrigate is *ābpāshi karna, pāni dena,* or *sīnchna. Pāni patāna* generally means the moistening of a field with water before ploughing. Irrigation is *ābpāshi, patwa, seka,* or *sinchāi. Panīwat* in Azamgarh is the place where irrigation is going on; and *leo* is the flooding of a field preparatory to planting rice. A water drawer is in the east districts *panihāra.* A man irrigating is *pāni denewāla* in the western districts, and to the east *pandiwaiya* or *panchalwaiya.* The man who distributes the water in the field is in Gorakhpur *hathwaiya,* from the *hātha* or wooden shovel which he uses, and in the Upper Doab *panbala.* The wages for irrigation are in Gorakhpur *panchalwai,* and in Azamgarh *paniwat* is a fee for leave to irrigate.[29] Sometimes cultivators combine to assist one another in irrigating. This is known in Gorakhpur as *janna,* which literally means giving a proportional number of labourers.

Section II—Kinds of Irrigation

439. There are three main kinds of irrigation:
(1) From canals (*nahr*), or canal distributaries (*rājbaha*).
(2) From wells (*chāh, kūan*).
(3) From tanks or ponds (*pokhar, pokhari, talāo,* etc.)

Section III—Irrigation From Canals

440. Irrigation from canals: Irrigation by *tor* or *katwa* is

[29] In Azamgarh the feminine noun *paniwat* had three meanings: '(i) A place where irrigation is going on, (2) Fees for leave to irrigate, (3) The customary course for water for irrigation to go', as in the phrase: *sab din se ihai paniwat hau,* s. v. in *Azamgarh Glossary.*

flush irrigation when the water is at a higher level than the field, and the cultivator has only to cut the bank of the water channel and allow the water to flow into the field. Irrigation by *dāl* or lift is when the water has to be raised from a lower level. A dam or *bāndh* is sometimes built across the stream to raise the water. In Azamgarh a *lāt* is a long straight or curved embankment thrown across a plain in which rice land is cultivated and there is a flow of surface water.

Section IV—Irrigation From Wells

441. Irrigation from wells: A well is generally *chāh* or *kūan*. They may be divided into three classes:

(a) Those lined with masonry.
(b) Wells without a masonry lining.
(c) Mere surface depressions containing water.

442. A masonry well is generally called *pakka*. *Bāoli* or *baori* is a large well sometimes with a *ghāt* or flight of steps running down to the water. *Indāra* or *nāra* (in the eastern districts) is a large masonry well, usually for drinking purposes.[30] A well with houses and flights of steps round it is *bāin kūan*.

443. A well without a masonry lining is generally called *kachcha;* in Oudh *barkuyān*, in Gorakhpur *matkuyān*, and in some places *mattia*.

444. Mere surface depressions containing water are *bihar* in Rohilkhand, *choya, choha, chonra* in the east districts, and in the Upper Doab *ogal* or *kacchi kuyān*. A clay well which has fallen in is *jhera* in the Doab; in other places *manrār*; and in Azamgarh *pāl* is the space formed inside a well by the collapse of the sides.

[30] *Inār*, or *inara*, rather than *indāra* seems to be the common form in Gorakhpur and Azamgarh. In Bara Banki, *indārās* are still to be found, usually in a grove.

Section V—Construction of Wells

445. The large circular excavation made before a masonry well is built is *dahal*, the spring is *sot* or *sota*; in the east districts *musara*; in Rae Bareli *musla*. *Jharna* or *jharni* in Azamgarh is the side spring in a well. When the water level is reached the phrase is *jigari pāni ā gya*. The hole through which the water rises when the spring is reached is *bam* or *sum*. *Bambh hona* is a phrase meaning that the water is inexhaustible. Wells are called *barhāi* when the spring is not reached, and they depend for their supply on the drainage of the subsoil. Such wells are also sometimes known as *choiya* or *garoa* (Central Doab). Wells supplied from a spring are *sotihai*. The place where the earth begins to become moist as a well is being sunk is *chūa* (Central Doab). In some cases there is a stratum of sand so fine that it falls in at once and chokes the well. This is known in Bareli as *lelwa*. The masonry cylinder of a well is *girgaz*. In Azamgarh the circular hoops of kiln-burnt earthenware used to support the sides of a well are called *kothi*. Sometimes a coil of twigs etc. is used for the same purpose. This is known as *bīnra* or *bīnr*. Wells protected in this way are *badjhār* and *ajār* in the Doab.

446. Wells are sometimes lined with a wooden cylinder called *kothi*. Such wells are called in the Doab *garāwari* or *kāthūān*.

447. When the cylinder of a well fails to sink, a second smaller cylinder is sometimes sunk inside. The well is then called *doband*.

448. To enable the well sinker to reach the spring a wooden frame is gradually sunk by undermining. This is known in the Doab as *rākh*. Above this, as a foundation for the masonry, is placed a wooden cylinder called in the Doab *jākan* or *jākhan*; in the east districts *jamuwat*,[31] in the Upper Doab *nīmchak* or *nichak*, and in other places *niwār*. A well so large that two buckets can work at the same time is *dolāwa* or

[31] *Jamuwat*: so called because ordinarily made of *jāmun* wood. See also *Bihar Peasant Life*, para 925.

dopairwa; one for three buckets is *tilāwa*; one for four *chaulāwa*, and so on.

449. A well sinker is *senhan*, or *chāhkan*. A well is cleaned with a dredge called *jhām*.[32]

(*Paras* ***450 to 452*** *appear in Appendix A*).

Section VI—The Lever used in Raising Water

453. This is known as *dhenkli, dhukli, dhikli,* and in the eastern districts *dhenkul*. The earthen pot in which the water is raised is in the Doab and Rohilkhand *karwāla*, or *karwāra*, in Cawnpur *thilya*, and in the eastern districts *kūnr*. An iron bucket similarly used is *dol*.[33] The stick placed across the mouth of the bucket to which the rope is fastened is *kiliya* in the Doab; in Gorakhpur *muthar* and in Azamgarh *makri*, or *danda*, where the string which fastens it to the pot is *gūrhan*. The rope of the lift is *barāri* or *bareri* or *bart* or *lāo*; in the eastern districts *rassa, barha,* or *nār* are used for the thick rope, and *chhor* is the short rope joining it to the bucket by a slipknot.

454. The beam of the lift is in the western districts *dhenkli*; in Gorakhpur *dhenkul* or *chhīp*; in Azamgarh *balla, barha,* or *pendar*. Sometimes a thin piece of wood is spliced to the end of the beam. This is in the east districts *agār* or *agāri*.

455. The lever is weighed down by clods of earth, etc. fixed to the end. These are called *chakka, chāk, thūa,* or *thamba* in the western districts, and to the east *lād, lāda* or *lādi*. The peg with which these are fastened to the beam is to the west *khūnta*, and to the east *killa*. The post or fulcrum is in the Doab and Rohilkhand *jara, filpāya, thūni, khambh, jangha;*

[32] I have provided additional material on the construction of masonry wells in Appendix A, and numbered the paragraphs 450 to 452.

[33] It would be worthwhile to investigate when the shift from the earthen pot to the conical iron bucket widely prevalent in eastern UP today took place. The *Azamgarh Settlement Report* of 1881 makes no mention of iron buckets, but refers in a matter-of-fact way to the earthenware pot (*kūnd*) with a capacity of somewhat less than two gallons. Grierson mentions both the earthen and the iron *dol* in passing (see paras 369 and 929 respectively).

and in the eastern districts *khambha* or *thamba*. In Azamgarh *kanna* means the two forks at the end for holding the axle. The cross-axle is to the west *paretha*, in Gorakhpur *killi*, and in Azamgarh *gulla*. The point where the lever works on the pillar is *maja*.

Section VII—The Skin Bag used for Drawing Water

456. This is called *charas*, or *charsa, pur* or *mot*. The iron ring round the neck is in the Upper Doab *māndal*; in other parts of the Doab *kūndar, kūr, kurra, kondra*, and in Azamgarh *merara*. The rope or cord which joins the bucket to this iron ring is in the Doab *kas* or *kasan*. The semi-circular pieces of bent wood fastened to the ring to keep the mouth of the bucket open are known in the Doab as *bāin* or *bāun*. To these are fastened two rings which, if made of wood, are called *kauli* or *kuili*, and if of iron *kariya* or *pakunchi*. The wooden handle which attaches the rope to the bucket is called in the Central Doab *khutti* or *bilāri* or *bahora*. The ropes attaching the rings to the handle are known in the Doab as *bandania* or *bandaṇi*, and the ropes which fasten the ring round the mouth of the bag to the hauling rope are in Azamgarh *ghorei*.

Section VIII—Other Well Appliances

457. The straw or rushes put at the mouth of the well to prevent splashing are called *chīk*, *chilwai* or *pārchha*. A well yoke with the two bars (*jua*) parallel is called *jūr* in the Upper Doab. When the rope is hauled up by men the centre part of the crossbar is in Azamgarh *mūrha* or *murra*, and the ends *tunguna*. In Azamgarh the yoke is *juāth*, the upper bar *balla*, the knob to which the rope is fastened *mahādeva*, the two bars which go outside the bullocks' necks *saila* or *gulla*, the similar bars inside *pachār*, and the lower bar *trāil*. The wooden framework at the mouth of a well to prevent people from falling in is *chaukhata, dahāna, kāthghara, jangala*. The wooden beam laid over the well on which the bucket is landed is in the Doab *patār*, in Gorakhpur *dharan*, and in Azamgarh *sardar*. The framework at the mouth of the well on which the pulley works is known in the Upper Doab as *adāna* and in the Central Doab as *mair*. The masonry work at the mouth of the well is *man* or *jagat*. The upright posts to support the pulley are known as *marwa* (Central Doab), *dhurahi* or *dhorahi* (Cawnpur), *fīlpāya, thūni, jangha, gahlat* (Upper Doab), *kohar*, and in Azamgarh *khambha, dhūhi* or *chhūhi*. The cross beam is *patiliya* in the Central Doab; in the Upper Doab *maiyāl*, in Azamgarh *balla* or *manjha*, and in other places *bharsaha, patāo* or *bhareth*. The bars to which the pulley axle is attached are known in the Doab as *guriya* or *sūja*, and in Azamgarh as *dhurei*. The axle on which the pulley works is in the Doab *gandla, gandra* or *garandu*. In Azamgarh it is *gurra*, in Gorakhpur *kulli*, and in some of the eastern districts *akauta*. The pulley itself is called *charkhi* or *charkh, garāri* (Benares, Bundelkhand, and Lower Doab), *garili, garri, girra, girri, chahli, chāk, bhon* (Delhi). When the trunk of a tree with two branches lopped short is used to support the pulley it is called in the Doab *kaur* or *kuhar*.

Section IX—The Pathway for the Bullocks etc.

458. The place where the bullocks turn from the well is in the Doab *bahoro* (which generally means the sloping pathway), and in the Upper Doab and Rohilkhand *gohan* or *gaun*. The sloping is *naichi* (Central Doab), *pairi, bahoro, dhalwān, gaun, paudar* (Azamgarh). In Cawnpur the run above ground is *lilāri*, the run below ground *khurīya*, and the fodder–through in the centre *paindha*, which in the eastern districts is *nādh, nānd* or *kunr*; a yoke of well-bullocks is *jawāra*.[34] Drawing water by cattle power is *purwat* or *paira*.

Section X—The Workmen Employed at the Well

459. The following labourers are employed at the well:

[34] The word *jawāra* is derived from *jua*, a yoke. Therefore the term also signifies 'as much land as can be ploughed by a pair of bullocks'. See Beames, *Supplemental Glossary*, ii, p. 367.

The bullock driver—*Kiliya* or *pairha*.

460. The man who empties the water-log—*Charsiya, purha, archha* or *parchhāwāla* in the Doab, and in Delhi *bāhara*. The place where he stands is *dāng*, and the place where he deposits the water *pārchha*.

461. The man who distributes the water in the field—*Panmela, panlaga* or *pankata* in the Doab.

462. The man who distributes the water in the field with the wooden shovel (*hātha*) is called in the eastern districts *hatḥwaiya*.

Section XI—The Persian Wheel

463. The Persian wheel is known as *arhat* or *rahat*. The upright posts are *khambh, sipāya, marwao,* and *jera*. The pole connecting the upright posts is *patāli* or *mānjhi*. The buckets used with the wheel are *jet, karwāla, dīnd* or *tind dabua*.

Section XII—The Swing Bag and Swing Basket

464. Irrigation from tanks and streams—Water is raised from tanks or streams by the leather swing-bag or swing-basket. The leather swing-bag is *paroha* or *dol*. When a hollow trunk of timber is swung in the same way by a lever it is called *don*.

465. The swing-basket is in the Doab *lenri* or *lehari*, or *boka* (Doab and Rohilkhand), *beri* or *benri* (eastern districts), *lihri, chhapa, dal* (Delhi), *dalea* or *dugla*. The *dauri* is smaller and lighter than the *dugla*.

Section XIII—Water Channels

466. The channel which conveys the water into the field is *pain* in Gorakhpur, and in the western districts *barha*. In the eastern districts the ascending scale is *barha, nalki, nāli, narua* and *gūl*. In Delhi water-courses are known as *bāha, kahāl* and *khāla*. In Azamgarh the terms used are *bāha, bāh, pain* or *gol*. In Azamgarh *ekwāi* is the irrigation rill along the sides of a field from which strips of only half the breadth of those watered from the central rill are irrigated.

Section XIV—Water-Lifts

467. The height up to which the water is lifted is in the east districts *bodar, thauka* or *rik.* The place where the men stand who work the basket is *bodar, paira* (Delhi), *pandar* (east districts), *anua, dāng* (Central Doab), *chaunrha* (Azamgarh), *paunrha* (Azamgarh).

468. The first reservoir is known as *nanda* (Cawnpur), *gonra* (Central and Lower Doab), *nyani, nandhu, nadhāo, theoki* (Gorakhpur), *anua* (Azamgarh). In Azamgarh the top of the lift is *tutha* or *chaunrha*. The catch-basin from which the water flows into the field is *jhular* (Cawnpur), *parcha, odh* or *ulaha*.

469. When there are more than two lifts the second from the bottom is *pachu, docha* or *dohcha* (west districts). The third is the *thauka, tehcha* or *thaicha* (Azamgarh). The fourth is *chauncha* (west districts). The raised bank between the two reservoirs is *odi.* Using the swing-basket is *baindi, chopna, ulchab dena, lihaindi*. In Azamgarh *chhopab* sometimes means to irrigate sugarcane with the wooden shovel. The man who works the swing-basket is *birwa* (East Oudh).

VII Agricultural Products

Section I—Wheat (Triticum sativum)

470. This is *gehūn* in the west districts and *gohūn* to the east. The chief varieties are *mundia*, a beardless first-class wheat (Rohilkhand and the Doab); *hansa*, a very white first-class beardless wheat (Rohilkhand); *samalia* or *samaria*, a white bearded wheat (Rohilkhand); *rattua* or *rattiya*, a fair small-grained bearded wheat (Rohilkhand); *kachera*, a small-grained red wheat (Rohilkhand); *kathiya* a red bearded wheat with a reddish grain (Doab); *pisiya* a small plant with few grains (Doab, Rohilkhand, and Bundelkhand); *lāi* or *laliya*, *bansiya*, and *jalaliya* are varieties of red wheats; *ujjar*, *situa*, *dhaula*, *pīli*, and *Dāūd khāni* are white wheats.

471. A grain of wheat is in the Upper Doab *gaddi*. When it germinates first it is called in Bundelkhand *kura;* in the Upper Doab the phrases used are *sūi nazar āne lagti*, *nīl*, *dikhāi deta*, and *jins pasar āya*. When the blade throws out shoots the phrases are *tīkra āne lagta*, and *jins tatar āya*.

472. When about six inches high it is *poi* in Bundelkhand. When it is ready to cut for fodder it is in the Upper Doab *khavīd* or *khūd*. When it is cut unripe it is known in the eastern districts as *ūmin* or *ūmi*. When the ear begins to form the phrase is in the Upper Doab *kābha* or *koth āne lagta*. The hair on the ear is *pūr* in the Upper Doab. The ear itself is to the west *bāl* or *bāli*, and to the east *bār*. When the ear is being formed, but is still unripe, the phrases *dūdh par jāta* or *jins gadar āya* are used in the Upper Doab. When the grain hardens they say in the Upper Doab *gola ho jāta*.[35]

[35] To the 'native ear' the phrases '*tikra āne lagta*', '*koth āne lagta*', '*gola ho jāta*' sound jarring. However, I have retained these specimens of the sahib's vernacular. Cf. *N.W.P. Gazetteer* (*Etah*), vol. VI, p. 29: 'Nearly all the crops have different names at different stages of their growth: thus, when

473. The ear of wheat and barley dry are respectively in the Upper Doab *gandam* and *jau*. Collected on the threshing floor it is *lānk*, and the chaff is *bhūsa*.

Section II—Mixed Crops

474. Wheat and barley grown together are *gojai, gojra, gojari, goji* or *adhgawān*, or *adhgehunwa*. A mixture of peas, gram, barley, or wheat, or any two or three of them is called *bejhar, bejhra, gojara,* or *jauchani, gauchani,* or *birra*. Barley grown with the small pea (*kirāo*) is in the eastern districts *jaukirāi*.

Section III—Barley (Bordeum vulgare)

475. Barley is *jau* which sometimes means the larger kind, while *jai* is the smaller. Oats are *wilayati jai* or *rāmjau*. *Jayi* or *jawāre* are shoots of barley artificially grown and given to friends at the festival of the Dasahrah. The prickly hairs on the ear is in the Upper Doab *tus*.

476. The varieties are *bādshāhi*—the best kind—and *tikuriha* or *tikurāri*—bearded—from *tikur*, the beard on the ear.

Section IV—Rice (Oryza sativum)

477. The crop is known as *dhān*. When unhusked it is called *dhān*; when husked *chāwal;* when boiled plain *bhāt* or *khushka*; when boiled with spices *khichri*. The straw is *pora* or *poara* in the eastern districts or *lirua*. The varieties of rice grown in the province are very numerous and not important. In the east districts there is a proverb—*dhān aur chhattrion ka ekhi hisāb hai*, i.e. there are as many kinds of rice as Rajputs.

---

young, the blades of wheat are called *kulha, poi, sui*; when older *khūnd*, and when the pod of the ear appears, *kānthi*; when the ear begins to appear it is described as *kutihana* or *galetha*, and when the ear is half in pod and half out as *kandhela*. When the ear is all out it is said to *chhatna*, and when the grain becomes developed, *nibauriya*; when half ripe *bhadera*, and when fully ripe *jhūra*.'

The chief distinction depends on the time of the sowing and cutting.

478. In East Oudh there are four main classes.

(a) *Kūari*, sown with the first fall of rain and cut in *Kūar* (September-October).

(b) *Jethi*, sown in April, and cut in *Jeth* (May-June).

(c) *Sāwani*, cut in *Sāwan* (July-August). This is also called *sāthi,* because it ripens in sixty (*sāth*) days.

(d) *Jarhan* or *lain*, sown in small seed beds and transplanted. This is the winter rice crop and is cut in *Aghan* (November-December), whence it is also known as *aghani*.

479. In North Oudh the distinction is—

(a) *Dhān*, the autumn rice crop.

(b) *Jarhan,* the winter crop. In Gorakhpur the autumn crop is also known as *bhadai*, as it is cut in *Bhādon* (August-September), and the winter crop as *jarhan* or *aghani*.

480. In Bareli the sowings are as follows:

(a) *Gaja*: The first sowings made in *Baisākh* (April-May), and cut in *Sāwan* (July-August).

(b) *Bijua*: Sown in *Baisākh* or *Jeth* (May-June), and cut in *Bhādon* (August-September).

(c) *Kundher*: Sown in *Phāgun* (February-March), and cut in *Asārh* (June-July).

(d) *Rutiha*, or *rusota*: The regular sowings at the usual season (*rut*). These sowings are either *khundhar*, where the water is banked up in the fields; or *sukhauna*, where the ground is ploughed and sown broadcast in the usual manner.

481. *Boro* in the eastern districts is a poor rice transplanted, in December and January, in the mud on the banks of streams and lakes.

482. *Chanau* in Gorakhpur is rice sown broadcast in the beds of tanks. Various kinds of wild rice are grown in low damp situations such as *pasai* in Bareli and the *tekna, sengar, usahan, dhūnsi* and *sokan* in the eastern districts.

483. Land which has been under a rice crop is known as

ghoti in Bundelkhand, the Lower Doab and Benares; and *dhankar* in the western districts. A field under preparation for rice cultivation is *biās* in Rohilkhand.

484. Fresh waste lands ploughed up for rice sowings are *kurhil* in the east districts. The preparation of a rice field is *gilli* in Azamgarh. A nursery for rice is in the east of the province *behnaur* or *behan*; in the western districts *panīr*, in Bundelkhand *jāyi*, and in Delhi *pīad*. The word *ber* is similarly used in Cawnpur. The seed, after being soaked and germinating before being sown in the nursery, is in Azamgarh *jarui*. Rice seedlings are *bīchra*, and the clumps of transplanted seedlings are *bān* in the eastern districts. To transplant rice is *ropna* or *baithāna*. The fresh shoots thrown up after the crop is cut are *gaunji*, and the first shoots when it springs up are *jarui*.

Section V—Indian Corn or Maize (Zea mays)

485. Maize is *makka* or *makai*. In the east districts *junhari* or *jundari* or *junhār*, which is properly applied to *juār* (*Holcus sorghum*), is used. In the Upper Doab the stalk is *pharra* or *phatera*, and in the east districts *laktha*. The broken stalk is in Gorakhpur *tiltha*. The unripe ear is in the Upper Doab *gūl*. When ripe it is generally called *bhutta*; in the west districts *kukri*; in Eta *bhutiya* or *andiya*; and in Bundelkhand *junhari*. The ear roasted is in Bundelkhand *gada* or *gadgade*. The empty cob after the grain is beaten out of it is in the Doab *gūli* or *gūliya*; and the grain beaten out of it is called *nanha nāj*. The hair on the ear is *bāl*, the male ear *chanwar* in the Upper Doab; the sheath of the cob is in the eastern districts *khūha*.

Section VI—Large Millet (Holcus sorghum)

486. This is generally *juār*; in the Central Doab *jundi* or *junhari*. The produce in the spring harvest (*rabi*) is *umra* (?) and in the autumn harvest (*kharif*) *sarheti* (?) The chief varieties are *joginia*, a large red kind; *baunia*, white and dwarf; *piria* or *sāer*, the head bends down and it ripens late; *bāsmati*, a fragrant variety; *jhalara*, a grey inferior variety with spread ears; *chāhcha*, the grain lies concealed in the husk which is hard; *latphikra* or *latughar*, like the *piria* but inferior; *jethi*, sown for fodder; *singhia*, with a long thin softish stalk and very white grain; *sūar munkki*, the head bends down. It is so called from its supposed likeness to a pig's head; *dogadda* or *daleria*, has two grains in one husk.

487. The stalks cut up for fodder are *chari* or *karbi*, and in Bundelkhand *karwi*. In Bundelkhand, when the plant first germinates it is called *kura*, and the young plants are *poiya*. The ears are in Bundelkhand *bhutiya*, in the Central Doab *bhutta*; in the Upper Doab *gupha* or *guphi*.

488. A large stack of the stalks collected for fodder is *chhaur* in Delhi. This comprises several smaller stacks called *syi*. In some districts, as in Rohilkhand, this is called *garri* and elsewhere *kundar* and *kharai*.

Section VII—The Small Bulrush Millet *(Holcus spicatus* or *Pencillarian spicata)*

489. This is generally *bājra*, also in parts of Oudh and the Doab *lahra*, in east Gorakhpur *masuria janer*. *Bājri* is a smaller species and ripens a month earlier; and also sometimes means the stalk used as fodder. The stalk in the Upper Doab *phatera*, and in Bundelkhand *patiya*. When the plant begins to throw out shoots the phrase is in the Upper Doab *kainas phūt āti hai* and in the Central Doab *ikuya*. When the ear begins to show itself the phrases are in the Upper Doab *kahiba nazar āta*; and in the Central Doab *gulhat hoti hai, khet guliha raha*, or *khet kuthiya raha hai*. The heads when blighted and grainless are in Cawnpur *kandwa*. The fluffy flowers are in the Upper Doab *būr* or *būra*.

Section VIII—The Small Millets

490. These are—

(1) *Kāun, kakuni*, or *kangri* (*Panicum italicum*).
(2) *Sānwān* or *shāmākh* (*Panicum mileaceum*).
(3) *Manrūa, minrua, makra*. In the eastern districts the

empty dry ears after the grain has been taken out are *khūha*; the stalks are *narai*, and *bhāka* the green ears roasted for food.

(4) *Chenwa, chīna, chena,* or *chen* (*Panicum frumentosum*).[36]

(5) *Kodon, kodo* (*Paspalum frumentaceum*).

Section IX—Pulses

491. Among the pulses are the following:

Arhar generally; in the eastern districts *rahar*;[37] in the Upper Doab *tuār* (*Cytisus cajan*). The dry stalks are generally in the eastern districts *rahtha* or in Azamgarh *rahretha*. The pod is in Bundelkhand *kons*, and in other places *chhīmī*. The chaff is in Gorakhpur *chhimaur*. This and the other pulses when

[36] 'The garden crop *chena* is sown in *Phāgun* (February-March) and reaped in *Chait* (March-April), usually. This being the hot weather, extensive irrigation is required and it is a precarious crop'. Hence:

Chena jī ka lena
Chaudah pāni dena,.
Byār chale to na lena na dena.

(You may irrigate your Chena as much as you like, but a blast will destroy it, and you get nothing for your pains.) See Register no. 7, Settlement Shelf, *c.* 1888, Gorakhpur Collectorate Records; and Beames, *Supplemental Glossary*, s.v. *chena*.

[37] *Arhar dāl*, or *rahari* in local parlance, is considered a delicacy in eastern U.P. Ram Gharib Chaube, the Gorakhpur ethnographer, cites the following stanza from the legendary rural poet Ghāgh in praise, *inter alia*, of *arhar*:

Rahari kai dāl, silhati bhāt;
kāgji nibua hoe jo tāt;
bhainsi kai dahi sakh as hoya;
banika nain parose joya;
ūnch atariya madhur batās;
kahen Ghāgh tahān bhog vilās.

(The pulse of arhar and the rice of Silhat; the small lime of good flavour. The curd of buffalo's milk as white as a conchshell; If a woman with bright eyes serves the dinner. A high storeyed [multi-storeyed] house and a pleasant breeze—Ghagh says this is real enjoyment). Chaube also provides a variant with *urad dāl* and piping hot *tarka* of *ghee* as the additional ingredients constituting '*bhog vilas*'. *See North Indian Notes and Queries*, vol. IV, no. 11 (Feb. 1895). no. 441.

sprouting are known as *dūla* or *dewala* in the Doab. Bread made from this, gram (*chana*) and *mung* is *bhatula, gankar, gākar, angākar, girdi, bhaura,* and *batti.*

492. *Mūng* (*Phaseolus mungo*)—The plants are in Bundelkhand *baula*, and the pods *kons*. The stalks used for fodder are *jhora*.

493. *Urad* or *māsh* (*Phaseolus radiatus*)—There are several varieties such as *kachchia, siāh, khūjūa* and *chikra*. The pods are *kons* in Bundelkhand. *Uradi* is a smaller similar grain.

494. *Moth* or *mothi* (*Phaseolus aconitifolius*)—The stalks used for fodder are *jhora* and in Delhi *ghara* or *kurar*.

495. *Masūr* (*Ervum hirsutum*).

496. Miscellaneous—Among these are *gawār* (*Cyamopsis psoraloides*), *darahri, bhaimāns, barhia* (eastern districts); *baijila* is a black pulse in the eastern districts.

Section X—Peas (Pisum sativum)

497. The larger variety is *matar. Kirāo* in the eastern districts is a smaller variety often sown with barley when the crop is called *jaukirāi*. The varieties in the eastern districts are the large white (*ujla* or *barka*) and the small black kind (*kāla* or *chhota* or *chhutka*). There is a variety known as *batra* in Jhansi. In Eta the varieties are *tora, kora, bara,* and *safed*. When the plant first appears above ground it is in Eta *akhua* or *ankhua*; when the pod appears the phrase is *choiya ho rahi hai*; and when the pod is fully formed it is called *phali*. The unripe pod is *ghenti*. In Azamgarh *phonka* are the young shoots used for pottage.

Section XI—Gram (Cicer arietinum)

498. Gram is generally *chana*, and to the east of the province *rahila* or *lona*, the latter of which is more properly the oxalic and acetic acid which forms on the leaves. In Bundelkhand *chhola* means gram, but this is usually the young pod of the plant. The varieties are *pīla*, with a yellow pointed grain (also known in the eastern districts as *rakswa, chaptāi* and *kasāri*); *kassa*, the superior kind; and *pachmel*, a mixture of *pīla* and *kassa*. There is also the smaller variety known as *chani* and *batūri*, and the *kābuli*. The young plant as it appears above ground is called in Eta *iksua*; in Bundelkhand *kura*; and in Gorakhpur *dopattiya*. The young leaves used as pot herbs are *sāg* or *bhāji*. The pod is *ghegra* or *gheghra* or *ghenti*; in Benares *dhūndi* (or more properly *dhenda, dhendha* or *dhinrha*); *ghitri* in Rohilkhand; *tāt* in Delhi; in Bundelkhand *dhauri*; and in other places *ghenti*. *Patpar, chatka, gheghra* and *satpar* are properly the pod when somewhat unripe. *Būt* in Bundelkhand is used for the ripe pod. When the flower appears the phrase is *patpari ho rahi hai* in Eta; and when the grain appears it is *nimona* or *gheghra ho rahi hai*. The husk of gram is *chhikar*, and to the east *bhūsi*. Gram injured by rain is in Delhi *birra*. Land under a crop of gram is in Rohilkhand *chaniyāda*; in Delhi *chaniāl* and *umri*; in the Lower Doab *onr*, and in other places *chanara*.

Section XII—Sugarcane (Saccharum officinarum)[38]

499. Sugarcane is known to the west of the province as *īkh* and *ganna*; and to the east *ūkh*. Among the varieties are *agaul* (Eta); *agkoli* (Bareli), a soft large whitish cane good for eating; *baraukha* (Rohilkhand, Central Doab and Benares), thin, with a reddish hard bark—the juice is sweet and thick; *bejhar* (Delhi); *bhūra surtha* (Doab); *chīn* (Rohilkhand and Doab); *chitura* (Cawnpur); or in Oudh *katāra*, a thick edible cane with a light-green coloured bark; *chun* (Bareli), a small hard red cane; *dantūr* (Bareli), a very soft cane, good for eating and makes first-class molasses; *dhaur, dhaul* (throughout the province), a hard thin whitish cane which stands water well; *dhūmar* (Doab); *digilchīn* (Eta); *gogla* (Eta); *gharari* (Delhi); *kāghazi* (Bareli), similar to the *agkoli*, *kālāganda* or

[38] The best late-nineteenth-century source on the crop and its products is S.M. Hadi, *The Sugar Industry of the United Provinces of Agra and Oudh* (Allahabad, 1902). For a recent discussion of the culture of sugarcane and the manufacture of indigenous sugars, see Shahid Amin, *Sugarcane and Sugar in Gorakhpur*, chapter III.

kālāgenra (Doab and Oudh); *kālāsurtha* (Delhi); *karba* (Doab); *katāra* (Rohilkhand and Benares); *kathori* (Doab); *khiwāhi* (Benares); *kināra* (Doab); *kitharwa* (Gorakhpur), an edible cane; *lakri* (Rohilkhand); *lalri* (Delhi); *manga, mango,* a biennial very luxuriant cane; *matna* (Doab), a thick cane with close knots giving thick juice; *mittan* (Bareli), similar to *agkoli; neuli, neula,* a soft sweet edible cane (Rohilkhand); *padara* (West Oudh and Rohilkhand), a non-edible cane grown merely for the juice; *pandia* (Bareli), a first-class cane much grown; *pansāi, pansāhi,* a thin cane, grown merely for the juice (Gorakhpur); *paunda,* the best edible cane, grown throughout the province; *rakhra, rakhri,* similar to the *dāntūr* (q.v.) but rather harder; *reora* (Benares); *sarauti* (Benares); *saretha* (Doab); *subia* (Cawnpur), same as *matna* (q.v.); *surtha* (Delhi); *tanka* (Cawnpur); *thun,* a very thick heavy cane (West Oudh and Rohilkhand).

500. A cane field is in the east of the province *ikhāri* or *ikhwāri*, and to the east *ukhāri* or *ukhwāri*. Land prepared for sugarcane is *bhadwār*; in parts of Rohilkhand, and the Doab *bhadwār parāl;* and in Shahjahanpur *pandri*. When the land is left fallow the autumn preceding the planting, the cane is said to be grown *paloch*. Sometimes an autumn crop is taken the season before planting the cane; this system is known as *khārog*. When cane is cultivated without irrigation a layer of leaves, grass, etc. is thrown over the seed, and acts as a sort of hot bed. This system is called *palwār* in Bundelkhand and in Cawnpur *paleo*. In Azamgarh the plough which leads the way in cane planting is called *chhinua*, the middle plough *paheia,* and the last *bhatua;* each row of seed is *mūr*, and the two first ploughs have a bundle of grass called *ledi* bound round them to widen the furrow (*harāi*). The first watering of cane is in the Upper Doab *palewa*, the second is *kora*, and the third *ākhiri*. Cane sprouting from the roots left since the previous season is known in Meerut as *moda* (which is properly the roots themselves), *mundha peri* (Doab and Rohilkhand), or *ratun*. When fresh seed is sown it is in Bareli *naulaf*. Sugarcane grown from cuttings is *bhatmai*. *Dusāhi, bastwa* or *karakh* is sugarcane sown after the autumn crop is cut. A nursery for cane is *hāpar*. The completion of the sugarcane harvest is *purvāi*. The earth is hoed once after the cane has sprouted. This is called in Bareli *andheria karna*. The chief hoeing is done in the month of *Asārh*, and is called in Bareli the *Asārhi kor*. When just sprouted the cane is called in Eta *kulha*, and in the eastern districts *poi*. The root is *thān* in Azamgarh; and *gohan* in the eastern districts are the sprouts when two or three feet high. At this stage it is in Eta *īkh* or *ikhāri*; when the knots become visible it is *ganna*, and when ready for cutting *gānda*. *Kothār* in the Upper Doab and *kāna* in Gorakhpur are applied to a plant attacked by the *sūndi* insect. The top of the cane cut up for seed is *agaund*, and in Bareli *phunkābīj*. In the Upper Doab the piece between two knots cut for eating is *gandka ganna*, and that cut for sowing *kānchi;* and in Gorakhpur *pataur*. The whole cane cut up for seed is *bel ka bīj*, *bīj barāi*, *painra* (Central Doab), in Gorakhpur *genri*, and in Azamgarh *painr* or *gānr*. The sprouting eyes in the cane are *ānkh*. *Gulla* is a piece of cane chewed at one time and *chenph* is the refuse thrown out of the mouth. The hole where the cane slips are kept before planting is *bīgadha* in Rohilkhand; in the Doab *bijara*, and in the eastern districts *khāta*.

501. The leaves at the top and the upper part of the cane are known as *pāt, āg, agāo, agaura, agīn, gaundi*.

502. In the eastern districts the green top cut for fodder is *genra* or *genr*. In Azamgarh *masganda* is the top of the cane. The dry leaves at the top are in Gorakhpur *patai*, and in the Upper Doab *pāti*.

503. A sprout of cane is *āk*. A branch springing from the bottom and injuring the plant is in the Upper Doab *karanjwa*, and at the latter stage *kanas*. The knots in the cane are in the Doab *poi* or *gānth*, and in other places *por* or *pora*.

504. A bundle of five canes is *painja* in the Doab. Twenty-one *painja* make one *phāndi*; a small bundle is *jūri*.

505. Among the preparations of sugar may be mentioned *rāb*, the undrained raw sugar; *gur, mithāi, bheli* or *dhosa* which

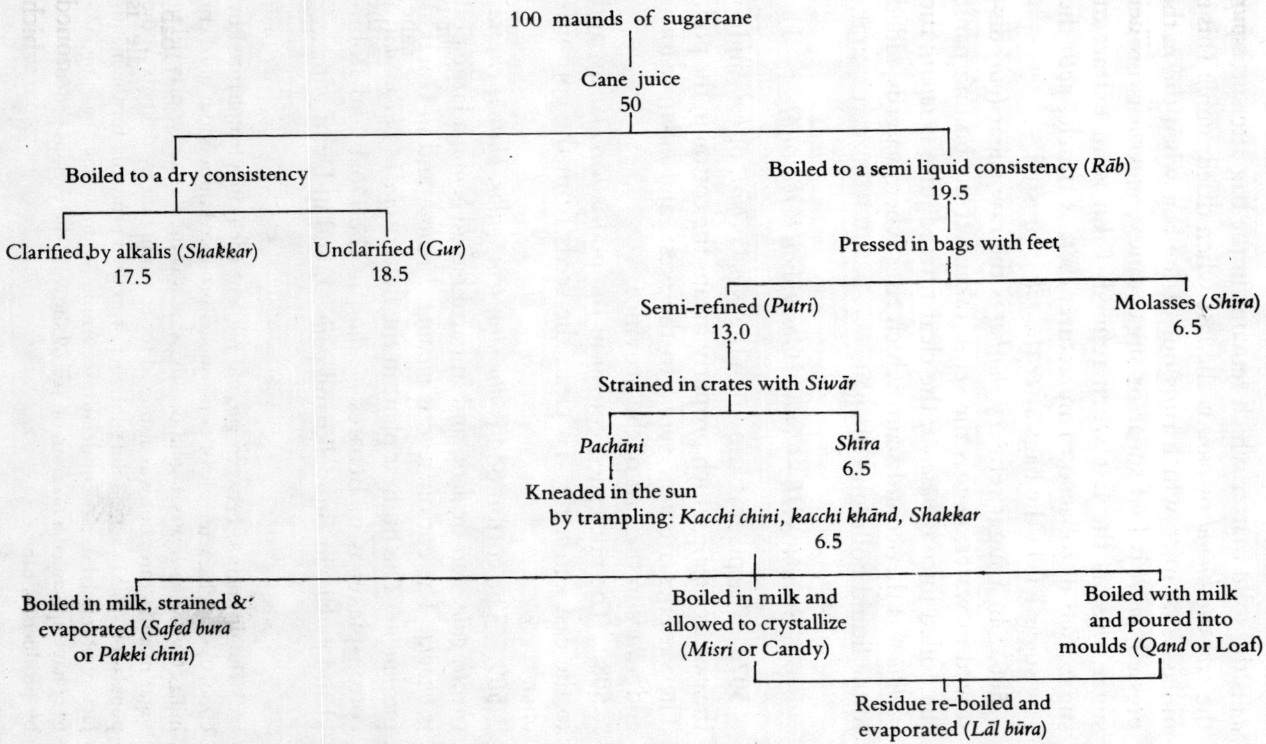

Source: Based on H. Z. Darrah, 'Note on Sugar Cultivation in NWP and Oudh', GOI: Rev. & Agr., Agr. A, May 1884, no. 35, NAI. The numerals below Cane juice, *Rāb*, etc. refer to the yield per 100 maunds of sugarcane. The work of the sugar refiner ends with converting *gur* or *rāb* into *chīni*, *khānd* or *shakkar*. *Safed bura*, *misri* and *qand*—the still more refined forms of sugar—are manufactured by confectioners (*halwaīs*).

are the *rāb* boiled down for a longer time.[39] In Eta the *choyanda* is the solid matter which remains in the bag after pressing the *rāb*; the *khānd* or *būra* is the last when dried; *shīrah* is the molasses or juice which runs out of the bag when the *rāb* is pressed; *misri* is loaf sugar or sugar candy; *shakkar* is brown sugar; *chīni* is the last when refined; *kakai* is an extract of sugar used in tobacco manufacture; *chota* is treacle; *potri* the raw sugar left in the bags after the *rāb* is pressed.

506. In a sugar refinery *sharbat* is the raw sugar (*gur*) dissolved in water; *maīl* is the scum taken off the boiling pans; the boiled juice is *pasāwa;* the clear filtered juice is *topāri*; the *pachhāni* is the second scum which rises when water is added to the liquid boiling in the pan.

Section XIII—Cotton (Gossypium herbaceum)

507. The plant is known in the west as *bāri*, or *ban*; and to the east as *kapās*, which properly means the cotton in the pod. The varieties are *desi*, *narma* to the west, and *kūkti, marwa,* and *jethwa* in the east of the province.

508. The uncleaned cotton in the pod is *bāri, kapās*, and to the east *kacchi rui*. To clean the seeds from the cotton is *otna*.

509. The cotton pod is *dhendra, tēnt, gūlar, bhitna, ghegra, ghenti, gāla, dori* or *dora,* and in Farukhabad *bonra*; a large pod is *bhogla*. The cotton seed is *binaula, binaura,* and in Gorakhpur *binaur*. The highest plant in the field is *sạrdār, bhogal dāi*; a cotton-picker is in Benares *binahar*; in the Doab and Rohilkhand *paikār*, in Bundelkhand *paihāra*, and in Delhi *pūi*.

[39] The distinction between *gur* and *rāb*, not adequately emphasized by Crooke, was characteristic of crude sugars produced throughout northern India. *Gur* or *bheli* was a solid dry mass; it was used as a raw material in sugar manufacture, but was also used for consumption by the bulk of the population. *Rāb* (a semi-solid substance) was used primarily for the manufacture of refined sugar. For details, see Amin, *Sugarcane and Sugar,* pp. 53–61. I have appended a diagram on p. 109 showing the various products and by-products of cane.

510. The stages in the growth of the plant are as follows:
When the first leaf shows—*Dīvala hona* in the Upper Doab.
The next stage—*Dopatti* in the Upper Doab.
The third stage—*Chaupatti* in the Upper Doab.
The pod bursting is *kapās khilna,* or *tent āna*, in the Upper Doab.

511. The flower is *pūri* or *puriya*; when the flower shows itself the phrases are *pūri lagna* or *bāri lagna*.

512. Raw cotton is *bạnga*. When the cleaned cotton is one-fourth of the uncleaned cotton (*kapās*), it is said in Rohilkhand to be *chauntāli*; when one-third *tihāi*; and when two-fifth *pachdūli*.

Section XIV—Tobacco (Nicotiana tobaccum)

513. Tobacco is *tambāku* or *tamāku*.

514. The varieties are *desāwari* or *desi*; *kalkatiya, katki* or *dhatūriya*; and *wilāyati*.

515. When manufactured there are the following varieties:

Surti, dry chewing tobacco; *galāwat*, the coarsest kind; *khundui*, broken tobacco; *karua*, second class; *dorasa*, a mixed tobacco of fair quality; *khamīrah,* scented and mixed with spices; *lāla shāhi*, the coarse kind used by the poorer classes in Oudh; *sādah,* plain or in common use; *nās*, snuff.

516. The stalks are in the Upper Doab *danthla*; the refuse, broken leaves and stalks are in Cawnpur *jhalla*; the blisters which come on the leaf when the plant is ripe are *dudri* in Cawnpur. The seed capsules are in the Doab *bonra; kanya* in the Doab are shoots which sometimes appear after the breaking-off of the head; the nipping of the leaf is in Azamgarh *badhiāna*, and a second crop raised from the roots is *dorja* or *dorji*.

Section XV—Opium Poppy (Papaver somniferum)

517. The poppy plant is *post* or *posta*. The advances made to the cultivators are *dādni* or *taqāvi*; the average produce per bigah *parta*; the rough measurement of the fields *lattha bandi*; the poppy petals *patti*; the poppy heads *bonri, dhondh, dhendri;* and in the eastern districts *dhendr*. The cakes of poppy petals are in the east districts *roti* or *thonta*. The instrument used for piercing the pod is *nashtar*, and to the east *naharni*;[40] to lance the pod is *pāchhna*. The milky juice which exudes is *dūdh*. The opium yield is *māl*.

518. The scraper used for collecting the coagulated opium off the pod is a shell called *sīpi* or *sutaha*. The gathering of the opium is *kāchhna*.

519. The grain of the prepared opium is *dāna*; the consistency *jharti*; the shell *kholāra*; and the oilcake prepared from the seed *pinna* or *pīni*.

520. The refuse opium, consisting of the washing of the vessels, is *dhoi* or *dhoan*. In the east districts the refuse scraped from the vessels is *khurchan*; the impurities in opium are *joga*; the juice which drains off the fresh opium is to the west *pasīna,* and to the east *paseo* and *pasewa*. This is inspissated on rags, and the product is *kafa*. The fluid opium used in pasting the leaves on the cakes is *lewa*, and the cakes themselves *goti*.

521. *Madak* is made by boiling down and inspissating the juice (*ras*) of pure opium or *kafa* for preference. This inspissated juice is in Gorakhpur *qimām*; with it is mixed cut-up

[40] The *naharni* 'consists of four lancets bound together in a packet with a space the thickness of the string between each lancet. The points are inserted at the top of the capsule half through the integument, and drawn down the capsule to the stalk. The operation takes place in the afternoon, and by the next morning the wound is covered with matter of a light-brown colour. This should be gathered (*kāchchna*, hence the name of the caste *kāchhi*) as soon as possible before noon. It is scraped off the capsule with a little iron scoop called *sutuha*. Those who have no *sutuhas* use shells or bits of bamboo. Two or three days after the first incision a second is made, and the gathering process is repeated. These incisions are generally sufficient to exhaust the plant's supply of sap. The matter having been collected, is worked up with the hand, divided into little lots of a ser or so each, and allowed to dry. It is then crude opium and is ready for delivery at the factory'. *Azamgarh Settlement Report*, para 468.

betel leaves known as *jāsu*, and when the preparation is intended to be extra strong *ainchi*, the sediment which accumulates in the stem of the pipe, is added. The pipe used for smoking *madak* is *mahru.* A small piece of *madak* known as *dāna* or *chhita* is ignited in the bowl of the pipe with a spill of charcoal called *qalam*, which is held by a small pair of tongs, *chimti*. *Chandu* is the distilled juice of pure opium and is smoked in an earthen bowl (*chilam*) attached to a stem (*nigāli*).

Section XVI—Hemp (Cannabis sativa)

522. The plant itself is *gānja*. The leaves are known under the names of *bhang, siddhi, patti* and *sabzi* or *sabji*; a favourite way of taking the drug is in the form of a sweetmeat, *mājūn* or *majūm*. *Charas* is the resin which exudes from the flowers and leaves. The male plant is *marda*, the female *mādi*, and the hermaphrodite plants *khasia*. The flat *gānja* is *chapta*, and the round *gānja gol; chūr* is the broken *gānja*.

Section XVII—Indigo (Indigofera tinctoria)

523. The cultivated plant is *nīl*. The wild indigo (*Wrightia tinctoria*) is *dudhi*, or *indarjāu* in Bundelkhand. In the Upper Doab *gaud* is native indigo. Indigo planted before the rains and irrigated by artificial means is *jamauwa*. If let to grow on to the second year it is *khūnti*. Indigo sown at the beginning of the rains is *asārhu* or *naudha*. In Bengal the chief sowing (*bāwag*) is the *Kātiki* in October; in Tirhut the *Phālguni* in February; and in the North-West Provinces and Oudh *Asārhi* or *Asārhu* in June.

524. The system of obtaining the plant from cultivators on advances is *bandi* to the west and *dādni* to the east. When the cultivator sows and sells the plant independently it is *khush kharīd*. The special cultivation carried out by the planters themselves is *zara'at*. The divisions of their estates are *zila*.

Section XVIII—Other Dyes

525. Among other dyes may be mentioned *āl (Morinda citrifolia)*, used for dyeing the coarse red *kharua* cloth.[41]

526. The root is divided into classes known in Cawnpur as *bāna*. The best and thinnest roots are in Jalaun *bhara*, in Jhansi and Cawnpur *bāra*, and in Cawnpur *hārgharka*. The second sized roots are in Jalaun *jharan*; in Jhansi *pachmer*; and in Cawnpur *lari*. The thickest roots are in Jalaun *ghatiya*; in Jhansi *lari*; and in Cawnpur *pachhkat*, or *katerāo*.

527. Safflower (*Carthamus tinctorius*) to the west is *kusum* and to the east *barre*. *Darhua* in Azamgarh is a means of distilling oil from the seeds.

528. *Dawāi* in Jalaun gives a brilliant red dye.

529. *Hara* (*Terminalia bellerica*) gives a yellow dye (Jalaun).

Section XIX—Oilseeds

530. Among the oilseeds are:

(1) *Sarson*—Mustard (*Sinapis dichotoma*).

(2) *Lāhi, rāi*—Mustard (*Sinapis ramosa*).

(3) *Til*, sesamum—(*Sesamum orientale*); *tilli* is a variety with a white grain which is sown with the autumn crop in the eastern districts. *Pinna* is oilcake produced especially from *til* and poppy.

(4) *Duān, seohān*—Colza. It is grown on the edges of fields and is hence called *mendha*.

(5) *Alsi* to the west and *tīsi* to the east—Linseed (*Linum usitatissimum*).

(6) *Kusum* to the west; *barre* to the east, safflower (*Carthamus tinctorius*). The seeds used for oil-making are *kur* in the Upper Doab.

[41] Crooke provided the botanical names of almost all the dyes, fibres, oil-seeds, crops and vegetables listed by him. However, given the fact that even Grierson admitted to some errors in his nomenclatures, botanical exactitude cannot be expected in Crooke. For *kharua* cloth, see Appendix B, para 745.

(7) *Arand, andi or anda* to the west; to the east *renr*—The castor-oil plant (*Ricinus communis*); a plantation is to the east *renrwar.*
(8) *Mahua (Bassia latifolia).*
(9) *Kurva* (*Argemone mexicana*)
(10) *Māl kangni (Celastrus paniculatus).*
(11) *Jamālgota*—Croton (*Croton tiglium*).[42]

Section XX—Fibres

531. *Bhang (Cannabis sativa)*, see Section XVI.
532. *San (Crotolaria juncea).* The stalk is *kondar*; a bundle of fibres is *lachhe.* If short stalks remain in the fibre it is called *arjha* or tangled. If then cleaned it is *tilohra.* In Jhansi the seed is *sanaiya*, the stalks *sansutali*, and after the bark has been removed *sanaura.* The coarse fibres used for basket making are in Banda *silaua.*
533. *Patsan* or *latia (Hibiscus cannabinus).* The fibre is *tilohra.*
534. *Khans (Imperata spontanea).*
535. *Dāb* or *dābk (Poa cynosuroides).*
536. *Bakhauta.*
537. *Bhābar* or *bhābari.*

Section XXI—Betel (Piper betel)

538. This is *pān.* The varieties are *kaker*, with a large leaf and mild flavour; *desāwari*, with a round leaf and a sweet taste; *kapūri*, a long leaf, mild but slightly bitter; *bangla*, sweet. The mound on which it is grown is *bhīt* or *bhīti*; a betel garden is to the west *barej* or *bareja*; and to the east *baraith.* The rows in the plantation are in Cawnpur *mandha*; in Partabgarh *antar*; in Azamgarh *mūr* or *khāt.* The intervening passages are in Azamgarh *pāh* or *pairah.* In each row there are in Cawnpur 30 *kuntra* or main props; in each *kuntra* 8 or 9 *gāt* or minor props; and in each *gāt* 6 *dhapiān* or lumps of clay in

[42] Better known as an extremely effective laxative.

which the plants are sown. The supports of the plants are in Azamgarh *sarei* or *kameia*. The supports of the shed are in the east districts *koro*; the walls *tatti*; and the roof *māro*. The young seedlings for planting are *bel* in Cawnpur. They are watered from an earthen vessel called *loti*.

539. A packet of 50 leaves is in Azamgarh *kaunri*; a bundle of 200 leaves is *dholi*; 60 *dholi* make a *leso*. A leaf of betel rolled up for chewing is *bīra* or *gilauri*. Betel is stored in the *choli*, *gadauka* or *dona*. The betelnut, the fruit of the *Areca catechu*, is *supāri*.

Section XXII—Garden Crops

540. These are divided into—(1) edible roots, (2) gourds, (3) miscellaneous.

541. EDIBLE ROOTS:

(1) Potatoes (*Solanum tuberosum*), *ālu*. The ridges on which they are grown are *khāwa* in Cawnpur.
(2) Yams (*Dioscorea sativa*), *ratālu*.
(3) Sweet potato (*Batatas edulis*), *shakarqand*.
(4) *Zaminqand (Dioscorea bulbefera)*.
(5) *Ghuiyān, arui, arwi, kachchu—Arum colocasia*.

542. GOURDS:

(1) *Tarbūz, tarbūza, kalindo* (Farukhabad), the water-melon (*Cucurbita citrullus*).
(2) *Kharbūz, kharbūza*, the melon (*Cucumis utilatiassimus*).
(3) *Karela*, the melon (*Momordica charantia*) [bitter gourd].
(4) *Lauka, lauki*, the bottle gourd (*Cucurbita logenaria*).
(5) *Taroi* (*Cucumis acutangulus*).
(6) *Phūt*, musk melon (*Cucumis momordica*).
(7) *Khīra*, cucumber (*Cucumis sativus*).

543. MISCELLANEOUS VEGETABLES:

(1) *Adrak*, ginger (*Zingiber officinale*).
(2) *Ajwāin*, aniseed (*Ligusticum ajowain* and *Ptychotis ajowan*.) (*Ajwāin khurāsāni* is *Hyosciamus niger*.)
(3) *Ajmūd*, parsley (*Apium involucratum* or *Petroselinum sativum*).

(4) *Bākla*, a kind of bean (*Faba major*?).
(5) *Baingan, baigan*, the egg plant (*Solanum melongena*) [aubergine]
(6) *Bhindi* [okra]
(7) *Chachenda*, the snake gourd (*Trichosanthes anguina*).
(8) *Chaulāi*, a pot herb (*Amaranthus frumentaceus*).
(9) *Gājar*, carrot (*Daucus carota*).
(10) *Gobhi*, cauliflower.
(11) *Haldi, hardi*, turmeric (*Curcuma longa*).
(12) *Isabghol* (*Phantogo isabghola*).
(13) *Kāhu (Lactuca sativa)*.
(14) *Karamkalla*, cabbage (*Brassica olereacea*).
(15) *Kasni* (*Cichorium endivia*).
(16) *Khurfa*, purslane (*Portulaca sativa*).
(17) *Lahsan*, leek or garlic (*Allium sativum*); a clove of leek is *pothi*.
(18) *Lobiā*, a bean (*Dolichos sinensis*).
(19) *Marsa* (*Amaranthus mangostanus*).
(20) *Methi*, fenugreek (*Tirgonella foenugraecum*).
(21) *Mirich*, capsicum (*Capsicum frutescens*).
(22) *Mūli*, radish (*Raphanus sativus*).
(23) *Pālak*, spinach (*Spinacea oleracea*).
(24) *Piyāz*, onion (*Allium coepa*).
(25) *Podīna, pudīna*, mint (*Mentha sativa*).
(26) *Ronsa*, a bean (*Dolichos sinensis*).
(27) *Sem*, a bean (*Phaseolus magnus*).
(28) *Shaljam, shalgham,* a turnip (*Brassica rapa*).
(29) *Singhāra*, the water caltrop (*Trapa bispinosa*).
(30) *Souf*, aniseed.
(31) *Soya*, a leafy vegetable, analogous to *pālak*.
(32) *Zīra,* cummin (*Cuminum cyminum*).

VIII Insects and Causes of Injury to Crops

Section I—Destructive Insects and Diseases

544. Among these are (in alphabetical order):

Agaya, a disease in rice by which the whole plant is burnt up, from *āg*, fire—Eta.

Agia, makari, a spider which attacks the buds of millets before the flower forms, chiefly due to want of rain—Cawnpur.

Āl, an insect which attacks safflower—Upper Doab.

Babhani, a blight in sugarcane—Azamgarh.

Badhiya, a disease affecting millets, sugarcane and Indian corn, which prevents the head from shooting.

Baguliya, a white spot appearing in the leaf of millets causing them to wither up, caused by non-rotation of crops or excessive or insufficient ploughing—Bareli.

Bahādura, a disease which attacks gram and pease.

Bahara, blight in cereals caused by the sharp west wind—Eta.

Bakuli, a green caterpillar destructive to rice.

Bāla, a grub which eats the young plants of wheat and barley when they are about six inches high—Benares.

Bambha, a blight which attacks the millet *sānwān (Panicum fumentaceum)*, cf. *bhanbha*—Azamgarh.

Bangka, banka, katua, an aquatic beetle which eats rice—east districts.

Barat, a disease which affects rice.

Bhābi, a kind of weevil destructive to wood and grain.

Bhanbha, vide bambha—Azamgarh.

Bhaunra, bhaunri, an insect which attacks millets in dry weather—Doab.

Bhori, a blight in opium—Azamgarh.

Bhungi, an insect which eats the leaves of sugarcane—Partabgarh.

Bhurli, eats leaves of the castor oil plant and pulses—Azamgarh.

Chanchana, an insect which burrows into the ribs of the leaf of the tobacco plant—Eta.

Charka, a blight on the transplanted rice—Azamgarh.

Chempah, a small dark-coloured insect which injures the *arhar (Cytisus cajan)* and tobacco—Eta.

Chheda, an insect like a weevil (*Calandria granaria*).

Chhipwa, an insect which eats the stalks of pulses and makes the leaves crumple up—Doab.

Chitya, a minute insect which attacks the *singhāra* plant, or water caltrop—Cawnpur.

Chinguran, a disease of the tobacco plant—Azamgarh.

Dakhana, a disease of sugarcane in which the tops wither—Gorakhpur.

Dhāra, a sort of mildew which dries up the grain in wheat—East Oudh and Gorakhpur.

Dehia, Dibiya, a disease in tobacco—Meerut.

Dhola, Dhora, an insect which attacks the leaves of the *til (Sesamum orientale)* and stored grain.

Dibiya, vide dehia.

Dīmak, the white ant.

Diwār, a grub which attacks the roots of sugarcane—Partabgarh.

Dudka, a disease of the rice plant.

Durkhi, an insect which ravages young indigo, tobacco, mustard and wheat.

Gadhela, gadahila, vide gindar.

Gandaila, vide gindar.

Gandhiya, vide gindar.

Gandhi, an insect injurious to rice caused by prevalence of south winds and excess of rain.

Gandhili, a blight in betel—Azamgarh.

Gandhuki, a small green fly which attacks those rices of

which the fronds come out of the leaves of *gandhi*—Cawnpur.

Gareri, a very small insect of whitish colour which ravages millets—Eta.

Gendwa, a worm which attacks millets—Meerut.

Ghuhan, a small yellow insect which attacks the *singhāra* or water caltrop—Cawnpur.

Ghonghi, *vide gindar*.

Ghun, a weevil destructive to wood and stored grain.

Ghungi, *vide gindar*.

Gindar, an insect very destructive to growing pulses.

Ginja, an insect like a centipede which is fatal to cattle if eaten.

Girwi, gerui, a disease of the cereals in which the plant dries up and assumes a reddish colour. It is caused by excess of winter rains and east wind. In *girwi* the plant turns red and the ear black; in *harda* the plant is yellow and the ear black.

Gobh, is produced by the prevalence of severe winds, and consists in the plant giving out little shoots which weaken it—Meerut.

Gobrawa, blight in betel—Azamgarh.

Guduri, an insect which attacks pease and gram—Azamgarh.

Gumta, a small white caterpillar which attacks the buds of cotton—Cawnpur.

Hadda, a white stem growing out of the root of the tobacco plant and throwing it far out of the soil—Eta.

Halda, harda, a disease in cereals in which the plant withers and assumes a yellow tinge, cf. *girwi*.

Jaunchi, a kind of smut in barley and wheat in which the ears produce no grain.

Jhānsi, an insect which attacks pulse and tobacco—east districts.

Jhola, a cold wind which affects wheat by drying up the ears—Upper Doab.

Jori, an insect which attacks gram in cold weather—Banda.

Jui or *jurai, vide gindar*.

Kajuri, a blight in opium—Azamgarh.

Kamra, the palmer worm, attacks pulses and cotton.

Kansi, a disease in rice.

Kapti, an insect which attacks young rice and tobacco—east districts.

Karanjwa, (1) a branch springing from the root of sugarcane and injuring it, (2) smut in barley—Meerut.

Kāri, a disease in sugarcane which dries up the juice and blackens the stalk—Partabgarh.

Katri, a disease of the rice plant.

Katua, *vide bangka*.

Katuwa, an insect which appears in years of drought and attacks the roots of wheat and gram—Banda.

Khaira, a blight which attacks rice and turns the ears an orange colour and destroys them—east districts.

Khandwa, a disease produced by floods in the autumn harvest—Meerut.

Khapra, (1) an insect which attacks stored grain; (2) destroys young gram—Jhansi.

Khapariya, a very small white insect which sometimes damages rice—Eta.

Kīri, an insect which attacks stored grain.

Korhiān, disease in tobacco caused apparently by fungi—Azamgarh.

Kudhia, a disease in rice and millets caused by west winds—Gorakhpur.

Kukhi, kukuhi, an insect which injures the cold weather crops.

Kuswa, a blight in transplanted rice—Azamgarh.

Lāhi, plant lice—east districts.

Lākha, an insect which attacks wheat and cane—Cawnpur.

Lapha, blight in betel—Azamgarh.

Lāsi, a black insect which attacks wheat.

Lenhra, smut in wheat or barley—Azamgarh.

Māho, māhūn, attacks mustard and cotton.

Makoha, a red insect about an inch long that in excessively dry weather attacks millets, sugarcane, etc.—Eta.

Orna, small red insect which injures the water caltrop (*singhāra*)—Cawnpur.

Pāi, an insect which injures stored grain—Azamgarh.

Pansiwān, an insect which attacks rice in drought—Gorakhpur.

Pāpa, an insect which attacks stored grain.

Papaha, an insect which, in excessive cold, attacks millets and rice—Banda.

Pātha, an insect which attacks stored grain.

Patui, disease of the castor oil plant—Azamgarh.

Paia, indifferent fructification of the rice flower resulting in empty ears—Azamgarh.

Petāri, an insect which attacks stored grain.

Purwāi, a disease of the rice plant.

Rāta, vide girwi.

Ratua, vide girwi.

Ratwai, vide girwi.

Rori, vide girwi.

Sajara, opium blight—Azamgarh.

Sanwal, a disease in wheat and barley, caused by east winds and excessive rain—Eta.

Sehi, a small black insect which injures wheat, etc.

Seūn, a blight in cereals on account of which no grain is produced in the ear—Eta.

Silai, a small insect with dark red and brown body, which injures sugarcane, maize, etc.—Meerut.

Sūndi, a red coloured insect which attacks cotton, gram, and the castor oil plant.

Sūra, a large black beetle found in granaries which does no harm and is reverenced by grain merchants—Meerut.[43]

Sursāri, tiny black insect which does great damage in granaries—Meerut.

Tāra, a small green insect, ravages wheat and eats the roots of sugarcane; similar to *diwār* (q.v.)

43 An interesting case of the malevolent not being malevolent, and so becoming the object of worship.

Tāri, an insect which attacks grain crops and trees—Banda.

Thontha, thuntha, an insect which eats the pith in millets maize and sugarcane.

Titli, an insect which attacks cereals and blights the grain—Gorakhpur.

Tiddi, tinri, the locust.

Tunki, an insect which attacks rice—Azamgarh.

Uhhta, withering of crops from excessive drought—Eta.

Section II—Noxious Weeds

545. Among the noxious weeds are:

Akra, appears in wheat—Bareli.

Bat, weed which chokes rice; the same as *dhonda*, *dhondi* or *dhauni*.

Baisurai, a weed which injures the spring crops—Aligarh.

Bānsari, chokes crops in the Doab.

Bansi, injures rice—Bareli.

Birana, birna khar, a tough coarse grass, spreading over uncultivated lands which are inundated yearly. It is only removed by digging.

Bhangra (*Verbesina prostrata*), a small creeping weed with a white flower which injures rice—Bareli.

Chaupatta, a weed in wheat—Bareli.

Dābh, a coarse grass injurious to crops.

Dhauni, vide bat.

Dhonda, dhondi, vide bat.

Gargawa, a weed which chokes rice.

Jharna, injures rice—Bareli.

Kāns (*Saccharum spontaneum*), a most destructive grass—Bundelkhand.

Khurkha, a weed in opium.

Lankhassia, a weed in wheat—Bareli.

Motha, a coarse grass which grows in uncultivated land and injures the autumn crops—east districts.

Murkha, a weed which grows in opium.

Rāri, a coarse hard grass, infesting poor soils.

Ras, a grass which overspreads fallow fields.
Tokra, a parasitic plant which injures the poppy.

Section III—Miscellaneous

546. A stunted crop is *bhaita*; a blighted ear is *agda*. *Paiya* in Azamgarh is used of blighted rice in which the seed has not formed. *Bankta* is an irretrievably spoiled crop. In Azamgarh *bhamahar* is used of blighted millets, and *bhābh* of blight in the early autumn crops. Crops withered from drought are *jhiri* (used specially of wheat), *admarjāi* and, in the east districts, *muār*. Crops trodden down by cattle are *paimāl* or *mismar*—failure of seed is *bījmār, nirbīj* or *abīj*. Crops are laid by driving squalls—*bauchhār*, and wheat is withered by a dry wind called *jhola* in the Upper Doab. Crops laid by wind are *mocha* or *sulāya*. Fogs are *tusār* to the west, and to the east *kohr* or *kohes*. Hailstones are to the west *ola*; to the east *patthar* or *patthal, binaura* or *binaula*; in Jhansi *loiya*. Frostbite is *pāla* or *tāri*.

IX Labour Advances, Wages and Perquisites

Section I—Pay and Advances to Labourers

547. A labourer is *mazdūr*. In Benares *arhwal* is a day labourer; in Gorakhpur *anhāi*. *Barsodiya* and *barsāliya* are servants engaged in cultivation who contract for a year. Forced labour is *begār*. In Gorakhpur the *tīnbighaiya* is a man who receives three *bighās* of land rent-free and works for his master without remuneration in the agricultural season; the *pāriwāla* sometimes works for his master and sometimes for himself, and the *harwāha* or *halwāha* works almost entirely for his master.[44] A labourer's pay is *mazdūri*. When paid daily it is

[44] I have not come across any detailed account of the *tīnbighaiya* of Gorakhpur, though Crooke's description corroborates the point made by many students of rural India (Dharma Kumar, Chris Baker and Neeladri Bhattacharya) that in terms of actual earnings there is very little to distinguish the sharecropper from the agricultural labourer.

The brief and vague description of the *pāriwāla* is taken from Buchanan's early-nineteenth-century account of Gorakhpur. It forms part of a more general discussion of the various types of 'ploughmen' and is well worth reproducing in full:

> The first type of ploughmen are chiefly strangers, that come here for employment from the territory of the Nawab Vazir. . . In general they remain here during the ploughing and sowing season, lasting about 5 months, and perform only these labours.
>
> They are commonly allowed either 2 rupees a month with an allowance of grain, but not enough for their entire maintenance; or a full diet, and from 1 to 1½ rupee a month.
>
> The other two kinds of servants are such as reside at all seasons, and have been tied down by advances (*Sāwak* or *Bhot*) which they are not able to liquidate, nor can they procure stock, otherwise they would take land of their own. The money advanced, and which thus holds them in bondage, is often only 5 Rupees, and seldom exceeds 10, until of late, when some in

rozīnha or *agora*; *darmāha* is monthly wages; yearly wages is *sāliāna*. In the eastern districts *koranja* is an allowance of grain made to a servant in lieu of pay. Advances of pay to labourers is *dādni* or *peshgi* to the west, and to the east *agti* or *agor*. In Benares *harauri* is an advance of grain or money given to a ploughman when he is engaged. *Ajauri* is an advance, particularly to agricultural labourers. In eastern Oudh and Benares *bhāta*, and in Rohilkhand *bhanta*, are advances to ploughmen without interest.

---

order to secure workingmen have been obliged to advance as far as 50 rupees for each. They pay no interest.

The one kind of this class called *Pariyas* or *Pāriwāla* is most common in the eastern part of the district. They are the same as the *Dhuriyās* of Bihar, and work 2 days on their masters' (*gosainya*) fields and one day on their own. This is only during the ploughing season, and they only plough and sow for their master. During the remainder of the year they weed, water and reap their own field, and whatever leisure time they have, they work for daily hire, or reap at the usual allowance. The whole value of the stock, that is cattle and implements, does not exceed 30 rupees, where there are four oxen, and the use of this for one day is the hire for working two. In some cases the servant furnishes one half of the stock, in which case he works 2 days on his own field, and one on that of his master.

Haraya or *Chhathiya*: Most common in the western parts of the district, [*Haraya* or *Chhathiya*] work the whole year for their master having no land of their own. They are allowed daily a quantity of grain more than they can eat, and which may feed one or two children besides themselves, and they usually get 1/6, although some are content with 1/7 part of the 'whole produce' of land which they have cultivated, after deducting what is given to those who reap the portion they are not able to accomplish, and the whole charges of the farm, such as keeper of oxen, blacksmith, carpenter, etc. They may plough and sow 6 months, hoe two months, and repair their master's house one month. In some places the *hariya* only plough for their master, in which case they get 1/7 of the grain, making similar deductions, and without any additional allowance.'

Source: Buchanan-Hamilton, 'An Account of the Northern Parts of the District of Gorakhpur', *c.* 1811-13, MS Eur. D.92, Book IV, pp. 75–7, India Office Library, London.

Section II—Advances to Tenants

These may be divided as follows:

548. Advances to buy food—These are in Rohilkhand *bījkhād*, and in the eastern districts *khauhat, khaiyān,* or *khawāi.*

549. Advances to purchase seed—In Rohilkhand *bījkhād*, in the eastern districts *beng, bengat* or *bisār.* In Gorakhpur the usual phrase is *bengbisār. Agti* is also used in the same sense to the east, and in the other places *manni.*

550. Advances for purchase of cattle and sinking wells—*Taqāvi* in Rohilkhand.

551. Advances for marriages—*Taqāvi* in Rohilkhand, in Gorakhpur *biāhi* or *tauja.*

552. In Oudh the *dehi nānkar* is an allowance in money from the chief proprietor (*tāluqdār)* to the sub-proprietors. *Nānkār tankhuāhi* was an allowance made to various village officials (*qanungo, chaudhuri*). *Chhorwa* or *chharauwa* was an allowance made to lessees. *Chahārum* (one-fourth) and *deswan* (one-tenth) were originally grants to persons who cleared the forest and afterwards came to mean grants to old proprietors and influential residents.

Section III—Dues Paid by Tenants

553. These may be divided into (a) those paid to the resident artisans and other non-cultivating residents in the village. Such people are known as *parja, pajhar, pauni*, or *paunia* in the east of the province, and (b) cesses paid to special village servants, etc.

554. General cesses—*Agwār*, which according to Elliot is the first corn taken from the heap for the village servants, in Gorakhpur means the light grains which are carried by the wind in the process of winnowing in advance of the heap of cleaned grain (*rās*). In Jalaun the *haraiti* is grain given to village artisans at the autumn sowing season. At sowing season in *Kuār* (September-October), they receive as much grain as the two hands can hold. This is called *anjul* or *anjuri* in Bundelkhand; and in Benares *ajauli*. These dues of grains are also known as *khalihāni* or *kharihāni haq* in Gorakhpur; *bukka* (properly a handful of grain) is used in the same sense in Gorakhpur; *jaunra* or *jeora* in eastern districts. *Ākhat* is grain placed on a sieve[45] and given to servants, etc. at marriages and other ceremonies; *kaula, kaulia*, or *kakhiāli* is an armful of grain given at harvests. In Gorakhpur the general terms for these dues are *gānwhāi* or *deohāri*, which are properly offerings to the local village gods.

555 Special cesses paid to particular persons—The blacksmith (*lohār*) receives a fee from a member of a marriage procession who gets any work done by him. This is *kārihak* or *khariyak*. His remuneration for the repairs of the implements, etc. is *pharwār* or *lehna* in Fyzabad, and in Gorakhpur *pharpitāi*, or welding of the ploughshare.

556. The carpenter (*barhai*)—In Bareli he gets 2½ sers of grain per plough known as *nibauni*, and one sheaf per plough called *phīri*. In Azamgarh he receives *kolhāwān* and *pācharāwan* for keeping the cane-press in order; and for repairing other implements *sāli, pāthi, lahna, puri, barūa*, and *kharihāni*.[46]

[45] This is properly speaking *sūp*, a winnowing sieve, as opposed to a *chalni*, a sieve with holes in it. Crooke in his printed Glossary gives line drawings of both *sūp* and *chalni* and states that the *chalni* is used for less coarse grain. The crucial difference is that with *sūp* one spreads the grain and then makes it jump up (*phatakna̤*) by the action of the hands and fingers, thus separating the grain from the chaff; while in a *chalni* the finer particles pass through the innumerable holes at the bottom with the bigger grains remaining on top. Crooke's Glossary does not make this clear. Interestingly, Crooke notes that 'the bottom of a *chalni* is made of grass or reed'. Should this be taken to mean that the standard iron *chalni* with innumerable holes had not spread widely in U.P. till at least the 1890s? That would also make the well-known proverb '*sūp bole to bole, chalni kya bole jismen bahattar ched*' an invention of the twentieth century! Crooke does not mention this saying.

[46] 'The offices of carpenter and blacksmith are often held by the same person. The carpenter's chief business is with the plough and sugar-press. For putting the latter into working order, fitting in the *pāchars* and *patnāri* and preparing and keeping in order the *jāth* and working gear, he receives

557. The *gorait* or village watchman's fees are *nekdāri* and in the eastern districts *pasra* or *parsa*, which is a share of the grain put aside in the first instance to propitiate the local ghosts (*bhūt, dāno, jākni*, etc.)

558. Dues given for religious purposes—In Benares *angaunga*, in Gorakhpur *angaung*; in the western districts *siyaudi* or *thāpa*; in Bundelkhand *anjuli*, in Upper Doab *ujari* and *syāwarh*. First fruits of grain given to Brahmans are in Meerut *soāri*. In Gorakhpur *pujaura* is the grain set aside for the family priest (*parohit*), and the religious instructor (*guru*); in Delhi *dohli* or *dohri* is the perquisite of religious mendicants (*faqīr*) at harvest; in Gorakhpur the share given to Brahmans is *bishnausa*, and that to the mendicant (*atīth*) is *sheonsa*. In Oudh these dues for religious purposes are known as *anjuri* or *hathuthwa*, and *pai* or *paipūja*. Cf. para 370 and note.

559. The weaver's perquisite—In Azamgarh *tāsan*.

560. The *chamārs* perquisite—*Chamrāwat*. The *chamārs* resident in the village who receive such dues are in the east districts *gauhān*, the opposite of which is *upaheiya*. *Adwanch* is the fee given to him for preparing leather buckets.

561. Perquisites given at ploughing—In the Upper Doab at the ploughing in the month of *Asārh* (June-July), *godka*

---

for each press in the season fees known as *kolhāwan* and *pācharāwān* which amount to about Re. 1–4–0. For making and repairing ploughs and yokes, wood for which is supplied to him, his various petty fees in kind are called *sāli* (or *pāthi*), *lahna* (or *puri*), *barūa*, and *kharihāni*. The total value of them is about five annas a year per plough.

The blacksmith derives nothing from the sugar-press except a petty fee for sharpening the *ganrās*; but for making and repairing (metal and fuel being supplied) ploughshares and hoes, fees called *acharāwān*, valued at about two annas a year per plough, are paid to him'. *Azamgarh Settlement Report*, para 498.

It may be noticed that the fees paid the carpenter for setting up the *kolhu*—*kolhāwan* (Re. 1–4–0) were about the same as the *kolhuāwan*, the tax paid by peasants for setting up a *kolhu* to the landlords in their village. This tax is mentioned in the village papers of the 1880s Settlement. For one such example, see the *Wājib-ul arz* of *mauza* Rampur Khanpur, *tappa* Patna, *tahsil* Hata, Gorakhpur District, 1885.

anāj; and in *Kārtik* (October-November), *mend kā anāj*.

562. The sweeper's perquisite—*Mihtarāi*.

563. The perquisite of the village accountant (*patwāri*)—*Odha, bojha*, and for weighing grain when the crops are being divided, *taulāi*.

564. The landlord (*zamīndār*) receives the following dues: his percentage on the village collections known in Bundelkhand as *mihnatāna*, *shukrāna* or *bhūmiāwat*, the unclaimed grain or straw on the threshing floor is called in Kheri *khaliyāni; bairag* in Azamgarh are dues and services given at special times; *agaira* the first sheaves of the crop; the perquisite of milk from his tenants' cows *dohāo*; his fee at the marriage of the daughter of one of his cultivators *ban, mūrāsa, mandwach, taka-bīra*, or *shādiāna*; in Kheri *dhora* is a fee paid by his tenants in acknowledgment of his proprietary rights; in Azamgarh *dhoa* is a customary present made by the tenants; from a hereditary tenant he receives *serīna*, and in Rohilkhand *ugāhi*; help given by the tenants to plough his lands is in the Lower Doab and east districts *hari*, and in Rohilkhand *sahel*; presents given to him when he visits the village are in the eastern districts *bhet* or *bhent* or *nazrāna*; his fee when a house is built or sold is *chahārum* (one-fourth); he collects cesses in the nature of a ground rent from the resident artisans and traders in the village: these are called *abwāb, chānti, bhitauri, dhiauri, parjāwat, prajāwat* or *parjot*; in Gorakhpur *ghar duāri*; and in other places *basauri*. In Oudh the Brahman landlord used to receive dues of grain known as *anjuri* from the tenants; in the same way he used to receive one *biswa* of land in each tenant's holding.

565. The cowherd receives a certain share of the milk of the cows he grazes. This is in Rohilkhand *bār* or *bāra*, and in Gorakhpur *pāri*. *Mendwāi* in Cawnpur is a fee for herding. (See also paras 415–17).

Section IV—Miscellaneous Cesses

566. *Dhāla* in Rohilkhand and other places *malba* (literally sweepings) are contributions to cover the ordinary village expenses. *Rakhwāi, rakhāi*, and in Kheri *pitya* or *shahnagi*, is a tax to pay a watchman. *Anwānsi* in the east districts is a sheaf given to a field watchman at harvest. In the Upper Doab *takina* is a contribution in lieu of fodder; the tax levied on a grain seller's [*bania's*] weights is *bartarāi*.

X Land Tenures

Section I—Tenures

567. Land tenures may be divided into: (i) Proprietary tenures, (ii) Tenures intermediate between proprietary and cultivating, and (iii) Cultivating tenures.

Section II—Proprietary Tenures

568. *Tāluqadāri*—This in Oudh shows the proprietary right vested in one person holding feudal privileges.

569. *Zamīndari*—Here the whole land of the community is held and managed in common. The rents, with all other profits from the estate, are thrown into a common stock, and after deducting the government revenue (*mālguzāri*) and other expenses (*gānw kharch*) the balance is divided among the proprietors (*hissahdār*) according to a fixed law or share. The government revenue is collected and paid in by one of the body called a *lambardār*. The inferior proprietors are in Azamgarh *mushakhsīdār*.

570. *Pattidāri*—Of this there are two kinds: *Pattidāri mukammal*, or perfect *pattidāri*—In this the lands are divided and held in severalty by the different proprietors, each person managing his own land and paying his share of the government revenue, the whole proprietary body being jointly responsible in the event of any sharer not fulfilling his engagements. One or more of the body are appointed to collect and pay in the revenue. This man is called *lambardār*. These divisions in the village are *patti* or *thok*. In the eastern districts an arrangement known as *phātbandi* is common. The rents payable by certain tenants are assigned to a particular *patti* or division and collected by its managers.

571. *Pattidāri ghair mukammal*, or imperfect *pattidāri*—

Here part of the land is held in severalty and part in common. The government revenue and village expenses are paid from the common stock, and any deficiency is made up by a contribution from the sharers according to their share or the custom of the villages. The contribution is called *bāchh*.

572. *Muqaddami*—This tenure was found in two villages in pargana South Haveli in Gorakhpur.[47] The *muqaddam* was found at settlement to be a sort of hereditary lessee or managing headman between the cultivator and the chief proprietor (*zamīndār*). He had the right of collecting rents from the cultivators and retaining a certain share himself.

573. *Birt*—In the large *tāluqa* estates which existed in eastern Oudh and the Benares division, there was a class of grants by which undoubtedly full proprietary rights were recognized to the holders, who were known as *birtiha*. These are of various kinds:

574. *Jīwan birt*—An assignment made by the *Rāja* to a younger son, of a certain number of villages in the estate for subsistence, to be held by such son and his descendants for ever.[48]

575. *Barchhibandi birt*—A grant to warlike tribes such as Rajputs, on the condition that they would carry the spear (*barcchi*) and fight for the *Rāja*.

576. *Marwat birt or khūn baha*—A grant given by the *Rāja* in compensation to the family of any man killed in his service in open fight. It was chargeable with half the rent demandable for a regular *birt* village.

577. *Sankalp* or *bishnpirt*—A religious grant to a Brahman in order to secure the merit of sacrifices and offerings

[47] Crooke's notice on the *muqaddami* tenure, limited to just two villages of Gorakhpur, shows his special interest in this region. See also the reference to *mandidāri* tenure in para 590.

[48] *Birt* was a fairly widespread 'subordinate tenure' created by the taluqdars of Gorakhpur in the period before the ṭakeover of the region by the East India Company in 1802. For an excellent discussion, see Asiya Siddiqi, *Agrarian Change in a Northern Indian State, Uttar Pradesh, 1819–1833* (Oxford, 1973), pp. 45ff.

performed by him. The terms correspond to *mūāfi* used among Muhammadans.

578. In Oudh they are of two kinds: (i) *Damkus*, or acquired by purchase, and (ii) *kusdam* or *kushhast*, or given by favour.

579. The part of the land left unassessed was known as *adand*. The rent-rate payable was called *barbasti*; and was arranged either *bighoti*, i.e. at so much per *bīgha*, or rarely *bīlmuqta*, i.e. in a lump sum. In the purchase tenure (also known as *bai birt*) the purchase money was called *baikti*. The rent-free tenures given by the Hindus in connection with religious ceremonies are known in Oudh as *Krishnarpan, sankalp, kushhast,* and *birt bishnprit.*[49]

580. *Bhaiyāchāra* is a term applied to villages owned by descendants of a common stock. The whole of the land is occupied by the proprietary brotherhood, and the revenue assessed at a rate (*bāchh*). If there be non-proprietary cultivators they are not responsible to the general body, but are introduced by some individual sharer, and pay him rent for land on which he pays by the *bāchh*. This resembles the *bīgha dām* tenure in Azamgarh, where *khuntaiti* is used of villages in which shares are expressed in shares of a given unit.

581. *Bhejbarār* or *bāchhbarār*—A tenure frequently met with in Bundelkhand in which the shares of the brotherhood are liable to periodical or occasional adjustment, and in which balances of revenue and village expenses occasioned by the fraud or insolvency of a sharer are made good by a rateable contribution or *bāchh* from the other co-sharers.

582. *Gātābandi*—This corresponds to *khetbat* and the

[49] Note the use of both the past and the present tense in this paragraph. This is an indirect indication of the fact that while *birt* as an integral part of the system of land control and agrarian relations had disappeared by the late nineteenth century, the system of religious grants (*bishnprit*, etc.) was still operational at the time when Crooke wrote. Revenue documents from Gorakhpur provide ample evidence of the decline of the *birt* system by the 1870s.

opposite is *pahābandi*—a tenure which prevails extensively in the Lower Doab, Bareli and Benares. The fields of individual proprietors are not in juxtaposition, but scattered through many villages.

583. *Chīrbatota* or *haq thākurān*—A tenure in Bundelkhand by which the semi-independent chiefs received from Sindhia tracts of land in lieu of their rights (*haq*). When the value did not exceed the chief's share it was considered *jāgīr* or rent-free. When the value was in excess of the chief's rights the difference was payable as *ubari* or quit-rent.

584. *Bhayāi*—These arose in Oudh from the grant by the chief proprietor (*tāluqdār*) of certain villages rent-free to his younger brothers or cadets of his family.

585. *Dih*—In Oudh the proprietor even after dispossession was understood to have rights in that portion of the village which was covered with houses, but which now either from decay or desertion of the buildings has become once again open waste, or has been taken up for cultivation. Such land is technically known as *dih*.

586. *Nānkār*—This in Oudh originally meant the drawback allowed to the proprietor (*zamīndār*) by the revenue authorities from the demand made on the state. In the case of a large estate or *tāluqa* it generally took the form of patches of rent-free land given to the sub-proprietors.

587. *Biswādāri*—A name given to the tenure of independent village communities holding [land] under a superior proprietor (*tāluqadār*), as in the districts of Aligarh, Mainpuri and Gorakhpur. In some parts, as in Delhi, it is equivalent to the *zamīndāri* or the *pattidāri* tenures.

588. *Garhiband*—A description of tenure in Bundelkhand where the former proprietors, by defying government, acquired their lands at almost nominal rates.

Section III—Intermediate Tenures

589. *Arāzīdāri*—In Gorakhpur and other eastern districts. Here, by purchase or gift, the holder has obtained possession of a plot which he holds rent-free, only paying his share of the government revenue.

590. *Māndīdāri*—In the eastern districts a high class of occupancy tenure which can be bequeathed or sold. This is found specially in pargana Bhauapar in Gorakhpur.

591. *Patāwān, patahuapan*—In this case the land is held as consideration for repayment of a loan, principal and interest. It is found chiefly in pargana Sidhua Jobna, Gorakhpur district.

Section IV—Shares and Sharers

592. A share in a village is *hissah, bakhra, hissah bakhra,* and in Azamgarh *khūnt*; a proprietor of a half share is *adhelia* or *adhia.* The shares of a brotherhood, especially in the lands of a village or township, are *bhai hissi* or *bhai pansi.* These terms are chiefly used in Bundelkhand, East Oudh, Benares and Lower Doab. *Bhaiwad* is to pay and receive on the footing of one of the brotherhood; making over one's share to another is in Benares and East Oudh *bolans. Bolansi* in Benares and East Oudh is the holder of such a share or an adopted heir. A father's share is *bapans* in Benares and East Oudh; and in the west districts and Bundelkhand *bapauti.* The government revenue is *māl, mālguzārī, jama, haq, sarkār.* The half-yearly instalment is *adhkari.* The distribution of the revenue over the sharers in villages held by a brotherhood is *bāchh, bachaunta, behri, dhārbāchh.* The amount of revenue payable by an individual sharer is in Delhi *bharat.* The value of the government share of produce is *baith.* A proprietor by purchase is *bāidār* or *kharīdār.* The subdivision of a village held by a proprietary body is *thok, patti*, or *taraf; dher* or *dheri* is a smaller subdivision. Of the spontaneous produce of a village—*bankar* is the produce from forest land, wood, gums, etc.; *jalkar* is the produce derived from lakes, streams, etc.; *phalkar* is the produce of fruits; *shikār māhi* are fishing rights. An estate comprising 84 villages is *chaurāsi*, or 52 *bāwani*, of 54 *chauwani.* Fields situated in one village and included in the area and belonging to the proprietors of another are known in Azamgarh as *chalāni* or *dākhili khāriji.*

Section V—Cultivating Tenures

593. Cultivating tenures. A cultivator is *asāmi, kāshtkār, jota, jotan, jotār* or *jotia.* A tenant with rights of occupancy is *maurūsi*—one without occupancy rights is *ghair maurūsi.* In Bareli, the *muqaddam, mahtia, mahto* or *pradhān, pardhān* is an intermediary between the proprietor and cultivator. He collects the rents, and receives in return some petty privileges and immunities.

594. The *jeth raiyat* is the head tenant; where there is a *muqaddam* the *jeth rāiyat* ranks below him, and is also known by the name of *chuqaddam*, but it is most usual to consider *muqaddam, jeth raiyat, mahton, mukhiya, mahteya* and *basit* as synonymous terms.

595. In Oudh the favourable cultivators are known as *amnek*; cultivators of the proprietor's family are *bhaiyāchāra* or *bhaiya*; in Oudh and the eastern districts high-caste cultivators are *ashrāf*, and low-caste tenants *arzal.* The remission in favour of such high-caste tenants is *kūr* or *charwa.* In Bareli the grade of cultivators intermediate between the *muqaddam* and the ordinary tenant is the *raqmi* or tenant, who for some reason holds at slightly lower rates than ordinary cultivators.

596. Cultivators are also divided into *chhaparband*, i.e. resident and cultivating in their village; and *pāhi*, who live in one village and cultivate in another.[50] The *adhiār* or *adhbār* or

[50] There is much discussion of the *pāhikāsht* in the writings on Mughal agrarian history. However the following couplet, attributed to Ghāgh, places the *pāhi* as maverick in a highly significant way:

'Bigar birāne jo rahai, māne tiriya kī sīkh;
yeh tīnon rah jāyenge, pāhi jo bove īkh'.

One who quarrels in his own house and leaves it to live in someone else's; one who follows the advice and instructions of his wife, all these three—i.e. the above named *and* the *pāhi* who cultivates sugarcane in another village—will come to grief.

adhwār (of Rohilkhand) is a man who passes half his time in one village and half in another. He differs from the *pāhi* in as much as the *adhiar̄* keeps up two establishments in different villages and the *pahī* only one. Below the ordinary cultivator again is the *shikmi* or sub-tenant of another cultivator. The *bolahdar* is an occupant of land under a verbal agreement with the proprietor or village community.

Section VI—Rents

597. Rent is *lagān, fotah, fot* or *pota, bhej*. Rent-rates are *dar, darbandi,* or *sharh* or *sharah lagān*. *Chukauta* is rent payable at a fixed or money rate. Rents paid in cash are *naqdi*; when paid in kind *batāi* or *jinsi*. Crops which are always assessed at money rates are in Rohilkhand *nichkāri* or *zabti*. Lands which pay in kind are *birrābarār* or *amali*. The tenure known as *naqshi* in West Oudh and Rohilkhand is distinguished by the rents being always paid in cash; they are paid not for the whole year but for each harvest; the landlord can claim no rent if the crop has been destroyed by floods, etc; the tenant, if he chooses, can leave the land fallow and pay no rent; and a certain proportion of the land is rent-free. This is called *chhūt*, and varies from one-sixth to one-tenth, in which latter case it is known as *dobiswi*. In Kheri *thahrāi* is a mixed tenure, half cash and half grain payments. No cash rent is fixed, but when the crop is ready for cutting the landlord and tenants inspect it together. The landlord's share of the crop is valued on the spot at a fixed sum and on payment of this the tenant removes the crop.

The couplet is interesting both in its form and content. The phrase, '*yeh tīnon rah jāyenge*', suggests that the third (till then unnamed character)—the *pāhi*—is the object of the couplet, in the form: 'Just as, just as, *similarly* . . .

It is worth remarking that it is the category of the householder and the husbandman which is the normative category, deviations from which in terms of change of residence, displacement of authority within the household *and* shift in the locale of agricultural operations are signs of impending doom.

598. When rents are paid in a lump for the entire holding and not by field or soil rates the terms used are *bil muqta*; in Bundelkhand *thansa* or *thanka*; in Mathura *katauta*; in Farukhabad *bidh bandi or bid bandi*; and in the eastern districts *chukti* or *chukauta*.

599. When the rents are collected at a fixed rate per plough it is called *halbarār, halbandi,* or *halsāri*. *Ankbandi* is the adjustment of the rents among the tenants by the landlord at the close of each harvest. In Bundelkhand, when the rent is calculated on the amount of seed required, it is known as *bījgania* or *bījūra*. In Azamgarh when rates per *bīgha* are fixed for the different kinds of crops, and the amount payable in each year varies with the crops sown, the custom is called *shudkar* or *jinspher*. In Bundelkhand an assessment by wells is *kuānbandi*; and in Azamgarh in the rice tracts, where the tenant pays only for the land under rice, and not for any land which may lie fallow, the phrase *uthti parti* is used.

600. A remission of rent on account of deficient produce is *bād*; in Rohilkhand *nābūd*; and in Azamgarh *dekhsun*.[51] In the western districts the landlord deducts as his right two *biswa* out of every *bīgha* (one-tenth) cultivated by under-tenants. This is known as *biswi* or *dobiswi*. In parts of Bundelkhand some of the wilder tribes squat in the forest, and burn down a portion each year for sowing. This mode of cultivation is *dhya, bhūndari, baunda* in Rohilkhand, and in other places *bhaundari*. *Bhūnda* or *bohndari* is land let without rent to village servants or indigent relations; *chākri* in Jhansi and in other places. *Jāgīr* is land given in lieu of service. The headmen are called *sardārs*, and the land under the tenure *tauzi* or *taujīh bat*.

[51] Lit.: to see and hear, an interesting term for deliberations about remission of rent.

XI The Native House

Section I—The Native House

601. A house is *ghar, makān* or *bāri*; an enclosure containing several houses is *ahātah* or *hātah* or *haweli*; a hut is *jhonpra* or *jhonpri*, and in the eastern districts *palāni* or *chhāni*; *kuti* is the hut of the religious mendicant (*faqīr*). *Marai* in the eastern districts is a grass hut, and *māro* is the hut in which the marriage ceremony is conducted.

602. *Obari* in the eastern districts is a little hut or hovel. A ruined house or enclosure is *khandar*, or *khandahar*. In Gorakhpur *chhāoni* is a house in the forest.[52]

603. The straw huts used by the lower castes in the Upper Doab are called *rāoti*, or *dochanna chappar*; a masonry house is *pakka*; when built partly of bricks and partly of mud it is *kaccha pakka*, and when entirely of mud *kaccha*; when it has three openings it is *sedara* or *tirpoliya* or *tirpauliya*; when twelve openings it is *bārah dari*; and when provided with lattices it is *jalīdār*.

Section II—Parts of the House

604. The courtyard—This is *sahn, āngan, angna* or *angnāi; awāl* is an enclosed space between cultivators' houses. The space in front of the house is *agwāra*, and that behind *pichhwāra; kawar*, in the eastern districts, is a space in front of the house.

605. The inner entrance room—*Dālān, dogahi.*[53]

[52] *Chhāoni*: any outhouse, also a farm house.

[53] Both Crooke and Grierson call *dālān* a room; cf. *N.W.P. Gazetteer*, *c.*1880 III, p. 271. *Dālān* in present-day parlance is a running corridor, normally in front of a row of rooms rather than an enclosed space with four

606. The upper storey—*Āta*, with its diminutive *atari* or *ūprauti kothri*.

607. The underground storey—*Tahkhāna, bhuindara* or *bhuinra*.

608. The verandah—*Sāyabān*. In the eastern districts *khamhia* is a low verandah.

609. The vestibule or portico—*Osāra* and in the eastern districts *dahlīji* (a corruption of the Persian *dahlīz*).[54]

610. The sitting platform—This is *chabutra; chauntra* in the Doab and Rohilkhand. The platform where the elders assemble to discuss village affairs is *chaupāl* or *chaupar*.

611. The roof or ceiling is *chhat*. The thatch is *chhāja* (eastern districts) or *chhapar*; a thatcher is *gharāmi*; when the thatch is only a 'lean-to' on one wall it is known as *ekpalla* or *parchhati*; if it rests on both walls with a ridge-pole in the middle, it is *dopalla*. In this latter case one side of the roof is in the eastern districts *pharka*; a small thatch put on the top of the wall to save it from rain is *parchhati* or *parcha*. The yearly repairs to a tiled roof are in the eastern districts *pherauti*; and *pusni* is the grass or mud put on a roof to make it water-tight.

612. The fireplace—*Chūlha*, of which the mouth is *mohān, chauka* or *thahur,* is the Hindu's cooking enclosure. *Borsi* or *gursi* is the moveable fireplace used by jewellers. *Angethi* is an iron moveable fireplace. In the eastern districts the *uthalla* or *uthauwa chūlha* is a fireplace made of sun-dried mud which can be moved.

613. The holes in the top of the fireplace in which the pots are placed are called *aila*. When there are places for four pots it is known as *charaila chūlha*. The partitions below are

---

walls. *Dogahi* in Gorakhpur had a technical sense as well. In an indigenous sugar refinery it was the corridor where *chīni* attained its final crystallized form. For a photograph, see Shahid Amin, *Sugarcane and Sugar in Gorakhpur*, illustration v.

[54] Informants in Gorakhpur maintain that *sāyābān, osāra* and *barāmda* all refer to the same thing, the middle term being considered more 'rustic' than the other two.

pūta in the eastern districts. The cooking house is *rasoi khāna, bāwārchi khana,* and to the east *chulhāni.*

614. The door—The door is *darwāzah* or *duār;* a gate is *phātak.* The main door is *sadar darwāzah.* A side-door or window is *khirki* or *bāri.* In the eastern districts *mukka* is a hole pierced in the gable or wall to give light and air. The two leaves of a door are *palla* or *kiwār* or *kiwāra. Beni* is the slip of wood nailed on one leaf to cover the chink. The threshold is *dāsa, dehri* or *deorhi.* The pivot used as a hinge is *chūl*; the door-frame *chaukhat*; the bar used for fastening the door *āgal, benta* or *kunda.* When a screen or hurdle (known in the eastern districts as *tatta* or *tatti* or *chachara*, and in the Upper Doab as *khirak*) is used, the spar to support it is called in the east districts *benora.* The door-bolt is *billi* or *chatkani.* The lock is *qufl* or *tāla*; the key is *kunji* and the bolt of the lock *jhāri* or *jhār.*

615. The wall—*Diwāl* or *diwār*, of which the foundation is *neo.* In the east of the province the lumps of damp mud used in building the wall are *londa*, and the stages in which it is built *radda.* In the eastern districts the back wall of a house or enclosure is *danwar* or *danrwāra*; the end or gable wall is *pākha*; and the space over the top of the wall is *bhīt.* To the west *barauntha* is the part of the wall between the top of the door and the roof; and in Azamgarh *doraundha* is the plank over the top of the doorway on which the wall is built.

616. The eaves—*Olti, ori, alauti* or *lauti*, to the west; and to the east *ohāri* or *auti, orauni* or *oriāni.* The eave-board is *muhabbat* or *mahāut*, and the pieces of wood left into the wall to support the eave-board are *chajja*; in Gorakhpur *tora*; and in Azamgarh *ghoria.* The slope of the root is *tāran* in the eastern districts.

617. The cupboard—This is generally *āla* or *tāq*, and in Azamgarh *gaunkha.* In the east districts *deorakha* is a wall-bracket for a lamp, and *gharaunchi, ghiraunchi, kharauti* or *kharkauti* is a hole in the wall for keeping toothpicks. (See also para 254.)

618. The men's and women's quarters etc.—The men's quarters are *mardāna* and those of women *zanāna*, and in the eastern districts the part between the two is *deorhi*. To the east of the province the *khalnga* or *darkhol* are rooms set apart for the reception of guests. In Bundelkhand the *munder* is the inner and the *barotha* the outer room.

Section III—Materials Used in the Construction of the House

619. The beams—The beams, pillars, supporting the roof, are *thūni, khamba*; in Azamgarh *kahmia, arwār, ār* (Marwari) and *thobli* (west districts). In the east districts *kauha* or *kauwa* is a truss formed of two poles to support the ridge pole. The *gaunkha* is a truss for supporting a thatched roof; and the *tarbāta* or *tarauta* is a strong bamboo under a thatch which supports it crossways. The *ota* is an earthen pillar for supporting a roof. The ridge pole is *balendi* to the west; and to the east *barer* or *bareri*. The *magari* is a ridge pole for a thatched roof. The corner beam of the roof is *kamarballa, baranga* or *barga*. The thicker rafters are *balla* and the thinner *koro*; in Bundelkhand *kurya*, and in the eastern districts *kurāi*. To the east the round poles built up inside the mud walls are *gol*. The *teoki*, or *tekan* is a support for a broken wall.

620. In Gorakhpur the beams of the *sākhu* or *sāl* tree (*Shorea robusta*) are divided into the *ekla*, which are small round beams; the *bareri* are similar but of a smaller size; the *gurha* are beams from trees two-thirds grown; the *chaukor* are squared and the *terhiya* are crooked beams. The *chaila* are splinters of roof, a layer of which is placed between the rafters and the tiling.

621. The tiles—These are distinguished into the flat tiles, *khapra* or *khaprel*, and in Azamgarh *thapua*, and the semicircular tiles, *naria*.[55] In Azamgarh *onhaua* is a rough mode of tiling when only flat tiles are used. Bits of broken tiles are *inkara*. Tiles are baked in a kiln, *āwa, parzāwa, pajāwa*. In the east districts the *tarāyal* or *tarāi* is the layer of loose grass in a

[55] The *naria* are arranged over the *thapua* in such a way that water flows down the latter and falls into the *olti* (see para 616). Both *thapua* and *naria* are made by Kumhars.

tiled roof between the rolls of the thatching grass and the tiles.

622. The bricks—These are *īnt* or *gūmān*. Among the varieties are *pakka* or kiln-burnt, *kaccha*, sun-dried, *kalān*, large table moulded, *khurd*, small table moulded, *bhuinpatti*, common small bricks, *nau terahi,* common country bricks, *lakhauri* (Bundelkhand), or *makheya* (Cawnpur) the smallest sized country bricks; *garh* are tile bricks forming a segment of a circle used in well building.[56] An overburnt brick is *jhānwān*. In the east districts *īntkoha, khoya,* or *kor* are pieces of half-fired bricks.

623. Stone is *patthar*. In Bundelkhand large slabs of building stone are *asāru*; small pieces for jambs and lintels are *turiya*; and smaller slabs or slates are *patiya*.

624. Lime and mortar—The calcareous nodular limestone used for lime making and road metal is *kankar*. When it appears in large blocks it is known as *chatān*, and in the east districts *ankta*.[57] The small pieces for road metal are in the west of the province *bichhua*, and to the east *ankti* or *ankri; chhara* in the east districts is coarse *kankar* gravel; *ankat* to the

[56] The phrase 'well burning' in the text is an obvious misprint for 'well building'. *Nau terahi* = 9″×13″. *Lakhauri* as a term for thin bricks is not confined to Bundelkhand; the term *lakhauri īnt* is used all over UP. Today specimens of this brickwork can be found in the dilapidated houses in the *qasbās* of UP. More than anything else, a *lakhauri īnt ka makān* is a sign of prosperity and the gentry status of yesteryears. It would be interesting to know when the transition from *lakhauri* to the standard-sized brick was made in northern India.

[57] Cf. *Ankatha Bīr*: 'In the village of Niamatpur is a shrine of *Ankatha Bīr* or the hero of the *kankar* heap. He is guardian of the village crops, and keeps off thieves.

His shrine is a great pile of calcareous nodules (*kankar*), to which worshippers add a piece as they pass. It is now some 6 feet high and 20 in diameter. Some of the larger pieces are smeared with red ochre. There is no day fixed for his worship. Sweets are the usual offerings, which are taken by a family of Shukl Brahmans of the Sarwariya tribe who live in the village. This is unusual, as such shrines have generally aboriginal or low caste priests'. William Crooke, *North Indian Notes and Queries*, vol. 1, no. 3 (June 1891), no. 308.

east is the *kankar* used in lime burning. Fine burnt lime is *chūna*. That eaten with the betel is *kali*, that used for whitewashing is *qalai*. The shells of the fresh water mussel burnt for lime are *sīpi*. Lime mortar is *masāla*; moistened clay used as mortar is *gāra, gonda* or *kapsa*. The broken brick used as a substitute for sand is *surkhi*.

XII Food

Section I—Meals

625. The morning meal is in the Doab *nāshta* or *kaleo*, and in the eastern districts *nahāri* or *kharmitāo*.[58] *Panpiāo* in the eastern districts and in other places *kor* or *akor* is food eaten by the labourer in the intervals of work in the field.

626. The midday meal is in the Doab *chāsht* or *khāua*; in Gorakhpur *dopahariya*; and in Azamgarh *charbanāo*.

627. The evening meal is in the Doab *byālu* or *esha*, and in Gorakhpur *sanjhaia* or *sanjhia*.

Section II—Preparation of Food

628. The following are some of the preparations of food:

Adauri—Little round cakes made of pulse.

Akhara—Barley ground without being first cleaned.

Ardāwa—Gram; also given to horses.

Āta—Flour or meal.

Avta auta—The juice of sugarcane fully boiled.

Avti auti—Sugarcane juice mixed with water and half boiled.

Baghār—Seasoning used with food.[59]

Bahuri—Unripe barley roasted.

Bajka—A dish of pease flour.

Bakhīr—Rice cooked in sugar and water.

Balūsāhi—A sweetmeat made of wheat.

[58] The expression in Gorakhpur is: '*Nahār munh nati raha, kharāi ho jāi*'. (Something should be eaten in the morning. If nothing else, peasants should eat a couple of black peppers and drink a *lutia* of water over it.)

[59] Rice with the *baghār* of *ghee* is *bagharua chāwal*, in opposition to *khushka* or plain rice.

Baphaura—Pulse flour cooked by steam.[60]

Barfi—A white sweetmeat made of wheat, flour, milk and sugar.

Barra—Balls of *urad* pulse fried in clarified butter.

Barri—Balls of *urad*, *mūng* or gram flour fried in clarified butter or oil.

Bāsi—Stale food reserved for the next day.

Batāsha—A spongy sweetmeat made of sugar.

Batāspheni—Similar to the last, made of sugar and flour.

Berhain—Pulse cakes.

Besan—Pulse flour.

Bhauri—Cakes fried in hot ashes.

Boran—Juicy food such as vegetables, etc., eaten with dry food.

Chabena, charban—Parched grain.

Chenua—Balls of rice steamed over a pot containing water.

Chhāch, chhāchh—Buttermilk.

Chhanauri—A dish of pulse.

Chīkas—Roasted barley ground up with unroasted barley.

Chirva, chūra—Rice partially boiled, then pounded and roasted.

Chiuri—Unripe barley parched.

Chokha—A mess of pounded roasted vegetables.[61]

Chopari roti—Cakes cooked with clarified butter or grease.

[60] *Baphaura* is also called *baphauri* in Gorakhpur. It could be described as steamed rather than deep-fried *pakoras* or *pakauris*. The procedure is as follows: A piece of cloth is tied to the mouth of a pot of boiling water. Bits of the paste of the *dāl* of gram or pease are then put on to this cloth and are steamed thereby.

[61] The description of food preparations in terms of their English equivalents sounds a bit odd. *Parātha, prātha*: 'Bread made like piecrust', does not describe adequately this common north-Indian wheat and *maida* preparation. I have refrained from giving 'proper' English equivalents. I cannot help commenting on the description of *chokha* as 'a mess of pounded roasted vegetables', for this fails to convey what is distinctive about this common delicacy of eastern UP, i.e. cooked in *kaccha* oil and with lots of chillies and spices. It is this that gives *ālu* or *baingan ka chokha* its name, and its pungent, strong taste.

Chūn—Flour.

Dabhaka—Partially parched pulse.

Daliya—Pounded maize boiled in milk and eaten with sugar.

Dālpīthi—(In Gorakhpur) balls of pulse flour boiled.

Dalla daria—Coarse grain of meal after being sifted.

Darra—Coarse meal.

Dhokha—A mess of ground gram and spices made to taste like meat.

Dhonga—A thick cake.

Dhoi, dhui—Soaked pulse.

Dhūnrhi—A round sweetmeat made of riceflour, sugar and clarified butter.

Dubki, dubhki—Pulse cooked in warm water.

Ghenga—A dish of rice and flour.

Ghewar—A sweetmeat made of wheat flour.

Ghughuri—A mess made of pulse, clarified butter, etc.[62]

Gojha, vide Gunjha.

Guldāna—A sweetmeat made of wheat.

Gunjha, gunjhia—A sweetcake of wheat.

Hābus—Green barley or wheat roasted for food.

Halwa—A sweetmeat made of eggs, flour and clarified butter.

Horha—Young ears of the pulses parched [usually of gram or pease].

Jābar, jabra, jabri—A mess of rice, vegetables, clarified butter, etc.

Jalebi—A sweetmeat in a coiled shape made of fine wheat flour, sugar etc.

Jāur—Rice, etc., boiled in milk.

Jawakhar—Ashes of burnt ears and stalks of barley used as cure for indigestion.

Jhānjha—A mixture of coarse sugar, hemp, clarified butter, etc.

[62] *Ghughuri*, also *ghunguni*: Deep fried fresh pease with onions and chillies. A common evening snack; used for *iftār* when the month of Ramzan falls in the early-Rabi months.

Kachauri—Cakes of flour filled with pulses, etc.

Khardar—Bread made of the fruit of the *mahua* tree (*Bassia latifolia*).

Karhua—Food saved from supper for the children.

Khaiba—Food saved from supper for the children's breakfast.

Khajūr—A sweetmeat made from wheatflour in the form of a date.

Khichri—Rice boiled with pulse and spices.

Khīl—Maize or rice slightly damped and then parched in very hot sand. Cf. *lāwa*.

Khīr—Rice boiled in milk.

Khurma—A sweetmeat in the form of a date made of wheatflour, sugar and clarified butter.

Khushka—Plain boiled rice without spices.

Khoncha—A thick cake of bread.

Konhrauri—Cakes made of ground pulse and pumpkin.

Koeli ki roti—(In Gorakhpur) bread made of crushed mango-stones.

Laddu—A sweetmeat made of coconut kernels, sugar and cream.

Lāi—Parched rice without sugar.

Lapsi—Thin sweet pastry.[63]

Lāta—A mess made of the flowers of the *mahua* (*Bassia latifolia*), molasses and parched grain flower.

Lāwa—Maize, rice, etc., damped and parched in hot sand. Cf. *Khīl*.

Loi—The lumps of dough out of which cakes are made.

Magdar—A sweetmeat made of pulse and sugar.

Maheri—A mess of rice and buttermilk.

Mahiāwar—Rice, turmeric, and salt boiled in buttermilk.

[63] A cookbook recipe for *lapsi* would read as follows: Stir fry some flour till brown; mix it with *gur* diluted in water, give it a *baghār* with cummin seed. Stir for ten minutes. When it thickens into a paste take it off the fire. *Lapsi* is also made of *mahua* flowers. If one were to fry diced unripe mangoes and mix this in the *lapsi*, the resultant preparation would be called *guramba*.

Mahuar—The flowers of *mahua* soaked overnight with grams, pease or linseed, crushed next morning and a cake made of the paste.

Maida—Fine sifted flour.

Makuni—Cakes made of pease flour.

Matha—Hot buttermilk.

Mathri—A sweetmeat made of wheat flour.

Mathjāur—Buttermilk boiled in water and a little rice, etc., added.

Merkhun—Broken pulse or rice.

Mungchhi—Balls of pulse flour boiled in clarified butter.

Nakhūdi—A preparation of gram.

Niguri—Barley from which the husk has been removed by pounding.

Pakaura—Wheat cakes filled with gram flour.

Palēthan—The dry flour rubbed on the dough as it is being made into cakes.[64]

Palla—Balls of flour and sugar fried in clarified butter.

Panahti, panhath, panethi—A thick cake of bread.

Pāpar—A crisp cake of pulse flour.

Pana—A roll of coarse flour cooked by steam in a pot with some water in the bottom and resting above on twigs.

Parauni—Little cakes of pulse flour.

Parmal—Parched maize or wheat.

Parthan—*Palēthan* (q.v.)

Pataura, patiaura—A mess of pulse flour cooked in the leaves of the arum (*arui*).

Petha—Candied gourd.

Pheni—A frothy sweetmeat made of wheat, flour and sugar.

[64] *Palethan* or *parethan* (see below), is properly speaking the rough flour left behind after the required number of *rotis* have been cooked. This is made into a thick tablet which is called *pichli roti* (= backward *roti*!), and is much coarser compared to the usual *rotis*. A common expression in Gorakhpur to chide someone for being 'thick' is: '*Kā ho! kā pichli roti khaile rahla*? (Did you eat *pichli roti* [and not the usual ones]?)

A surprising omission from the list of 'breads' is *litti*, a thick ball of roasted bread.

Phutehra—Parched gram and pease.

Pīch—Rice gruel.

Pīthi—Pulse flour.

Prātha, parātha—Bread made like piecrust.

Pūa—Wheat flour and molasses mixed and cooked in clarified butter.

Pūran—Pulse flour cooked into a wheat cake.

Pūri—Thin cakes boiled [deep fried] in clarified butter.

Sāgpīthi—Pulse boiled with vegetable.

Samosa—Balls of flour with fruit, etc., inside cooked in clarified butter.

Sattu—Parched gram ground into flour.[65]

Seo—A sweetmeat in the form of an apple [also a saltish snack].

Shakarpāra—A sweetmeat of wheat flour.

Sūji—The flour from the centre of the wheat grain.

Thurra, thurri—Grain which has not burst while being parched.

Toran—Cakes of dry bread which must be broken before being eaten.

Tūka—The fourth part of a round cake.

Ujhila—Cooked mustard seed or blossoms of the *Bassia latifolia (mahua)*.

Ulta—Pease pudding.

Ūmi—Unripe ears of barley and wheat cut in the spring harvest (*rabi*), and of the millets *sāṅwān, tāngan*, cut in the autumn *(kharīf)*.

[65] *Sattu*: 'Parched gram ground into flour', is more an ingredient than a preparation of food. It is the most common portable food of the countryside. A peasant while travelling would tie a pound or so of *sattu* in his *gamcha* and make a 'dish' by mixing it with the right amount of water and kneading it into dough. This is then eaten, garnished with green chillies and/or some onions. A few pounds of *sattu* is enough for a peasant to survive for a couple of days. Hence the phrase: *Sattu bāndh ke pīche par jāna*.

XIII Ceremonies of Rural Life

Section I—Marriage

629. Marriage is *biyāh* or *shādi*. *Nikāh* is the less regular form of marriage among Mohammadans.[66]

630. The bridegroom is *banra* or *dūlha*, the bride *dulhin*. The dowry is *dahej*, or *daija or jahez; mahar* is the marriage settlement among Mohammadans.

631. The husband is *bar, pī, bhatār, khāwind, khasam* or *shauhar*.[67] In the eastern districts a woman calls her husband *mard* or *marda*.

632. A wife is *joru* or *jurwa* or *istri*; among the Jats of the Upper Doab the word *birbāni*, and in the Upper Doab *bām*, are also used. In the eastern districts *mehrāru, maug,* or *maugi*, or *dhania, bahu* or *parāni* are met with.

633. When there are two wives each is *saut* or *sautin, sauk* or *saukan* to the other; and the first wife is *biyāhta*.[68] A woman whose husband is alive is *suhāgan*, and in the eastern districts *ahibāti* or *ahiwāti*.

634. A widower is *randūa* or *randor*. A widower who marries a second time is in the eastern district *duāh*, and a man three times married is *tiāh*. A widow is *bewa, rānd* or *randori*. The second marriage of a Hindu woman is *dharauna* or *dharanwa*, and the second husband of such a woman is *dharicha*.

635. Among some castes the concubinage of a widow with generally one of her late husband's relations is legalized and is called in the Doab and Rohilkhand *karāo, sagāi* or

[66] It is not clear to me what Crooke means by *nikāh* being 'the less regular form of marriage among Mohammadans.'

[67] Witness the saying, *'Bānjh ke ghar bhatār dularua'*, i.e. in the house of the barren woman it is the husband who is the darling!

[68] The child from the first wife is referred to as *'Biyahtha ki aulād'*.

madākhila. Children brought forth by the woman previous to this ceremony, except when the late husband's brother is the father, are called *kadhelar* or *kadhelara*.

636. A woman who lives with a man without marriage is to the east of the province *gharkaili, dhenmani*, or *rakheli*.

Section II—Wedding Ceremonies[69]

637. The proposal for a girl in marriage by the boy's relations is *mangni*. This is done by the *agwa* or matchmaker. To the east *taurab* means to search for a boy in marriage. The bethrothal is *sagāi*, the marriage procession *barāt*. In the eastern districts *marjād* means the marriage procession remaining at the house of the bride for a day after the wedding, and *dolākārh, dolkarh* or *dolkarhi* is a woman who has gone to her husband's house without a marriage procession.

638. The ceremony of bringing the bride to her husband's house to consummate the marriage is *gauna*, and in Rohilkhand *rauna*. The newly-arrived bride and her party are to the east *gaunahri*, and her escort is *pathaunia, anwaia* or *anwanihān*. The second visit is to the west *challa* or *dūsra*, and to the east *donga*, and the third *tenga* to the east and *tīsra* to the west. Her subsequent visits to her father's and husband's house to the east are *anauni pathauni*.

639. The husband and wife each call the houses of their respective fathers-in-law *susrāl*. The wife knows her parents' house as *naihar* or *maika*. The husband calls the house of his father's mother *nanihāl*. *Dādiaura* or *dadihāl* and *dādka* are the paternal grandmother's house. *Piusar* is the husband's father's home and *mamiāur* is that of the maternal uncle's. *Ajiaura* is the paternal grandfather's house. The permission given to the bride to visit her parents' home is *rukhsat, bida* or *chhutti*.

[69] This forms a long paragraph in Crooke, which I have split into shorter sub-sections. However, I have not sought to rearrange the rituals described into a proper temporal sequence. This means that *ganna banna*, or the matching of the horoscopes of the bride and the bridegroom, for instance (para 642), comes after a discussion of the wedding breakfast!

640. At the wedding, wreaths of mango leaves, flowers, etc., known as *bandhanwār, bandanbāri* (Farukhabad), and to the east *banwār* or *bandnewār*, are hung over the door. The marking of the bridegroom's forehead before marriage is *tilak*. This is done by a man called the *tilkahru*. The *gath bandhan* is the part of the ceremony when the clothes of the bride and the bridegroom are tied in a knot. The *gānth* is a silver pendant attached by a thread to the arms or the corner of the shawl of a newly-married woman. The *sāt pheri* or *sāt bhaunri* is the ceremony of turning the bride and the bridegroom seven times round the sacrificial fire.

641. The wedding breakfast is *pangat*. *Bhatwān* is the feast at the house of both parties the day before the marriage procession. *Ubtan, abtan* or *bukwa* is the cosmetic of turmeric, meal, oil, etc., rubbed on the bride and bridegroom for about ten days before marriage. *Tel charhāna* is a similar application of oil.

642. The *janampatr* or *janampattri* is the horoscope of the boy and the girl. If they agree the phrase *ganna banna* is used.

643. The *phaldān* is the money, etc., given by the girl's relations to those of the boy's as a pledge of carrying out the marriage engagement. This is carried by a man known as the *chhenkahru* in the east of the province. After this the boy's father performs a rite known as the *tilak*, and from this date the *lagan* or period of the marriage ceremonies commences.

644. The *parchhan, ārta* or *ārti*, and *sewal* are ceremonies nearly all of the same kind, the essence of them being that a married woman of the family takes a brass pan (*thāli*) with a small lamp and gives them to the boy; and then holding two corners of her mantle (*dopatta*), touches them with the pan, then the boy's forehead, and then her own.

645. The day after the wedding is *barhār*. On that day the ceremony of feeding the bridegroom is solemnized; the food is known in Gorakhpur as *basiaura khāna*, or *khichri khawāi*. The *chauthi* is the ceremony of untying the wedding bracelet (*nāra* or *kangana*) from the wrist of the bridegroom.

646. When the auspicious day for the marriage has been

fixed, an announcing letter is sent to the boy's father. This is known in some places as *tewa* and in Gorakhpur as *lagan pattri*. The regular invitation to the wedding is *neota*.

647. The rite performed by the bride's brother of raising the bridegroom by the ear and dropping him three times is *uthāwal baisāwal*. *Athal* is the bathing of the bridegroom and the bride on the third day after marriage respectively by eight men and women. *Bhāji* or *jeonār* is the food given to the brotherhood at the wedding. The *maur* is the head-dress worn by the bridegroom. The bride wears the *mauri*.

648. The presents given by the brotherhood to the parents of the bride and bridegroom are *neota, purhath*; and *neochhāwar* are presents made to dependants. *Gaudān* is the present of a cow made by the girl's father to the family priest (*parohit*). The *gurehthab* or *pratishtha* are presents made to the bride by the elder brother of the bridegroom.

649. *Kanyādān* is the ceremony of making over the bride to the bridegroom. As the bridegroom's party go away after the wedding, the men embrace. This is known in Azamgarh as *angmalika*, and in Gorakhpur as *milan*. The *anchardharua* is when the bridegroom before leaving with the bride seizes the hem of the garments of the old women of the family and demands money.

650. The day after the evening of the arrival of the bridegroom's party is *janwānsa*. The *dāl, dālbari, dālmauni, bari* or *charhauwa* are the wedding presents sent by the bridegroom before the arrival of the procession.

651. The *piari* is the bride's yellow dress, and the *kanhāwar* a red handkerchief or sheet used in the ceremony. There is a ceremony in which cooked rice is given to the bridegroom and other unmarried boys. This is known as *konhrat ka bhāt* or *konhrat ki patari*. In the *chumāwan* rite the women put rice in the hand of the bridegroom and flowers on his feet. The *duār pūja* is the ceremony at the door of the bride's house when the party of the bridegroom arrives.

652. When the bride comes to the house of her husband, it is the custom for her to pass from her litter to the door, putting her foot into a basket at each step. This custom is known as *dauri men gor dālna*.

653. The *dhurchhak* is a rite peculiar to Agarwala Banias in which on the arrival of the bridegroom the bride's friends meet his party with presents.

654. The *nahchhu* is the ceremony of cutting the boy's nails for the first time at marriage, and the *pair puja* is the washing of the bridegroom's feet by the representative of the bride when the marriage arrangements are complete.

Section III—Births

655. The feast given and rites performed in the seventh month of pregnancy are known as *satmāsa, satwāsa*, or *satwānsa*. The *baras gānth*, or *sālgirah* is the ceremony of tying a knot in a string on the child's birthday. The *chhati* is the rite on the sixth day after delivery. On that day the child is named. *Chilla* is the ceremony of purification performed on the fortieth day after the birth of the child. The ceremony of first feeding of the child with grain is *annprāsan, pāsni,* or *chatāna*.

656. An adopted child is *mutabanna* or *rās nashīn*. To adopt a child is *godlena, rāsbaithāna*, or *rāslena*.

657. When a woman for some reason cannot suck [suckle] her child the terms *thantūt, dūdh khattu*, or *sutaura* are used.

658. A seven month's child is *satwānsa*, an eight month's child *athwānsa*.

659. When a woman has a child every year the phrases *barsāin,* or *sūarbiyān*, are used.[70]

660. A woman with only one child is *ekaunj*, or *ekwanj* in the east districts. A barren woman is *bānjh*.[71]

[70] Cf. *Barsāin* in *Azamgarh Glossary:* (i) Yearly (of an allowance, of a birth. etc.) (ii) Giving birth to a young every year (iii) A year old or more (chiefly of cattle). *Sūarbiyān*: 'breeding like a pig'.

[71] Two proverbs in praise of multiple children (and specially male offspring) are worth noticing:

Bānjh ka munh dekh lo ekaunj ka nahīn (Look a barren woman in the face, but not a woman with one child.)

661. A woman after delivery until the purificatory ceremonies are performed is in the east of the province *alwanti*. The *achhwāni* is aromatic food given to a woman after childbirth.

662. The lying-in room is *obar*. In this a fire known as *pasanghi* is kept burning for ten days after the woman's delivery.

663. The *biaua* or *sadhāwar* in the eastern districts are presents (given) at pregnancy.

664. *Khatnah* or *kanūri* is circumcision among Mohammadans.

Section IV—Disposal of the Dead

665. The burning of a corpse is *dāgh dena* or *dagadh*. The bier on which the corpse of a Hindu is removed is *arthi*, which becomes *ranthi* in the east, and *rathi* among the Marwaris, or *tikthi*. The cremation place is *chihāi, chihāna, chihāra, marghat, bhoidagdha, samsān* or *smasān, chitka*, and in the eastern districts *harohar*. The funeral pile is *chita*, or *chitākha*. When the body is nearly burnt the friends each throw five sticks known as *pachkathia* into the fire.

666. The offerings made to the manes during cremation are *chita pinda*. The *pinda* are offerings made at the obsequial ceremonies. The celebrations in the month of *Kuār* is known as *kanāgat, pitra paksha, shrādh* or *nauhanr*.[72]

667. The ceremony on the second or third day after death is the *uthāwani*, when food consisting of rice, milk and *urad* pulse known as *dūdh mukh* is distributed to the relatives. For ten days after death the rite of the *dīpdān*, or hanging a lamp

---

Na sau rupaya ko rupaya kaho, na ek bete ko beta (Don't call a hundred rupees 'money'; nor a single male child 'son'.)

[72] *Kanāgat* or *kanākat:* 'The dark fortnight of Kuar (Sept-Oct.) when sacrificial feasts are held by Hindus in honour of deceased ancestors'. Hence: *Āye kanākat phutke khās, Ḅābhan baithe chūlhe pās'*. (When *kanakat* approaches *khās/kāns* sprouts and Brahmins are feasted.)

SOURCE: Register no. 7, Settlement Shelf, *c.* 1888, Gorakhpur Collectorate Records.

to a fig or other tree to light the soul of the deceased to the other world, is performed. A vessel with water known as a *ghant* is hung from the tree, and the relatives each day up to the tenth throw handfuls of water mixed with sesamum (*til*), one the first day, two the second, and so on. This is called *tilānjul*.

668. When all the ceremonies are performed in the orthodox way it is called *krya karm*. When the body is merely thrown into a running stream, it is *jalprabāh* or *jalparwāh*. There are five days in the year during which if a death occurs the body must be thrown into a stream, not burnt. These are called to the east *pachka*, and to the west *panchak*.

669. The visit of the women to condole after a death is *angna*.

670. The *khorsi* is the ceremony on the 16th day. On the 10th day is performed the *khaur*, or *kāgkrya*, and the *ghāt* or ceremonial bathing. This day is also known as the *dasgātar, dasgatra* or *daswān*, and the widow assumes white clothes: *ranrsār*.

Section V—Ceremonies at Ploughing and Sowing

671. The *mahūrat* of Rohilkhand and the *akhtīj*, which is performed on 18th *Baisākh*, are modes of fixing lucky seasons for the commencement of agricultural operations. The ceremony is intended to propitiate the *sheshnāg* or world serpent.[73]

[73] Cf. Elliot: *Akhtīj:* 'The 18th day of the month Baisakh, upon which frequently the obligations incurred by the Agriculturalists to enable them to provide for the cultivation of the *Rubbee* season are adjusted....[Under the *Akhtīj ka bhāo*] when money is borrowed by a cultivator, he agrees to re-pay it in corn, with the *oop* [*ūp*] or interest, at the price prevailing on the day of the *Akhtīj*. The grain merchant can scarcely ever lose under this engagement, as in consequence of the season of the year the average necessarily ranges high....

The *Akhtīj* is to the *Rubbee*, what the *Dewalee* is to the *Khureef*—the day appointed for settling the accounts of the past harvest.

It is proper to commence the manufacture of agricultural implements, and to feed Brahmins on the *Akhtīj*, as well as to eat new grain, which

672. In the eastern districts the rite of throwing a handful of grain into the field at the begining of the months *Asārh* or *Kārtik* is known as *mūnth*. The grain is sown in the north-east corner of the field, which is called the *munthewa kon* in Gorakhpur. During sowing the surplus grain is distributed each evening to the workmen. This is called *ubarwa* in Gorakhpur; in Rohilkhand *bījwār*, and in the Upper Doab *bijāi*.

673. In the Upper Doab the ceremony of testing the direction in which the wind blows before the cane is planted is called *paun parichchha*. The day on which the cane is sown is called *ikhraj, ūkhraj, ūkh bhoj,* or *ukharhaj,* or *nimauni*. The worship of the plough after the cane is planted is *ūkhar*, or *okhar* in the Upper Doab.

674. The conclusion of the sowing season which is a time of festivity is known as *daliya jhār* (the brushing out of the sowing basket), *kunr mundla, hariar, baibhari, kunr bhoji,* and in the eastern districts *kurmundan*.

675. The *nāg bel puja* in the eastern districts is performed with lamps filled with clarified butter and *urad* pulse. It is principally carried out in planting betel (*pān*).

Section VI—Harvest Ceremonies

676. The ceremony at the first cutting of the sugarcane is *deothan* (Rohilkhand), *dithwan, dataund, daiten, dashtun,* or *dutāon* and *bodini*. It takes place on the 11th of the bright half of *Kārtik* (*Kārtik badi ekādasi*).[74]

---

scrupulous men generally forbear doing till the return of this auspicious festival. A plough is also slightly passed over the fields, as the ceremony is supposed to secure good luck...' See H.M. Elliot, *Supplemental Glossary of Terms Used in the North Western Provinces* (Allahabad, 1844), pp. 13, 135.

Akhtīj, also known as *Khartijiya* in Gorakhpur, marks the auspicious beginning of *Kharīf* cultivation. See Appendix F para 797, and para 683.

[74] Cf. *Dithwan* or *Deothan* in Elliot, pp. 280–1: 'The standing up of the God'. This falls on the *ekādasi*, or the 11th day of the bright half of the month of *Kātik* (Oct.-Nov.) 'On this day a ceremony is observed in celebration of Vishnu's return from his slumber of four months...

677. In Rohilkhand there is also a ceremony in *Kārtik* to avert from the cane the *sūnri* insect. This is known as the *sūi ka pūja*. When the cane is cut, a red string called *kalāwa* is tied round the first bundle.

678. On the first day of the cane pressing, the ceremony of distributing the juice is known in the Upper Doab as *raswāi*; in the Central Doab *rasyāwal*, and in the eastern districts *khappar jār*, or *bhanraro*. The ceremony at the first boiling of the juice is in the Upper Doab *farīdi*; in the Central Doab *jalāwan* by Hindus, and *sinni* by Mohammadans; and in Gorakhpur *jhartha bhartha*. The ceremony at the last distribution of the cooked juice is in the Upper Doab *īkh barhi*.[75]

No marriages and but few festive ceremonies have taken place in the meantime, and the *Dithwun* is the signal for their commencement. Houses are cleaned, and smeared fresh with cow-dung, and the fruit of the *Singhāra* and *Ber*, and *Chunaka-sāg*, and other dainties of the season may be lawfully enjoyed.

But amongst Agriculturalists it is more especially celebrated for its connexion with the cutting of the Sugar Cane. All Hindoos of correct habits will carefully abstain till this day from touching the crop; but on the *Dithwan* a little is taken from the corner of the field, brought home, and spread out for the reception of the *Sāligram*, which, in due form, is lifted up several times; an action significant of Vishnu's rising from his slumber.' Elliot, pp. 280–1. See also *Bareilly Settlement Report* (1874), p. 136.

[75] The obverse of this was the right to beg and the duty of the peasants to donate grain or sugar when a surplus was readily available and at the site where it was being processed, i.e. at the *Khalihān* or the *Kolhuār*. An obligation was placed on peasants manufacturing *gur* at the *Kolhuār* to part with some of the sweetstuff: to turn a beggar away from a place where so much sugar was being made was an undesirable act which would seldom go unpunished. Grierson's account of the worship of Makkar or Makar Bīr is worth recalling in this context: 'Near the place where the cane is cut into slips the men make a round idol of the deity called *makar bīr*... He is said to have been originally a Dom who once came to a sugar manufactory in the olden time and asked for juice, which the people refused to give him. Thereupon he jumped into the boiler and was boiled to death. His spirit became deified and is worshipped by the workmen...'. See *Bihar Peasant Life*, pp. 55–6. The theme of suicide leading to the wrongdoer accepting his fault and then propitiating and worshipping the deceased is a running one in Indian folklore.

679. When the crops are cut, some of the new grain is taken home and eaten with certain ceremonies. This is known to the east of the province as *nawān*; and in the west *arwan, dadri, alo, awāsi, kawal*, or *kawari*.

680. When the grain is collected on the threshing floor, certain ceremonies are performed to propitiate the ghosts and penates of the village known as *dih, bhūt, bamār deo* and *jākni*, or *dāna*. In Gorakhpur the offerings of a clay horse or elephant, a woman's forehead ornament (*tikuli*), vermilion (*sendūr*), and an ear ornament (*tarki*), are called *pujaura*.

Section VII—Miscellaneous Ceremonies

681. Among these may be mentioned the *dam madār*, or *dhammal*, feast in honour of Badi-ud-din Shāh Madār, which is also known as *chhari, medni, chirāghan*, and *badi*.

682. The *barra* is a rope made of the *makra* grass which is pulled by the inhabitants of adjoining villages on the *bānta chaudas*, or 14th of the light half of the month *kuār*.

683. The *akhtīj* is the feast on 18th *Baisākh* on which the obligations of the spring harvest (*rabi*) are cleared off. This is in the east districts, the *ākhir tithia*, or *kāti kūti*.

684. On the *ekādasi*, or 26th *Jeth*, is the *deosoni* when the women mark the houses with lines of cowdung, fast during the day and eat sweetmeats during the evening.

685. In the eastern districts, the rite performed at the selection of the site of a new village is the *dih bandhwāi*, which is performed by two men, the *pattiwa* and *mattiwa*, the latter of whom pretends to be seized by the local ghost.

686. The *godhan* is a woman's rite in which they make cowdung figures of snakes, scorpions, etc., and beat them.

Changing the context and the time period, the refusal of an Ahir in Nanusakh village (Azamgarh) to offer some *gur* to a hungry sadhu who came begging to his *Kolhuār* (on 1 March 1921) was rumoured to have resulted within half an hour in the gur and the two buffaloes of the Ahir being destroyed by fire. See Shahid Amin, 'Gandhi as Mahatma: Gorakhpur District, Eastern UP, 1921–2', in Ranajit Guha ed., *Subaltern Studies III: Writings on South Asian History and Society* (Delhi, 1984), p. 47.

687. The *jiuṭia* is a fast and worship with women on the 8th day of the dark half of *Kuār*, for the benefit of their children.

Section VIII—Arbitration, Oaths [Deified Persons, Evil Spirits, Disease, etc].[76]

688. A body of arbitrators is *panchāyat*. The chief arbitrator is *sarpanch, pradhān,* or *pardhān*.

689. In deciding a disputed boundary the arbitrator walks along it with a raw cowskin on his head and holds five sticks in his hand to imply that he represents the body of arbitrators. This is known as *chhaur* in the western districts and *dill* in Benares. When one party in a case challenges the opposite party or a particular person to an oath, the phrase used is *hasr karna*. The oath is taken on the *harbans pothi* or *purāna*, and the person taking the oath wears a yellow loincloth, *pīli dhoti*. The oath taken on the cow in the eastern districts is *gaukiria*. *Gururu* is a circle drawn on the ground in which the man who takes an oath stands, or from which he takes the thing claimed.

690. Excommunication from caste is *hukkāh pañi band*. The headman among the Bania caste is *chaudhuri*, or *chokrāit*; among Telis and Chamars *mehtar*, and among the Gujars of the Upper Doab *pardhān, padhān,* or *pradhān*.

691. A magician in the eastern districts is *sokha* or *ojha*, and to the west *jādūgar* or *syāna*. His incantations are *jādu* to the west and to the east *sokhāi* or *ojhāi*.

692. An omen is *shagun* or *shugun*; if auspicious it is *nek shugun* or *sagnauti*; and if inauspicious *kusagun* or *badshagun; khom* is an evil omen connected with certain days and places.

693. There are a vast number of local divinities (*dīwār, dihwar, thānāpati, gram deota*, or *bhūmia*) worshipped in these provinces. A *kāli asthān* or mound in honour of the wife of

[76] For details one has to turn to William Crooke's classic, *The Popular Religion and Folklore of Northern India* (London, 1896, and various Indian reprints).

Shiva is generally erected outside each village. The mound erected to a deceased Brahman or holy man is to the east *Brahm*. Among the local divinities may be mentioned *Katesari, Barnaicha, Hanwat, Bhīm Sen, Chanwar, Kāshināth, Mansārām, Hardaur, Ratnu, Harirām, Jharkhand Iswar, Kall Sen, Bishari, Hardewal* or *Hardeo, Ratan Pānde, Mānik Pānde, Mari Bhawāni* (the goddess of death), *Nakt Bīr* (a divinity among the Nat caste), the *Agya Baitāl,* also called the *Dāno* or *Dān Sāhib* (a hideous demon which lurks in trees, lives on dung betels, and siezes wayfarers at night), *Samāy* or *Banspati Māi* (the dreaded forest goddess, to whom a heap of wood is raised beside the road, and every passer-by adds a stick), *Rāja Kidār,* or *Khwāja Khizr* (the patron god of the boatman—*mallāh*—caste), *Nāthu Kahār* (the protector of bearers (*Kahār*) and boatmen (*Mallāh*)).

694. A male and female ghost, the *jāk* and *jākni*, protect adjacent villages, and are propitiated by gifts of grain at harvest.[77] *Totka, tutka*, or *tona*, are spells or charms generally with an evil object. The *āparwāns, ūpariha, ūpari, batās* or *bayār* are various kinds of evil spirits in which villagers believe, The *ghoghar, ghogho,* or *dodo*, is a ghost invoked to frighten children. *Bihia* is a witch in the eastern districts. In Gorakhpur she is known as *bhānmat* or *bhānmati*. In Gorakhpur the *dukhra bhūt* is a sort of vampire that goes about at night sucking children's blood and milking cows. A stick from a crow's nest (*gad ki lakri*) is supposed to have great magical powers. The *pujāpa* is an animal, etc., offered to *Kāli* as a sort of scapegoat. This is also known as *khelauna*.

695. In cases of sickness (particularly small-pox) some rubbish is exposed on the road in a saucer. This, called *jog*, is supposed to communicate the infection to the first person who touches it. A little masonry terrace is sometimes erected near a village, and twice a year jars of water are placed on it to

[77] For a thoughtful discussion of spirit cults, including—*preta, dāk*, etc., see Gyan Prakash, 'Reproducing Inequality: Spirit Cults and Labour Relations in Colonial Eastern India', *Modern Asian Studies*, vol. 20, no. 2 (1986).

lay the ghost of a childless person. This is known as *aūd* in Mathura. The oblong mounds studded with flags to avert epidemics, especially cholera, are *hardaur*. The deities which bring disease are propitiated with an offering of various liquids poured on the ground which is called *chhāk*. The *khatola* is a miniature bedstead hung on a tree as a propitiatory offering.

696. The *ojhaini pūja* in Gorakhpur is the worship of a deified Ahir named *Kāshi Dās*. It is performed in the month of *Sāwan* by the lower castes. The *Kheti Bhawāni* is worshipped by Koiris, who then plant and cut their vegetables. Similarly the Mohammadan vegetable-sellers (*Kunjra*) recite the *fātiha* or opening chapter of the Quran. *Rāhu deota* is worshipped by Doms and Dosādhs in Gorakhpur; the ceremonies are a sort of fire worship, and are described in the District Gazetteer.[78]

697. The *banotsarg* is the emblematical marriage of a grove to a well without which preliminary observance it is unlawful to partake of the fruit. The *brikhotsarg* is the ceremony of marriage performed in the name of a bullock let loose on the 11th day of mourning for a near relative. The *jalotsarg* is the emblematical marriage ceremony on completion of a well or a tank.[79]

698. Water brought from a sacred river, spring, or place of pilgrimage (*tirath*) is much used in religious ceremonies, and is carried by men called *kāmārthi* or *kanwārathi*.

[78] The Gazetteer of Gorakhpur (Vol. VI of the NWP Gazetteer, 1881) contains no description of Rahu worship—in fact it devotes very little space to the Doms. The Basti Gazetteer (p. 628), on the other hand, has a longer notice on the Doms, and characterizes their 'funambulistic dance' (rope-walking) as a form of Rahu worship. For a detailed treatment of Rahu, see Ranajit Guha, 'The Career of an Anti-God in Heaven and on Earth', in Asok Mitra, ed. *The Truth Unites* (Calcutta, 1986).

[79] The *jalotsarg* ceremony is discussed in some detail in Appendix A, para 452.

XIV Trade and Money-Dealing

Section I—Trade and Accounts

699. Trade is *lenden, beohār, byopār* or *bepār, banaj* or *banij, bohrgat, dādsitad.* A moneylender is *mahājan, bepāri* or *beopāri, sāh* or *sāhu, sāhūkār* or *bohra. Rīniha* in the east districts is a lender or borrower. An account book is *bahi* or *siyāha.* Each page is *bāriz,* or more generally *panna.* According to Elliot, 'the page is divided into two equal parts called *zila*; each *zila* is divided into two *rukan* or *rukn.* The right hand *zila* is called the *hāsho.* The first right hand quarter (some say half) of the left *zila* is appropriated to the *bāriz,* and the remaining portion is called *irāda.* The *bāriz* contains the sum finally brought to account after the necessary deductions have been made from the gross amount in the *irāda* and *hāsho.*'[80] In the eastern districts the ordinary village moneylenders keep only one book, the day-book, *roznāmah* or *roznāmchah.* Each page of this is called *panna.* The left hand or credit side is known as *jama* or credit, and the right or debit side *nām.* Very small traders do not keep up even this book. They have a separate slip of paper containing each customer's account, which is called *sarkhat.*

700. Wealthy traders who only carry on one trade or deal in only one class of goods can do with three books—

1. The *roznāmchah* or *roznāmah bahi*—The day-book, as above described, with two pages (*panna*), the *jama* or credit and *nām,* debit. They are not very careful about this book, and erasures do not much matter.

2. The *rokar bahi*—This is in exactly the same form as the

[80] J. Beames in his revised edition made virtually no addition to the detailed entry of Elliot under *Bāriz.* See Elliot (1844), pp. 51–2, and Beames, II, pp. 229–30.

rōznāmah. There is only this difference, that it is balanced after each transaction. For example, the book shows Rs 1,000 on the credit side; Rs. 100 are disbursed on a certain account. This is entered on the debit or *nām* side and the book is balanced showing Rs 900 still to credit. This is called *bāqi tahvīl* and is brought forward again to credit. A man who carries on several distinct trades keeps up a separate *rokar bahi* for each.

3. The *khāta bahi*—This is made up as time allows out of the *roznāmah bahi*, of which it is in fact an abstract. It contains each creditor's account separately with a reference to the page of the *roznāmah bahi* on which each item has been entered day by day. Some traders keep up a separate *khāta bahi* for each of their trades or speculations. Others have only a general *khāta*.

701. Besides these there is the *jama kharch*. It is only an abstract *khatauni* or *khatiauni* or the *roznāmah bahi*, showing the totals of the receipts and payments on each page, *panna*.

Section II—Interest, Discount, Commission

702. Discount and commission are *dharta, batta, chota*, and in the eastern districts *batkar*. Interest is *sūd*. *Barhi* is interest in kind paid on seed-grain. *Biāj* is interest on money. *Biāju* is the capital put out to interest. *Barhotari* is profit or interest. *Udhār* is a loan when the exact thing lent is to be returned. *Qarz* is a money loan; also *paincha* or *paona*. A temporary loan is *dast gardān*, or to the east *tauja*.[81] A debtor is to the east *khaduka; khāubīr* is a defaulting debtor; *gayāla khāta*, a bad debt. When an animal or other property is pledged for a debt it is to the east *lāin* or *lāwan butāwan*.

Section III—Rates of Interest

703. The following are the rates of interest charged:

1. *Deorha* or 50 per cent, e.g. a man borrows 5 maunds of grain at sowing time and repays 7½ maunds at harvest with-

[81] *Tauja* is defined in the *Azamgarh Glossary* as 'a loan taken for a few days without interest'.

out reference to the selling price at the time of borrowing or repayment.

2. *Deorha nirkh kātke* or *bisār*—A man borrows 5 maunds of grain worth say Rs 10 at sowing time. He repays after harvest Rs 15 worth of grain.

3. *Bhao ūp siwaia*—A man borrows 5 maunds of grain at sowing time, the value being, say, Rs 10. He repays Rs 12-8-0 worth at harvest at current rates.

4. *Siwaia*—Twenty-five per cent. This is considered a fair rate, provided the substitution of grain and price is not made.

5. *Ughāi*—A form of moneylending. Rs 10 is borrowed, and is to be repaid in a year at Re 1 per mensem. This is known as *chhoti ughāi*. Rs 20 for a loan of Rs 16 also to be repaid in twelve months at Re 1 per mensem is *lambi ughāi*.

6. *Bhao bitka lena, bhao bitka dena*—A cultivator returns at harvest an equivalent in grain to the real money value of the grain lent at the time of borrowing, no interest being charged.

7. *Takāsi*—In the east districts is money interest at 2 pice or 1 *taka* per rupee.

704. The first money received by a shopkeeper during the day is *dastlābh* or *bohni*. A pledge or deposit is *giro* or *girai*. *Gathaund* is properly a deposit tied up in a bag. *Jākar* or *jānkar* is a pledge in deposit until goods which are taken away are finally approved of.

Section IV—Mortgages

705. A mortgage is *rahn* or *bandhak*: the mortgage or *rāhin* and the mortgagee *murtahin*. In Bundelkhand the *gurkhāi* mortgage binds the mortgager to pay three-fourths of the revenue of the mortgaged land. An usufructory mortgage is *patāwān* in the east districts, and in other places *bhog bandhak* or *pat bandhak*. *Bhog lābha* is the usufruct in lieu of interest. A redeemable mortgage is *būra* in the eastern districts. *Disht bandhak* is a simple mortgage without occupancy. A conditional mortgage is to the east of the province *jamog*.

Section V—Miscellaneous

706. An invoice or manifest is *bījak*. Insurance is *bīma*. A handsel or something additional given to a purchaser is, when given in kind, *ghelauni, ruk, phao*; and in the east districts *ghālu* or *ghalwa*.[82] *Jug* is similarly used by women in making petty purchases. A money-box is *golak*.

707. To test coin is *parakhana*. A money-tester is *parkhaiya* or *pajkhiya*. To test the correctness of scales is in the Upper Doab *hār lena*; *tār lena* in Rohilkhand, and in the eastern districts *sādh lena*.[83]

708. Capital is *pūnji* or *bisāt*. *Biāju* is properly capital out on interest.

709. The adjustment of accounts is *bujhārat*. To test the entries is *jānch lena*. A release in full of a debt is *bharpāi, bharauti, fārigh-khati* or *farkhati* or *chhor chitti*. The phrases in the eastern districts are *kāghaz sun ho gaya* or *daurān ho gaya*.

710. Money advanced on the security of standing crops is in the Upper Doab *īnch*. To become bankrupt is *dīwālā nikalna*.

711. A bill of exchange is *hundi, tīp* or *pāth*. The duplicate of the bill is *paith, painth, par paith* or *par painth*. A bill payable at sight is *darshani*; if payable at a future date it is *miādi*. The salutatory heading of the banker's letter of advice is *jog*. A bill paid and discharged is *khokha*. The phrase in Gorakhpur is *bhugtān ho jāna*. To accept a bill is *sakārna*. The number of days after the date is fixed by making it payable on such and such is a *mitti*.

[82] *Ghalwa* is pronounced *ghelua* in Gorakhpur.

[83] *Tār lena,* in everyday parlance, has an element of intuition attached to it. It doesn't refer to just 'finding out', but rather 'to discern despite appearances'.

XV Weights and Measures

Section I—Measures of Length

712. The *ungal* and *angul* is a finger-breadth equal to eight barleycorns; twelve *ungal* make one span.

713. The *angusht* in Meerut is the length of two barleycorns. The *bhāo* is the breadth of 5⅓ threads (*sūt*). The *bitta*, generally a span or hand's breadth, is in Hamirpur 16 *angul* or ½ a *hāth*. *Chaua* to the east of the province, or *chiya* in Meerut is 4 *angusht*; and 6 *chiya* make one *hāth*. The *dand* in Aligarh is equal to two *ilāhi gaz*, and 2500 *dand* make one *kos*.

714. In Gorakhpur the *dhāp* is about half a *kos*; but in Azamgarh it is a footstep, and three go to the *lattha*. The *dori* in Banda is equal to one hundred *hāth*, and one hundred *dori* go to the *kos*; and in Hamirpur one hundred *dori* make one *khet*. The *gattha* is one-twentieth part of the *jarīb* of 55 yards and contains three *idāhi gaz*. The *gatthwānsi* is the twentieth part of a *gattha*. The *gaukos* in the Upper Doab is a vague measure of distance, as far as a cow's bellow can be heard.[84]

715. The *girah* is one-sixteenth of a yard. The *hāth* is the cubit, and varies from 18 to 20 inches in length. The *ilāhi gaz* is Akbar's standard *gaz* of 41 fingers, the length of which was

[84] E. P. Thompson in his pathbreaking analysis of time and work in the transition to factory discipline refers to several identically vague measures of time in the pre-industrial world. 'In seventeenth-century Chile time was often measured in "credos": an earthquake was described in 1647 as lasting two credos; while the cooking-time of an egg could be judged by an Ave Maria said aloud. ... The *Oxford English Dictionary* gives us English examples—"pater noster wyle", "miserere wyle" (1450), and (in the *New English Dictionary* but not the *Oxford English Dictionary*) "pissing while"—a somewhat arbitrary measurement'. See E. P. Thompson, 'Time, Work-Discipline, and Industrial Capitalism', *Past & Present*, 38 (December 1967), p. 58.

fixed at 33 inches. In Hamirpur the *khet* is 100 *hāth*, and 100 *khet* make 1 *kos*. The *kos* varies in length in different districts. It properly consists of 5000 *gaz*, and the average is 2 miles 4 furlongs 158 yards. The *lattha* is one-tenth of the *jarib*, or 5½yards.

716. In the east-districts *deg* or *parag*, and in the west *qadam*, is a pace. *Sūt* is a thread-breadth. *Tarha* is a cubit used in measuring work in earth-digging and well-sinking. The *tasu* is 12 thread-breadths, and 24 *tasu* make one yard.

Section II—Superficial Measures

717. The *pakka bīgha* is fixed at 3025 square yards—i.e. one square *jarīb* of 60 *gaz*, or 5/8 of an English acre; or 3 roods 5 perches.

718. The sub-division in the Upper Doab is—20 *nanwāsi*=1 *kachwānsi*, 20 *kachwānsi*=1 *biswānsi*, 20 *biswānsi*=1 *biswa*, 20 *biswa*=1 *bīgha*.

719. The local or *kachcha bīgha* varies throughout the province, and is on an average about one-third or one-fourth of an acre.

720. The *dhur* in the east districts equals the *biswa*; and a *manda* is two *biswa*.

Section III—Measures of Weight

721. Twenty-five *dām* are counted to the pice (*paisa*). The *damri* is a nominal coin equal to 3⅛ or 3¼ *dām*. The *taka* equals 50 *dām*. The *adhela*, 12½ *dām*.The *dukra*, 6¼ *dām*, or one *chhadām*. A pice to the east is called *kachcha*. The *kanwāi* is 2/16 of the *ānna*. The *tāli* is eight annas.

722. In weighing, the *ratti* of 1875 grains troy is the basis of the metrical scheme:

8 *ratti*=1 *māsha*=15 grains troy.
12 *māsha*=1 *tola*=7 dwt. 12 grs. troy.
5 *tola*=1 *chhatānk*=1 ounce 17 dwt. 12 grs. troy.
1 ounce troy=2.667 *tolās*, or 2 *tolās* 8 *māshas*.
7½ dwts.=1 *tola*.
1 dwt.=0.133 *tola*.

723. The standard *man* of 40 *sers of 80 tolās* each weighs exactly 100 lb. troy and 82.286 lb. avoirdupois. 1 ton=27.222 *man*.

724. In weighing gold, jewels, etc., the standard is a seed known as *ghungchi (Abrus precatorius), ratti, chhantili, chirmithi, surkh, gunja, gumchi,* or *kūnch*. Its weight is about 1.933 grains. The *kaurena* in the east districts is a standard used by *sonārs* or jewellers.

725. The following are some of the local weights used in the province:

1. *Adharo*—In Jalaun half a *ser*; in Hamirpur about one *ser*.
2. *Adheli*—Varies from ½ to ¼ *ser*.
3. *Ādh pau, ādhpāi*—1/8th of a *ser*.
4. *Adh ser, aserwa*—½ a *ser*.
5. *Arhāya, arhāi ser*—2½ *sers*.
6. *Bandeia ser*—A *ser* in which wages in kind are weighed out—about three-fourths of the Govt. *ser*.
7. *Barya*—A *ser*, Lalitpur.
8. *Chahuri*—Banda. (See Diagram 2 on p. 172.)

The *pāth* varies in size all over the district.

9. *Chaukari*—One fourth of a *chauthiya*—about ¼ *ser*.
10. *Chauri*—About a *ser* (Hamirpur).
11. *Chauthiya*—A grain measure used in Bundelkhand about equal to a *ser* of wheat.
12. *Chola*—A grain measure about ¼ lb. (Bundelkhand).
13. *Chūra*—A grain measure equal to one *ser* (Jalaun).
14. *Dhāra*—A weight of four *ser* (east districts).
15. *Don*—A grain weight in Gorakhpur; 16 *ser* go to a *māni*, and 16 *māni* to a *don*.
16. *Duāni*—*Vide Chahuri*, no. 8 above.
17. *Gon*—A weight equal to 8 *mānu* (Hamirpur).
18. *Kanwa*—1/16th of a *ser*.
19. *Karuwa/kuruwa*—*Vide Chahuri*, no. 8 above; about a *ser* in Lalitpur.
20. *Khanri*—A weight equal to 20 *kuro*, or 100 *chauthiya*, no. 11 above.
21. *Kuro*—a weight equal to 5 *chauthiya*, no. 11 above.

Diagram II: Measures Used for Grain in Banda District

					Chahuri
				Kuruwa	4
			Paila	4	16
		Duāni or *Paili*	2	8	32
	Mān	2	4	16	64
Pāth	16	32	64	256	1,024

22. *Mān*—In Banda—*Vide chahuri*, no. 8 above.

23. *Māni*—A weight of 16 *sei*, equal about 16 *ser* (Gorakhpur).

24. *Mānu*—A weight equal to 4 *paila* (Hamirpur).

25. *Paseri, panseri*—Properly 5 *sers*, but it varies throughout the province according to the size of the local *ser*.

26. *Pāth*—In Banda—*Vide chahuri*, no. 8 above.

27. *Pāu, pawa*—1/4 *ser*.

28. *Poli*—Half a Ser (Lalitpur).

29. *Rajia*—A measure of capacity in Gorakhpur. It varies in size and averages about 1 1/4 Government *ser*.

30. *Sawa ser*—1 1/4 *ser*.

31. *Tīnpāu*—3/4 *ser*.

Appendix A: On the Construction of Masonry Wells and Ceremonies Associated with it in Kanpur and Gorakhpur

A Villager Gets His Well Built (Kanpur) *

450. 'When any one proposes to build a well he sets about collecting material for the kiln (*bhattha āwa*). If a zamindar, he cuts wood from any scrub jungle (of *reeān, chinkur*) he may have; if a cultivator, he either gets the zamindar's permission to do the same, cuts down the dead tree in his grove, or, failing both these resources, he has to buy. Dung-cakes (*kanda*) are collected or purchased, and a sufficient amount of refuse manure (*ghura, pans*) is begged from his neighbours. A brickmaker (*kumhār*) being found, a lucky day (*sāit*) is selected, on which a contract is concluded with him for bricks. This may either be for all the work connected with bricks—making, burning, and laying—or more often is for making the bricks, arranging them in the kiln (well-owner finding fuel), and laying in the well. The bricks almost universally used are '*patiyas*', large radiating bricks according to the size of the well it is intended to build. This class of bricks is preferred because it stands without masonry, the pressure of the surrounding earth maintaining the circle unbroken; the smaller bricks (*nau terahi*, 9″×13″) have to be laid in lime, or they fall out, and a breach in the works is formed which will eventually lead to its destruction.' Unbaked bricks cost Re 1 per *koth*—or sufficient for one yard of well (about 320 in

* *Source:* Report by F. N. Wright, 'On the construction of state wells in pargana Ghatampur, zila Kanpur,' 10.2.1879, GOI: Agr. & Hort. A Progrs., Oct. 1879, no. 17.

number). Baked bricks cost Rs 5 per *koth*. 'In this case the brick-layer gets six-annas per diem, or a contract is given as above for the whole well—Rs 20 to Rs 30, according to the depth and the owner finds the fuel. . . If the bricks turn out of the kiln well-burnt the *kumhār* gets a present.'

'Material now being all ready, again a lucky day for commencing to dig is ascertained from the *pandit*; and the evening before, the owner and the *pandit* go to the selected spot and draw a circle on the ground, within which they place nine small earthen vessels full of water to the brim on places about a foot apart, representing shrine of the *deotās* (generally the *naugirah* or planets), one of the nine being in the centre. In the morning the vessels are examined, and that which is found still quite full is accepted as indicating the centre of the proposed well and where the spring will certainly be found. It is an article of faith with the simple villager that only one—but certainly one—vessel will be found full. The *pandit* is fed, and some *gur* given to him, and the *kuiyās* [well diggers] and friends also receive small presents of *gur* or grain. During the progress of digging below water level the *pandit* attends daily, and each day reads a service (*pāt*) in honour of Debi, being paid at the rate of Rs 4 or 5 per mensem'.

'The first digging to the water level is often given on contract to a village *chamār*, but according to the depth and assistance given by the well-owner, the sum paid varies from Rs 4 upwards. The water level (*panihās, chān*) reached, the bricks are carted to the spot, and the difficulties commence. The *kuiyās*, or men who dig below the water level (generally *kāchhis* in the tract examined), get good wages, five and six annas per diem and their food. Their names are often registered at the *thana* to absolve any one from blame if an accident should occur. As the *kuiya* digs he supports the earth with ropes (*binde*) of *arhar* stalks (*khāre*), fastened in with iron pegs (*dāt*). Above he is assisted by all available hands in the village, with eight or ten yokes of oxen hauling up the water and the earth as quickly as possible. It is absolutely necessary to keep the water down, or the *kuiya* could not dig below a certain depth.'

451. 'If all goes well the spring is reached. The *kuiya*, who knows when it is near, by experience, lays the curb (the curb is passed down wrapped in cloth, which is the perquisite of the digger), and proceeds to build up the steining. The circle of earth being kept in position by earth, small *kunker*, broken bricks, etc., are poured down between the cylinder and the soil through a *sūnr* (pipe, literally elephant's trunk) of *tāt* or gunny. If by accident the spring is tapped before the masonry is completed up to a safe level, the water often rushes up at imminent risk to the digger. All hands in the village turn out, and haul away for dear life. In one instance work was stopped till the spring was choked by earth, etc., poured into it through the *sūnr*. Even here there is the fear that the yielding sand may force in the binders, bury the diggers, or destroy the well . . . Once above the water level all is safe; and it only depends on the funds of the owner or the object of the well as to how it is finished off. Sometimes, when the spring has not been reached, the cultivator sinks a small cylinder (*pit-kuiyān*) still lower. This, however necessitates driving'. All this 'clearly bring[s] out how wonderful it is, not that so few wells are dug, but that so many are dug as actually exist. The risk of failure attends the owner at every step. . . '.

Well-Construction in Gorakhpur—Ritual and Communal Aspects *

452. 'When a man intends to sink a well he enquires an auspicious moment from the Pandit to commence it. When that hour comes, he worships Gauri, Ganesh, Shesh Nag, earth, the *kudāri* (spade), and the nine planets. After worship-

* *Source:* Notes by Ram Gharib Chaube, *North Indian Notes & Queries*, March 1894, no. 437, and March 1895, no. 437; *NWP Gazetteer*, VI (Allahabad, 1881), p. 595; Rept. on Pergunnah Rasoolpore Ghaus, Appx. L, in *Goruckpore-Bustee Settlement Report*, I (Allahabad, 1871).

ping these deities the person himself begins to dig with the *kudāri* five times, facing the direction the Pandit has prescribed. Then the labourers begin their work. When they have sunk, so far as to make water appear, an auspicious moment is obtained to put the *jamuat* or wooden support on whom [*sic*] the brick structure of the well rests in the well. At the auspicious moment the person to whom the well belongs smears the *jamuat* with red powder in five places and ties grass (*dūb*) and thread (*raksha*) on it, and then it is lowered down in the well. On this occasion a fire sacrifice (*homa/hawan*) is performed and Brahmans are fed. When the well has been sunk, cow-dung, cow-milk, cow-urine, cow-ghee, Ganges water, leaves of *tulsi* plant and honey are put in it before its water is made use of. Then a fire sacrifice (*homa*) is performed and Brahmans are fed'.

In Gorakhpur, according to Ram Gharib Chaube, a mango tree was usually 'married' to a well. Accounts from neighbouring Basti district suggest that the construction of a pukka well was both a communal and a ritual act. Neighbouring zamindars sent men, women and children to collect wood for the firing and baking of bricks, and the *sattu, gur* and liquor received by them were regarded 'in the light rather of a marriage feast than of remuneration.' The 'marriage' of the well to an image (*jalotsarg*) was preceded by the carpenter spreading a *chaddar* (sheet) on the wooden frame. Into this the members of the brotherhood would throw coins of various denomination ranging from one paisa to one rupee, depending on their means and liberality. It was a measure of the importance of ritual in the construction of pukka wells in this region that the 'regular cost' of constructing a well, eight feet wide and nineteen feet deep, was reckoned to have been Rs 43 in the late 1860s, while nearly twice as much was spent on ceremonial expenses. The settlement officer reported from Rasulpur Ghaus, 'On account of the expense, the ceremony is often delayed one or two years, during which time the family of the builder makes no use of the water.'

The break up of expenses was as follows:*

Regular Expenses	Rs	annas
Digging (by contract)	8	0
Price of wooden (*jammaut*) frame	6	8
Wages to blacksmiths, including price of iron	2	0
Kaccha bricks including cost of burning	7	0
Mason for building	8	0
Sinking the well (*churhaee*)	6	0
Ramming down earth	3	0
Finishing off the top	2	8
	43	0
Ceremonial Expenses		
Offering to family god	1	0
Given to Brahmins: 5 dhotis and 5 rupees	9	0
Given to head *beldār*, 1 dhoti and 1 rupee	1	12
Liquor for remaining *beldārs*	0	4
Feast to Brahmins (5 to 20)	11	0
Given to Brahmins and workmen, 5 rupees and 5 dhotis	9	0
Marriage ceremony from 10 rupees to an unlimited amount	50	0
	82	0
Total:	125	0

*Source: Appx.L, *Goruckpore-Bustee Settlement Report*, I (1871). The ceremonial expenses are referred to as '*Abwab*' in the original document.

Appendix B: On Cloth and the Clothes of the Natives of Eastern United Provinces*

726. *Mārkīn*: It is a corruption of the English word 'marked', meaning 'that with the mark'. It is customary among Hindi speaking people to use the suffix '*īn*' or '*kīn*', to a noun to make adjectives. E.g. '*lāl-kīn*' is the general term for 'red cloths'. *Mārkīn* is said to be made of cotton and jute thread. It is rather rough when not washed; its width is between 12–15 *girah*. A *thān* consists of 36 yards. It is used by the 'poorer classes' in making their *dhotis*, *angochās* (big handkerchiefs) which function as a head gear in the fields. 'As it [the *angocha*] is not sewn, high castes may cover their bodies with it when at their meals. It is very necessary for a Hindu. In a village from a boy to an old decrepit everyone uses an *angocha*.' Women also make sarees, but generally of the poorer classes who also make their *chaddar* from this cloth. The poorer classes are 'chiefly the users' of *mārkīn*.

727. *Nain-sukh kora*: 'That which gives pleasure to the eye.' 'Extensively used by well-to-do people in the villages' when in *kora* (unwashed or rougher) form for making *dhoti* and *angocha*. The reason is that its width is wider, 16–22 *girah*, and the thread fine and well set. Poorer people use it for *chaddar*, but used basically for *dhoti* and *angocha* by the well-to-do. When washed, it becomes 'wall white and smooth.' 'To wear a loin-cloth which reaches the ankles is a mark of respectabil-

* This appendix is based on a long letter written by Ram Gharib Chaube of Gopalpur, District Gorakhpur, to Crooke, at the latter's request. I have paraphrased this long document, retaining several key passages from Chaube.

Source: Ram Gharib Chaube to William Crooke, 14/19 (?) December 1900, Crooke Papers, MS 139, Museum of Mankind, London.

ity among us and it is the chief reason why this cloth is used for the purpose.'

728. *Dhoa nainsukh*: Washed *nainsukh*. It is used by 'the gentry in making their *anga* (long coats), *kurta, chaddar* and sometimes *dhotis* for the summer. It is 'considered a respectable cloth'. It is durable, fine, strong, smooth and well set, and is of good width. While *mar̄kīn* sells from 11 pies to 2–3 annas a yard, *kora nainsukh* from 11 pies to 3–4 annas, this cloth sells from 4 annas to 8–10 annas a yard. *Razāis, dulāis* [quilts of varying thickness] are also made after the cloth has been dyed by the *rangrez*, but the *nainsukh* used is the ordinary one. *Pāyjāmas* for the summer are also made 'by the gentry. But it must be noted that the village gentry do not often use *pāyjāmas*. They content themselves with well-washed *nainsukh dhotis* hanging down the ankles. It looks more beautiful and becoming to us than the Muhamadan tight (*chūri-dār*) *pāyjāma*.' Its *thān* is of 18 yards.

729. *Malmal*: 'Now comes *malmal*, a word apparently formed from action. It is very soft to touch. Means "rub and rub".' Dhaka *malmal* is soft, that imported from England is also soft and fine, but 'except for the beaus [*sic*] of cities none in India uses it for *anga* etc.' However, it is often used for *kurta* 'by court going men, by gentry of the city and by every respectable man. They also make *chaddars* of it which, while in public, they put upon their shoulders or half wear upon their body above their loins.' They make *sirband* (as distinguished from *pagri* which is used by old fashioned men). Handkerchiefs are also made, of various prices, both for 'the high and low classes'. The price ranges from 3 annas to Re 1 a yard. 'Musalman poor make their *anga*, and all except *pāyjāma* of this cloth generally in summer, as they can become gentlemen by spending a rupee or so on this cloth.' Its *thān* is probably of 18 yards.

730. *Tan-zēb:* 'Body; ornament'—'Chief of the fine cloths that are used by the gentry and the nobility of this country.' It is manufactured both in Europe and India. The *tan-zēb* of Mau [Azamgarh district] is famous for its durability. It is used for *anga, kurta, dupatta* (sheets), *topi, ek patta* (the cloth put on the shoulders). 'It is a respectable cloth. The best *tan-zēb* goes under the designation of *addhi* (or half a rupee per yard). Its width is large and becoming; its threads very fine and smooth. This cloth though fine is durable. When washed it becomes very beautiful.' Its price ranges from 4 annas to a rupee a yard, 'but that *tan-zēb* is considered good which is sold at 8 annas and upwards. This cloth is used by the rich men only.' The *thān* is of 18 yards.

731. *Doriya*: From '*dora*'=thread. It is used for *kurtas* and *angās*. It has straight lines drawn closely together from one side to another in width. 'It is not very dear. Middle class men put it on. . . Used for making summer dress.' It sells from 3 annas to 6 annas a yard according to the ground cloth on which lines are drawn.

732. *Doriya sūsi*: Named after a place in Central Provinces. Same as above.

733. *Sītin*: A kind of *mārkīn*, with red lines on both sides—*angul-bhar* (finger-breadth) wide. Its breadth is 8 *angul*, and is used by girls for saris. 'Much in demand in villages.' Of English derivation, but unclear.

734. *Jin-dhoi*: 'Thick cotton cloth, which is used by Europeans as well as natives, who have received English education, for their coats and pants.' Corruption of *zīn*: saddle-cloth. Its price varies from 3–4 to 8 annas a yard.

735. *Dhoti-Jora*: A pair of loincloths, sold together for Rs 1½ to Rs 2 per pair. Made of *mārkīn, kora nain-sukh* or *malmal*, and have black, or red or *butēdār* borders of an inch or more wide. Some have silken borders, and are expensive.

736. *Tikra*: From *tīn*=three—Three zenana-saris woven together, with a dividing mark for each sari. Can be purchased treble or singly. These saris are generally 6 yards long and cost about Re 1 a sari. 'Ordinary women put them on.'

737. *Paniāla*: Water coloured. 'It is black generally. It resembles the colour of a deep water. It seems to be *zīn* of an ordinary kind dyed in *kachha* dye. Poor men purchase it for their winter *anga, kurta, kot,* etc. When used thus they use an undercloth, *bhitauli,* with it.' It does not cost more than 4–5 annas a yard.

738. *Chīnt,* or *calicoes*: From '*chīntna*'=to spread, broadcast. It is a 'noteworthy fact that in winter High or Low, rich or power [poor] all in India use calicoes of different kinds and values for their garments. The best calicoes earlier were French (*Farāsisi-chīnt*). They then sold very dear, but are now replaced by English calicoes of different kinds, named *ūni* (woollen), *bel-dar* (i.e. with creeper like stamps), *makhmali* (velvety), *nīm-patti, khāki, khaira rang* and so on.' Are used for *angās, kurtās, dulāis,* etc. (the upper cloth of *dulāis* and winter *anga* is usually of *chīnt*). The price ranges from 3 annas to 15 annas a yard: 'According to their means people purchase them.'

739. *Ek-ranga*: Of one colour. 'A red cloth in the market principally used for three purposes. Women make saris (6 yards) to go bathing in sacred stream or to *mela.* But the women who use *ek-ranga* saris are low caste. In going from *naihar* to *susrāl* or vice versa they use these saris also. At Chunar station in Mirzapur your worship saw a woman of this class and jokesely [jokingly] pointed her out to a gentleman with the remark: "How far above cattle are this class of native women?" Their hair pasted together with an objectionable seasumum [*sic*] paste, their forehead up to the nose painted like the elephant, the hands, the feet with silver handcuffs and chains on, their nose pierced and clumsily adorned with a heavy nose-ring, their necks weighed down by heavy silver weights, their face covered with a long, hanging veil, these daughters of India really excite laughter—than pity in the hearts of all thinking men.'

Second, the cloth is also used for the *bhitauli* of *dulāis,* winter *angās,* etc.

Third: *Angās* of children are generally made of it. 'It seems to be *nain-sukh* dyed red.' It is *pakka* of colour, costs 3 to 3½ annas a yard, with a good width.

740. *Chār-khāna*: Cloth with coloured square lines,

generally woven by 'native weavers' at Mau, Tanda, Fyzabad and Ludhiana; the Ludhiana one is of a superior kind. 'It is much in demand. Some men, who have received English education and sympathize with that fast-disappearing class of men, known among the officials as professional agitators, make their coats, pants, etc. of *chār-khāna*, believing perhaps that they are, thereby, serving the interests of their country. . . . *chār-khāna* of the worst kind are also used by men of common run for their *angās, kurtās*, etc., simply because they are cheap and in their eyes fashionable. Sometimes men of no party and of Govt. service put on coats and *pāyjāmās* of *chār-khāna* at the time when they are on tour, because that cloth does not get soon dirty [*sic*].' Its price ranges from 2½ annas to 6 annas a yard.

741. *Nan-gilāt*: A corruption of English 'Longcloth'. There seems to be some difference of opinion as to what *nan-gilāt* is: 'Among villagers *mārkīn* also sometimes goes under the designation of *nan-gilāt*. But those who are educated and have much to do with good cloths call a soft, well-washed, strong cloth, superior to *nain sukh nan-gilāt*. It is used by missionaries, by well-paid teachers of English schools and colleges, English-educated officers (natives) for their coats and *pāyjāmas* in summer. Men of position in Hindu society sometimes make their *dhotis* of it.' Its price varies from 6 annas to 12 annas a yard. 'It is respectable cloth. Its breadth is large.'

742. *Nainu*: Corruption of *nawanīt*, meaning butter, [q.v. *Azamgarh Glossary*: '1. Butter 2. A kind of embroidered cloth.'] *Nainu* has 'for its ground what is called *malmal* of a superior kind and on it *bel* and *būta*, i.e. *naks*[*h*] and *nigār* of the moslem are laid out. These are not of silk but of cotton.' The chief 'uses of it are confined to *chaddars* of men and women. Young men of native education of an inferior kind use *nainu chaddars* at the time of a marriage party or when they visit their relatives. Widowed women use white *nainu chaddars*, while married ones use the coloured ones.' The best *nainu chaddars* are called *Dhaka pātan ki chaddar*. 'Comparatively high priced', it costs Rs 2 for a piece 4 yards long and 1 yard broad. The superior varieties cost much more. Coloured *nainu chaddars* are generally red. There is another variety—*nainu kauriya būti*, with *butās* of small shell-like design. It is used for making *angas* of 'grown up boys of village gentry. Caps are also made of it.'

743. *Jām dāmi ki chaddar*: It resembles the one described above. The *butās* on it are big, resembling a cup (*jām*) and *dāni* (grains). 'As its name indicates it is used by females as their *dharāu* (to be kept for use at grand occasions) *chaddars*.

744. *Chālti*: Seems to be derived from *chhāl*, bark; so called because in thickness it resembles the bark of a tree. 'It is a thick cloth, the threads of which in the length are prominent like the *doriya* cloth', with the difference that it is absolutely white. 'It is used by men of the new school for their coats, and *pāy jāmas*, or coats and pants. Its breadth is good.' It sells from 6–8 annas a yard. 'But it is not much in demand. My village, with the neighbourhood market Gola, is a big station. But I have seen only one person putting on an *anga* of this cloth.'

745. *Kharua*: Is used mainly for making *jhārans* [dusters] of Chaprasis in Govt. offices, *bastās* for native chiefs and *gaddās* and *masnads* (beds and thick pillows). 'The coverings of guitar (sitar), musical instruments of European man, [*sic*] chests, clocks and the like are made of this cloth; the upper side is made of *kharua* and the lower of *mārkīn*. The satchel of children, the *jholīs* (wallets) of religious mendicants, and the *pujahīs* (the wallet in which the articles of the worship of an image are kept) are made of this cloth. The book binder uses this cloth in binding a Hindi or Urdu or Persian book.' It is a very useful cloth for rough purposes. It appears to be made somewhere in Central India, and something like catechu is applied to make it thick.

746. *Toshak*: A cloth stamped on the native *gaji* (the thick cloth woven by native *jolāhās*) by *chippīs*. So called because it is used in making beds ('The native bed is sometimes called *toshak*'). 'Poor men use this cloth for their winter wrapper, known as *doga*, for they keep the same cloth on both sides. It is so manufactured.'

747. *Fard or Lihāf*: A wrapper. A single sheet in Persian phraseology is *fard*. When 2 yards wide and 3 yards long a sheet is stamped exclusively for the purpose of *razāi* or *dulāi* it is called *fard*. 'Men of substance purchase a good *fard* for the upper part of a *razāi* for 2–2½ rupees. The lower part of the *razāi* is made of *ek-ranga* or some other coloured cloth. But it should always be thin so that it may catch cotton.' *Fards* can be made for lower prices as well. 'The price depends on the quality of the cloth on which the *chīnt* with *bels* on the margin have been printed. Also on the length and the breadth.'

748. *Galta*: It is manufactured at Mau and other places in India. The word means 'rotten'. 'The cloth, when seen at first sight appears as if it is rotten. Hence the name.'[85] It is a silken cloth. 'Those of the old school, who are well-to-do, get their *angia* made of it. . . for winter use. This cloth is kept on the upper side and *ek-ranga* on the lower side. It is considered a good kind of cloth.'

749. *Chikan*: 'The cloth on which needlework of the superior kind is done by the moslem women of Lucknow.' It is derived from '*chikkan*,' i.e. soft. 'The cloth by needlework becomes the reverse of *chikkan*, yet the name is given to it possibly according to the custom of the country, which finds vent in the following couplet of Baba Kabir Das, the weaver philosopher who flourished during the reign of Sikandar Lody the Emperor, whose reign is famous also for the fact that the first European ships came to India during his reign.'

Chalti ko gāri kahai, bane dūdh ko khoa,
Sahi ko bahi kahai, yeh suni Kabira roya

'Many Lucknow women of good family make a fortune through this industry.' The cloth is generally used for *anga*, *kurta*, sometimes for *chaddar*.

[85] Local informants maintain that the term, properly speaking, is *ghalta*, from *ghalat*=mixed.

750. 'Musalmans of means generally use this cloth. Then Kayastha. Other castes have no wish for it. The price of *chikan* goes from 8 annas upwards. For my own part, I have a great liking for it, as I have for several other Mahometan fashions. The only reason for this liking is that I have lived long in the company of Musalmans.'

751. *Imli-patti*: 'Any extraordinarily fine cloth, whether it is first class *tan-zēb* or *mal* [*mal*] is called in the phraseology of the village people, *Imli-patti*. . . . "Old-fashioned men" who get their *angiās, mirzais* (an *anga* which is only knee-long or less—or as long as the English coat), etc., get *imli* leaves decorations on *nain-sukh* made and sown round the neck. They joke with a beau at the sight of him thus: "*Imīl-patti-kai angarkha pahiri-ke kahān ghumat hawwa*"!'

752. *Chuhali or mata-phulan*: 'This is the worst kind of cloth used in covering the dead body at the time of cremation. Only poor men use this cloth for their dead. Rich men use *Pītāmbar*, i.e. yellow or red silken cloth.'

753. *Kashmīra*: 'All woollen cloths, mixed with a certain amount of cotton threads or sometimes pure; but as a rule having streaks [stripes!], sometimes like *chār-khāna* and sometimes of straight ones in the length go under the name of *Kashmīra*—from the kingdom of Kashmir, where they were originally manufactured.' Used mostly in making long *angās* or small coats, native *pāy jamās* or English pants and native *fatuhi* or *sadari* (waistcoat put under the *anga* and above the *kurta*) or English waistcoat corrupted into *Basket*. Price ranges from Rs 1½ to 3 per yard.

754. *Malīda*: 'A woollen *chaddar* or cloth, white or brown in colour and very soft to touch is called *malīda* from the resemblance it bears to the Musalman bread or loaf, made of wheat flour, sugar and *mewah*, i.e. *kismis, chohāra, gari* and *badām* and called *malīda*.[86] The *malīda chaddar* sells for Rs 18 and upwards a piece.' Some people make coats/pants with it.

[86] *Malīda* is not a 'Musalman bread'. Platt's Dictionary refines it as 'a cake made of pounded meal (or of flour), milk, butter and sugar', and gives the secondary meaning as 'a kind of fine woollen cloth (made of Kashmir

755. *Dhussa*: 'Another kind of woollen cloth, which is much used by the ordinary native. . . . It is a kind of wrapper. It sells for 8 or 9 rupees a piece. It is so called from the wear and tear which it stays. In native phraseology "*dhūs dālna*" means to use a thing mercilessly.'

756. *Shāl* or *du shāla*: Fine Woollen *chaddar*, single or double.

757. *The silk cloths of Benares* (not directly investigated by Ram Gharib Chaube): These are of the following kinds: *Makhmal, Atlas, Choli, Dariyai, Pitambar, Mukuta, Kora, Gulbadan, Mashru, Kamkhāb, Khes, Multāni, Dhūp Chānh, Suikar.*

758. *Sāri*: Women make saris of 'ordinary or fine cloths or thick cloth. . . according to their means. But well-to-do women generally, ordinary women sometimes, use saris sold in the market.' The determinants of the price are the quality of the cloth and the border (*kināra*). 'If the cloth is superior *nain-sukh* and the *kināra* silken, with *bel* and *buta*, the price will be high. If the cloth is *mārkīn*, the *kināra* narrow and only red or black, the price will be low. The ground of the saris is generally white. Women dye them red, yellow, green or what they please, at home. Widows wear only white saris in good families. Some women of high families prefer saris of very thin border. Such *kinārās* are called *nakhūni*. A sari of *tan-zēb* of good length and breadth, of *nakhūni kināra*, red or black, is put on by women of high rank in Hindu society.' Saris called *Frāsisi* or of French manufacture (of fine cloths, with stamps fine and beautiful) are now going out of fashion; 'only old women like it'. The price of a good sari varies from Rs 2–5.

759. *Muraila-anchara-ki-sari*: Made of calico with 'the stamp of a peacock on the part of the garment which covers

---

lamb's wool).' The adjectival phrase 'Musalman bread' underscores the powerful distinctive signification that the term 'musalman' had acquired in eastern UP in the 1880s and 1890s. One can almost hear the demotic sectarian strains of the *gaurakshani sabhas* in the ornate English prose of Ram Gharib Chaube. See paras 750, 762.

the breast,' are worn by 'women of inferior order. . . It sells very cheap.' Its opposite, the *rēshmi* sari is very expensive.

760. *Lahanga*: A long skirt, used mostly in western UP. In eastern UP, it is not much in use, although it forms a part of the *dāl*—the clothes and ornaments sent from the bridegroom's house to the bride. 'In the western districts I have seldom seen women without a *lahanga*. But to us Easterners *lahanga* does not look well. We make our wives put on themselves a good sari and a waist-coat (a coloured *jhulla*). This looks very beautiful.'

761. *Dupatta*: *Du*=two; *pat*=cloth [Chaube discusses the *dupatta* basically as a part of male formal attire]. 'In reality *dupattas* are special favourites of Pandits in general and Bengalis in particular.' It is sometimes of plain *tan-zēb*, and sometimes embroidered. Its price ranges from Rs 3 upwards. 'A *dupatta* is generally 3 yards long and 2 yards wide. Some people put them on their shoulders cross ways and some in an ordinary way. The custom of putting it crossways is ancient.' Hence Baba Tulsi Das: *'Piyar dupatta kankha soti'*—A yellow *dupatta* worn on the shoulders crossways.

762. 'In ancient times high-caste Hindus used *dupattas* universally. . . Now I find people of Benares and of Bengal using *dupattas* universally as part of their suit. NWP men, influenced as they are by moslems, have generally forgotten their ancient Aryan ways. Persians are said to be Aryans but Indian musalmans seemed to have availed of the praiseworthy ways of Persians very little, though they study Persian poems, with a tenacity which is simply wonderful. Their religion (i.e. the religion of the Prophet of Mecca) is responsible in a great degree for their deteriorated ways and manners. They prefer Persian poems because Persian poets of the comparatively modern date. wrote generally on "love" of the inferior kind and they have their special relish for this theme.'

Appendix C: Durations of Time and the Agricultural Year*

763. *Nakhat* or *nakshatra* is a lunar mansion or constellation in the moon's path, a star or asterism. Astrologers (*najūmi*) besides the common division of the zodiac (*rāsi-chakr*) into 12 signs, divide it into 27 *nakshatras*, two and a quarter are included in each sign. These range from 13 days and 20 *dands* in the dry, to 15 days in length in the wet months. The longest is *hathiya* which is 16 lunar days. For the peasants the *nakhats* are extremely important subdivisions of the year; every agricultural operation commences in a certain *nakshatra.*

The sun's progress is also sub-divided into 12 *lagans* or parts or months. 1 *lagan*=30 *ans*; 1 *ans*=60 *dands*; 1 *dand*=60 *pals*; 1 *pal*=60 *bipal* and 1 *bipal*=60 *sisals*. This makes up the solar year of 360 days and gives 12 months of 30 days each.

'The Muhammadan year is purely lunar, consisting of 12 months, each commencing with the appearance of the new moon, without any intercalation to bring the commencement of the year to the same season; but in chronology and all documents, the Muhammadans use months of 30 days and 29 days alternately, adding one day to the last month 11 times in 30 years, thus making up a year of 355 days; the average year is therefore $354^{11}/_{30}$ days, the 12th of which is $29^{191}/_{360}$, differing from the true lunation little more than 3 seconds.

764. The Hindus compute time according to both solar months (*sūraj mās*), of 30 days each, and lunar months (*chandrmās*), which vary from 29 days to 31 days in different parts

* *Source:* Patrick Carnegy, *Kachahri Technicalities* (Allahabad, 1877), pp. 214–18, with minor amendments.

of India, and on different ceremonial occasions. The lunar is 10 days shorter than the solar year, and to equalize them, an intercalary month of 30 days, called *laund* or *malemās*, has to be introduced after every third year into the *Hindi* calendar.

765. The year is in Sanskrit divided into 6 seasons thus, *sard, him, basant, sisir, grīkham* and *barkha*; but practically the only sub-divisions known, are the hot, wet and cold seasons, or *garmi, barkha* and *jāra*. The hot months are considered to be *Phāgun, Chait, Baisākh, Jeth,* the wet months are *Asārh, Sāwan, Bhādon, Kuār,* and the cold months are *Kātik, Aghan, Pūs* and *Māgh*.

766. It may as well be noted here that the Hindus also divide their months into two parts, each consisting of 15 days. The *andhēr pachh* or dark portion, is the first half from *parewa badi* (Ist day of the dark half), to *amāwas* (or 15th). The *ujer pachh* or bright portion, is the second half from *parewa sudi* (Ist day of the bright half), to *purnmāshi*, full moon (or 15th).

767. Cultivation is commenced in *Baisākh*. In *Jeth* the fields are manured. If during the *mrigsira nakhat*, which now occurs, the weather is hot, a copious and regular rainy season is looked for, thus

Tapai nakhat mrigsira joe,
Tab barkha pūran jag hoe.

768. *Mrigsira* is followed by *aradra*, during which mansion the rains begin and with them the early sowing of the *kharīf* crops, *dhān, juār, makra, kodon, kākun,* etc., and trees look their best. . . .

769. If the rains are late it may be *puranbas* or *pukh*, the 7th and 8th mansions, before paddy and *bājra* are sown; in the last of these *jarhan* transplanting usually takes place.

Pukh, puranbas bowe dhān,
Magha Sarekha kheti ān.

Sow paddy in *pukh* and *puranbas*, but in *magha* and *aslekha* sow miscellaneously.

Ardara dhān puranbas paiya,
Gā kisān jo boe chiraiya.

Paddy sown in *ardara nakhat* turns into plenty, sown in *puranbas* it turns into chaff, and sown in *chiraiya* it turns into nothing.

770. *Aslekha*, the 4th *nakhat* of the rainy season, follows, and then the *aghani* crops, *māsh* and *mothi*, are sown. In the 5th *nakhat, māgha*, of the rainy season, such grains are sown as were not sown in *aslekha*, owing to either want or the superabundance of rain. The miscellaneous grains mentioned. . . above are *māsh, bājra, mothi*, etc. *Pūrba* is the 6th and *utra* the 7th *nakhat* of the rainy season. Gram is sown in *hast*, the 8th *nakhat*, more commonly known as *hathiya*, and wheat in *chitra* the 9th , but should the rain continue, the sowing of wheat is postponed to the *swāti nakhat*. *Hast* is reckoned the last *nakhat* of the rainy season by the people. . . which lasts for 16 days, all the rest of the rainy *nakhats* last 15 days each.

771. The advantages or otherwise to the crops by the fall of rain in these various *nakhats*, are thus described:

Charhṭe barse aradra, utrat barse hast,
*Kitnau Rāja dānre, rahe anand girhast**

Notwithstanding the high demand of the raja, tenants profit by the fall of rain in the first part of *aradra nakhat*, as also in the latter part of the *hast nakhat*.

772. *Hathiya barse tīn hot hain, shakkar, shāli, māsh,*
Hathiya barse tīn jāt hain, tilli, kodo, kapās.

* A variant on this heard in Gorakhpur goes as follows:

Āt na ādar dījiye, jāt na dīje hast,
Kā karen ghar-pāhuna, kā karen girhast.

If you don't show respect when the guest comes (if it does not rain in *Ardara nakhat*), and if you don't hand something over when the guest is leaving (and if it does not rain during the *hast nakhat*), then what would the guest do (and what the farmer (*grishasht*) do)?

Rain in the *hathiya nakhat* produces sugarcane, paddy and *māsh*, but destroys *tilli, kodo* and *kapās*.

773. *Chitra barse māti māre,*
Āge bhai girwi kī kāre.

Rain in *Chitra nakhat* destroys the power of the soil, and is likely to produce blight (*girwi*).

774. *Ek pāni jo barse swāti,*
Kurmin pahine sone ki pāti.

Rain in *swāti nakhat* enriches the people so much, that Kurmi women get golden earrings to wear.

775. *Pāni barse ādha pūs*
Ādha gehūn ādha bhūs.

Rain in half of *Pūs* will give you wheat and chaff in equal portions.

Diagram 3

North-Indian Calendars

	Hindi				Muhammadan	
	Name	Commences when the sun enters	Astrological	*Nakhat*	Arabic	Ordinary
April–May	1. *Baisākh*	Aries	*Mekh*	*Aswini, Bharni,* ¼ of *Krittika*	*Jamād-ul-auwal*	5. *Madār*
May–June	2. *Jeth*	Taurus	*Brikh*	¾ *Krittika, Rohni,* ½ *Mrigsira*	*Jamād-us- sāni*	6. *Khwāja Muinuddin*
June–July	3. *Asārh*	Gemini	*Mithun*	½ *Mrigsira, Aradra,* ¾ *Punarbas*	*Rajjab*	7. *Māhrajjab*
July–August	4. *Sāwan*	Cancer	*Kark*	¼ *Punarbas, Pukh* or *Chiraiya, Aslekha*	*Shabān*	8. *Shabrāt*
August–September	5. *Bhādon*	Leo	*Singh*	*Magha, Purba Phālguni,* ¼ *Utara Phālguni*	*Ramzān*	9. *Ramzān*
September–October	6. *Kuār* or *Asin*	Virgo	*Kanya*	¾ *Utara Phālguni, Hast* or *Hathiya,* ½ *Chitra*	*Shauwāl*	10. *Id*

North-Indian Calendars (Contd.)

	Hindi				Muhammadan	
	Name	Commences when the sun enters	Astrological	*Nakhat*	Arabic	Ordinary
October–November	7. *Kātik*	Libra	*Tula*	½ *Chitra, Swāti,* ¾ *Bisākha*	*Zīkad*	11. *Khāli*
November–December	8. *Aghan*	Scorpio	*Brischik*	¼ *Bisākha, Anurādha, Jeshta*	*Zilhij*	12. *Bakrāid*
December–January	9. *Pūs*	Sagittarius	*Dhan*	*Mūl, Purba Khārh,* ¼ *Utara Khārh.*	*Moharram*	1. *Moharram*
January–February	10. *Māgh*	Capricornus	*Makar*	¾ *Utara Khārh, Srawan,* ½ *Dhanishtha*	*Safar*	2. *Tezi*
February–March	11. *Phāgun*	Aquarius	*Kumbh*	½ *Dhanishta, Satbikh,* ¾ *Purb Bhādrapad*	*Rabi-ul-auwal*	3. *Barāh-wafāt*
March–April	12. *Chait*	Pisces	*Mīn*	¼ *Purb Bhadrapad, Utara Bhādrapad, Reoti.*	*Rabi-us-sāni*	4. *Mirānji*

Note: As the Islamic months are entirely lunar their correspondence to 'English' or 'Hindi' months in the table is purely coincidental.

Appendix D: A Calendar of Agricultural Sayings

Kuār or Aswin

776. *Asin kahe kisan jo mujh mein nulai,*
Phin paidawar sawaiya dekh ho jai,
Jot ke turat anaj saraiya (?) bijai,
Sarhe ke bahan mein bab bahut diyai,
Sardi ka jab baith suru bona kar diyai.

'If you weed your fields in me' says Asin, there will at once be very great increase in the produce. If it rains do not let the water run out of your fields. Plough them well and you will have a good crop. Best to sow when the cold weather has fairly set in.'

Kātik

777. *Katik kahe kisan, baat meri sun taiya,*
Pakhware pahile mein rabi bo sari diyai
Makki, chatora dhan inhe sagwa tu bijai,
Chana dofasli boi tu inmen diyai,
Tere bail baju chasm hain bhai,
Inke hare tujhe thikana nahai.

Katik says, 'Cultivator listen to my advice. Sow all the spring crops in my first fortnight. Harvest your maize, your coarse and fine rice. Sow gram as a second crop. Mind friend, your oxen are your arms and eyes. If they are disabled you have no chance of getting on.'

778. *Katik lage boai, Aghan mein marai,*
Muttha karab menr par dharai.

Sow in Katik and irrigate in Aghan and you will pile the sheaves on the edge of your fields—a good harvest.

779. *Katik bove Aghan bharai,*
Tako Hakim phir kya kare.

He who sows in Katik and waters in Aghan is so well off that no official can harm him.

Kātik (Chitra nakshatra)

780. *Chitra genhun, adra dhan,*
Na unke gerui na inke gham.

Wheat sown in Chitra, the paddy of Adra (*nakshatra*), no rust eats this, no heat injures that.

Aghan

781. *Sabai kisani hete, Aghania paani jethe.*

All cultivation is backward but that watered in Aghan is superior.

782. *Mangsar kahe kisan ho ja mardaana,*
Teri paki aai Kharif ise san gawana,
Khene jugta rakh tu ghar mein tiyai,
Rakhte ko de bech tayyar jab baki kiyai,
Kar genhun mein dene ki taiyari,
Yeh mahnat ka wakt hai tere bhari.

Mangsar says, 'Cultivator now be a man! Your autumn crop is ripe. Now is the time to harvest it. Keep as much as is required for food in your household. Sell the rest and prepare to pay the rent. Now prepare to give the first light watering to your wheat fields. This is the time when you must work hard'.

783. *Aghan bova, kahun man kahun sawa.*

Wait for Aghan to sow your spring crops and in some you will get a maund, in some 1¼ maunds yield a bigha.

Pūs: (Purba or *Pob nakshatra)*

784. *Pob kahe kisan baat main tujhe bataun,*
Barse jo jagdish naaj ko kujam jamaun,

Lakhon man barhe naaj, baaj nahron se chutaun,
Bail bachen kisan mard kaamon se bachaun,
Hokar kai nighram ikh sab apna pelai,
Ek ek peri beech kitne hi phailawi.

Hear what I have to say, says Pob: 'If the creator vouchsafes rain in me, I will even make the helpless seed grain grow. Your crop will increase a thousand fold and you will escape paying canal dues. Both oxen and cultivator will be spared their toil. Thus relieved the husbandman can crush his sugarcane and each root of cane will give off several shoots for a second year's crop.'

Māgh

785. *Magh kahe kisan sun yeh albela,*
Baras din ki kamai ikh yab maine pela,
Diye paani hetu kuan sambhalo,
Kolhu ko do chor genhun tum barh ke maro,
Jo barsai bhagwan mauj phir teri aave,
Man man bigha kham tumre barh jaave.

Magh says, 'Listen to me jolly cultivator. The sugarcane has given you as much as will support you for 12 months. Now set your well in order for the second watering of your wheat. Leave your cane mill and drive the water full into your fields. If God be pleased to give rain you will be truly blessed. For every small bigha you will have an additional maund of produce'.

Phāgun

786. *Phagun hahe kisan baawla mat ho jai,*
Tal-rag mast hoke khet ki baat na sujhai,
Pus-Magh mein ghas barhat hai, naaj barhan samaiye,
De-de isemn pani naaj sawaiya ho jaihe,
Rakh tandwal khet ke ujran mat diyai,
Jo chahe bhagwan naaj naaj man chana ujai.

Phagun says, 'Cultivator don't let the merriment of Holi

make you forget about your fields. The watering in Pus-Magh helped the growth of stalks. Now is the time for the grain to swell. Irrigate it now and you will have a quarter as much. Take care of the fields. Don't let it all be wasted. If God wills, you will have a bumper crop.'

Chait

787. *Chait kahe kisan chana ho mujhmen doona,*
Sar uska mat tootan dije, rakhiye mat soona

Says Chait, 'Oh kisan you can have a bumper gram crop in me, provided you irrigate properly and not let its top half break.'

Chait

788. *Ikh paundra bo le tu jo chahe hua nihal,*
Bhar-bhar gari khaad dal de phaila, kod de kudal,
Bar-bar de paani usmen bandh bahut si suthri dhal,
Meethi lakri sab koi khave baitha de phauran rakhwal.

If you want to be happy, verging on the ecstatic, sow your *paunda* sugarcane (after a year's fallow). Spread cart-loads of manure and hoe repeatedly with the *kudali.* Irrigate the field regularly, and fence it with a hedge of *Hibiscus cannabinus.* Everyone (man and beast) likes the sweet-stick; have a watchman ready.

Baisākh

789. *Baisakh kahe kisan bawla khet-khet par phera maar,*
Dekh-dekh kar sagwa kheti jo-jo hoga taiyyar,
Jau aur chana kaat le pahile nahin jhar jawe saara khar,
Gehun katne ki jaldi kar jagah-jagah se kattha kar,
Olon ki dahsat rahti hai jhar na jaave sab pak kar.

Baisakh says, 'Oh peasant now is the time to make the rounds of your ripe (*rabi*) fields. First reap *jau* and *chana* and then get ready to harvest your wheat. There is always the danger of hail, and the grains may get overripe and fall to the ground.'

Jeth

790. *Jeth kahe kisan denth kar dhoop tapat mein kar pairi*
Mehnat karke jaldi utha le ho na ja barsha jaari,
Pachuwa looh mein turai jo pairi ho jawe do-do din mein,
Purwa plate jo aake phir hone ki nahin cheh din mein,
Purwa mein tu bijai uraya dhoop-dhoop sare kheja,
Jitni jaldi ho sake bhoos anaaj ghar mein le ja.

Jeth says to the cultivator: 'Be undaunted by the heat of the season. Make ready your threshing floor; work hard and gather the produce before the rains set in. If you begin your threshing in the hot west wind (*pachuwa*), you can finish in two days what you cannot do in six days if the wind veers round to the east (*purwa*). You can winnow in the east wind. Patiently endure the heat and carry the chaff and grain home as quickly as you can.'

Asārh (Nakshatras: Mrigsira, Aradra, Punarbas)

791. *Asarh kahe kisan suno ek baat hamaari,*
Kar hal-bail taiyyar baab de saari kiyari,
Bari Sanwak, Guwar boi tu mujh mein diyai,
Aur saali ke paudh, paache se charon na kiyai,
Jis ka ghori har isi samay par jaave,
Haare woh kisan saal bhar raas na aave.

Asarh says, 'Oh cultivator listen to me. Get your plough and oxen ready and plough up the whole field. Sow in me *sanvak*, cotton and *guvar* as well as paddy for transplanting. Take care never to let these four be late. Ruined is that cultivator whose oxen break down at this time of the year.

792. *Rohini, Mrigasir boiye makka,*
Urd, marua de nahin takka,
Mrigasir mein jo boe chena,
Zamindar ko kuch nahin dena,
Boe bajra aaya pukh,
Phir man maar bhogo sukh.

Sow maize and *urd* in the asterisms (*nakshatras*) of Rohini and Mrigshir (Jeth and Asarh respectively), and you will not be able to pay a penny of your rent. Sow *chena* in Mrigshir and you cannot pay your landlord. Sow *bajra* as *pukh nakshatra* (in Sāwan) comes, and you will never have peace; i.e. you cannot survive by sowing inferior grains.

Sāwan (Nakshatras: Punarbas, Pukh or Chiraiya, Asres or Aslekha)

793. *Pukh, Punarbas boiye dhan,*
Ashlekha kodon parmaan,
Magha mashina dije pel,
Phir dije Parhal mein pel.

Sow rice in the asterism of Pukh and Punarbas, Kodon certainly in Ashlekha, plenty of pulses in Magh and give them another push in Parhal.

Sawan kahe kisan baat tu sun le meri,
Pagri bandhat hot pacheti kheti teri,
Dhan chahora gahre boiye unchi urd juar,
Bo makki pichle pakhware dhundh sab se eksau kiyar,
Saari sawani bo le mujh mein aur sarahi mein de le baab,
Saathi saath hari ho jave ghas-naaj ki kamti naath.

Hear me says Sawan, your cultivation will be late if you wait even so long as to tie your turban. Sow coarse-fine rice in the lowlands; *urd*, pulse and *juar* millet on the highlands. Sow maize in the last fornight of this month and look out for an absolutely level field for it. Sow all the autumn crops in me and go on ploughing for the spring crop and then you will have lots of fodder and no lack of grain.

Bhādon

794. *Bhādon kahe kisan tant kheti mein paaya,*
Barah mein sardar khud hari ne banaya,
Jo kiyari tappar pari rahti mujhmanhi,

Phaile aisi dub danab ik hota naahin,
Wahi hai put-saput mujhe jo khub kamawe,
Main na barson kharab donon faslen ho jawe.

Bhadon says that the Lord himself has made him the boss of the twelve months. A field left vacant in me will get overgrown with grass and shall yield no grain. He is a man who tills well in me; both the Kharif and the Rabi are spoilt if I do not rain.*

*Compiled from Register no. 7 (1888), Settlement Shelf, Gorakhpur Collector's Record Room. This register, which was prepared as a part of the settlement work, contains a large number of agricultural sayings in Roman script. The handwriting appears to be of A. W. Cruickshank, the Settlement Officer. Cruickshank followed a system of diacritical marks which does not conform with the one used in the present *Glossary*. I have therefore preferred to omit diacritics altogether in the proverbs. These are provided only in the lunar months.

Appendix E: The Harvest Calendar in the Gorakhpur Region

795. The principal crops grown in the Gorakhpur region were (1) *bhadai*: (early *kharif*), consisting of *manrua* (*Eleusine coracana*), *kodon* (*Paspalum scrobiculatum*), *juār* (*Holcus sorghum*), early broadcast rice and other inferior grains. These were sown in *Jeth-Asārh* (late May–early July) and harvested in *Bhādon-Kātik* (September–October); (2) *jarhan* or *aghani* (late) rice, which was transplanted in late June–early July and collected in late November–early December; (3) sugarcane, which was planted in March–April depending on the crop rotation and crushed from January to March; (4) *rabi*: some wheat, but basically gram and other inferior grains which were sown in *Kuār-Kātik* (late September–early November), cut in middle and the later half of March, and threshed and stored in April–May.

796. The harvest calendar of the majority of the peasants was based on the crops mentioned above. In this system of *fasli* production the crucial role played by consumption loans, rental instalments and *gur* loans, to quote J. R. Reid, the Settlement Officer of Azamgarh, was as follows:

> If the rice and the rabi crops of the preceding year had been good, the agriculturalist has generally grain in his house; to feed—from April to the middle of August—himself and his family; and if he employs someone in watering his sugarcane, or in ploughing his land, to pay in kind for the hired labour. He may have rice to use as seed, but is not likely to have seed for the *rabi* crops, and will probably have to borrow in addition to the *rabi* seeds grain for food during September. When the *bhadai* crops are ready he is in need for grain for domestic use, and little or none of his crop will be sold. Through poor eating it will somehow carry him and his family on till the rice is cut and threshed. Meanwhile he needs cash to pay the first and second instalments of his rent, and this he borrows. When

the rice crop is ready, he perhaps repays part of the money and grain he has borrowed. But rice is a favourite foodgrain, and sells generally very cheap at harvest time. Besides the crop must supply food for himself and his family for three or four months at least. The cultivator therefore parts with as little of his crop as possible. Then comes the sugarcane season. The price that he gets for his *gur* is set against his old debts for grain and cash and out of it he pays his *rabi* instalments, and his banker realizes debts that have been caused during the past year by marriages, domestic trouble, and the like. Out of his *rabi* grain the cultivator saves as much as he can but part of it he will have to sell in order to pay the last instalment of his rent, or square his account with his banker; for grain that he borrows the agriculturalist pays in kind 37 per cent, for cash and grain repaid in cash, he pays interest at 25 per cent.*

* *Source:* S. O. Azamgarh to Bd. Revenue, 3 Aug. 1870, N.W.P. Rev. A Progs., May 1873, no. 12.

Appendix F: Agricultural Ceremonies in Eastern U.P.

797. In some places after getting the Pandit to fix an auspicious day they make a mixture called *mayān*, which consists of rice and turmeric ground together in water. This is put in a dish (*thāli*) and some red lead (*sendur*) is placed on a little box with a silver necklace (*hansali*). The yoke, plough and the back of the ploughman are marked with the *mayān*. Carefully abstaining from the south or unlucky part of the field he ploughs in a circle, and inside this cow-dung images of Gauri and Pārbati and Ganesa are worshipped with the *naugraha* or nine planets. After this the goddess Dharti Māta and the family god (*kuldeva*) are worshipped. Then a fire sacrifice (*hom*) is made with *ghi* and coarse sugar, and the field is ploughed five times and some seed sown. When they come home they eat choice food, and give curds and sweetmeats to the oxen. On that day they will not give alms or fire to any one.

798. In some places the custom is that after referring to a Pandit for a lucky day they plaster a part of the courtyard with cow-dung in the form of a square (*chauk*). In this they put a bludgeon (*lāthi*), a mattock, five plates (*thāli*) filled with *dūb* grass, a wooden stool (*pīrha*), and a large bamboo basket filled with a mixture of grains—*sānwān*, paddy, maize and barley. A rupee is also placed on one of the plates. Then the Pandit fixes on one member of the family as the proper person, and he comes forward dressed in white with a turban on his head, and his wife puts in the fold of his waist cloth (*phānr*) some of the grain. He then puts the bludgeon on his shoulder, takes a *lota* filled with water and the mattock in his hands, and veiling his face with a cloth so that he may see no inauspicious person or thing on the road, he goes straight to the field, where he stands in the centre, sows the grain out of his loincloth, sprinkles it with water out of the *lota*, rubs a little earth on his forehead in honour of mother earth (*dharti māta*) and comes home. He takes the remainder of the grain out of his loincloth, puts it in the basket, and sitting in the courtyard eats a little curd and molasses, first dedicating a little to Vishnu. The women cook special food on that day, which all the family eat, dedicating a portion to Thakurji or Vishnu.

799. Ploughing should begin on 18th Baisakh. On that day cultivators go to the field by night, and selecting the northern side, dig the ground with a piece of mango wood. Afterwards when there is a fall of rain the field is sown on an auspicious day. On returning from the field after sowing they eat coarse sugar (*gur*) and *ghi*. They enjoy themselves on this day, and never engage in quarrel with anyone. From that day they commence removing manure to the field and burning weeds in it.

800. When sugarcane is being sown a square (*chauk*) is made with cow-dung in the courtyard and sprinkled over with flour. The phrase for doing this is *āta se chauk pūrna*. Inside are placed some pieces of burnt tile. On that day choice food is cooked in the family.

801. Others when they sow corn, make five lamps (*chirāgh*) of cow-dung and fill them with corn. A small quantity of grain is taken from each lamp and sown in the field. On returning home they worship the family deity (*kuldeva*) and eat specially good food. Much the same is done at cotton sowing.

802. When they go to pick the cotton they first make a fire sacrifice (*hom*) with *ghi* and coarse sugar, and after worshipping the family god they take the cotton picked on the first day to the market and exchange it for salt, which is distributed to the members of the household. . . .

803. In Mathura the people worship the Gobardhan Hill on 15th Kātik, which is necessary to secure fertility in the soil. In other places the people take to the field in a tray a silver necklace and other jewelry. First they worship the ripe sugarcane, extract some of the juice, and with it make marks (*chāpa*) on the plough, yoke and cane mill, and after dedicating some to the deity the rest of the sugarcane is brought into use.

804. On the 25th Jeth some people collect dry grass and leaves, and burn them in the field at night to improve its fertility. When the Ardra asterism (*nakshatra*) falls in Asārh they plough round the field five times and commence sowing. On that day it is forbidden to give charity or to give fire from the house (see para 797 above). To do this involves ruin during the coming year. When the seed grows up they do worship to the eight-armed Devi of Vindhyāchal, and on that day eat cakes (*pūri, kachauri*), and rice boiled with sugar (*mītha bhāt*). On the 20th Sāwan they worship the snake-god and his wife (Nāg, Nāgin) On that day oil and salt is given to the oxen, and their heads and horns are anointed with oil. Ploughmen are also fed, and the cattle get a rest from work.

805. When the corn is collected on the threshing-floor the piled grain (*rās*) is worshipped. A certain portion is dedicated to Vishnu and Siva, which falls to the share of the family priest, or the Bairagi in whose circle the village lies.*

* *Source:* Ram Gharib Chaube, *North Indian Notes and Queries*, vol. 7, no. 6 (Sept. 1893), no. 203.

Appendix G: A Rural Glossary for Gorakhpur District, 1839*

A

Agowar	Perquisite of ploughmen in kind.
Angwara	Reciprocal assistance in tillage.
Arar	Outsheds for cattle.
Akhnee	flail.
Ar	Ladle used in sugar factories.
Ateyr	Mat (b)rush.
Agowree	Advances.
Akore	Bribe.
Aoree	Bank of a pond or rivulet to the water's edge.
Ahree	Salt pit—also trough for watering cattle.
Akra	Called elsewhere lutree or grain mixed with grass.
Anar dana	Spice of millet.
Ageya	The smut.
Agowasee	Called Konpee, the body of the ploughshare.
Angonga	Perquisite of the Brahmin from the threshing floor.
Aryee	Good.
Aaolee	Mode of estimating by the ascertained produce of a Biswa that of a Beegah.
Aokaon	Crop straw and grain heaped up.
Atturpul	Land alternately fallow and sown.
Abmass	Land constantly ploughed from Assar to Magh.

* *Source*: E. A. Reade, Gorakhpur Collectorship, 30 April 1839, Unnumbered Register of Collector's Correspondence for 1839, Gorakhpur Collector's Records Room. I have retained the non-standardized transcription and queried those words which are only mildly legible in the manuscript. See also Introduction, pp. xxiv and xxv above.

Ajaolee	Perquisite of the lower castes from the threshing floor.
Awaee	Pickaxe.
Amudnee	Revenue payment.
Abadcar	Settler on waste or forest land.

B

Bhatta	Ploughman's wages in kind.
Buthan	Pasture ground.
Busgit	Homestead.
Bala	Blight
Bishoonprut	Land gratuitously assigned to Hindoo priests.
Birt	Right of property and village management.
Burumpoojah	Service land to Hindoo priests resumable at will.
Brik Birt	Ancient Birt.
Beyd Birt	Birt acquired by sale.
Bhat	Advance to ploughmen without demand of interest.
Bowdur	Stages upon which water is raised by sling basket for irrigation.
Beesur	Gleanings left for the lower orders in the fields.
Boora	Resumable mortgage.
Bheyt	Present made in cash.
Behree	Sling basket.
Bareyt	Rope used at lever wells.
Boro	Marsh rice.
Burheya	A species of pulse.
Burha	Water channel in irrigation.
Buswaree	Bamboo garden.
Bithook	Ant-hills.
Breda	Mounds.
Bowrun dugda	Gifts at marriage and funerals.
Beesar	Loan of seed upon stipulation of ample refund after harvest.
Beyng	The same as above.

Bumhnee	Light red soil.
Beyra	Seed of lotus.
Behta	Mounds of a tank.
Birra	Ceremony of building a house.
Bussend	An edible root in jheels.
Bayaee	Weighman's perquisite.
Bar	Perquisite of the Ahir in milk.
Bunkass	A grass used in making ropes.
Buchownchee	Zamindar's fee in kind on the purchase of cattle.
Bhujwa	Stalk without ear.
Bawag	Seed time.
Bukheyl	Bark twine.
Bhutaee	Division of crop in the field or harvest floor.
Behree	Cultivator's instalments.
Bogbandhuk	Mortgage with occupancy of mortagagee.
Baht	Salt soil not requiring irrigation.
Bangur	Silicious soil dependent on irrigation.
Bandh	Called also Bundhik—mortgage.
Bounra	Winnowing sheet.
Beegmot	Ant-hill—often mentioned in determining boundaries.
Bunour	Cotton seeds.
Bulooa	Light or sandy soil.
Banda	Tree creepers.
Bidhnee	Process of extirpating weeds or rank grass.
Budhwar	Lands left fallow in Bhadon.
Beyar	Places from where transplantings [of rice] are made.
Bissara	Borrowing of seed upon condition of profits on repayment.
Baha	Irrigation channels.
Beyhun	Transplanted rice.
Bunjur	Soil of first year's tillage or sowing.
Bonhree	Perquisite of Fakeers at reaping time. Sale of necessaries by travelling merchants at the door of purchasers.

Bulsoondur	Mixed soil of light character.
Bukolee	Green caterpillar. Destructive of rice crops.

C

Churwaee	Wages of herdsmen in kind.
Chowr	Large tract of low land.
Chikarwaee	Wages for weeding.
Cheeta	Rice crop obtained by sprinkling [*chhīntna*].
Chowmass	Land tilled from Assar to Kooar.
Chowkoor	Division of crop where the zamindar only gets one-fourth.
Chundeya	Deep places.
Chuhkoor	Division of crop where the zamindar gets only one-sixth.
Choongee	Illegal abstractions of handfuls of market produce.
Chumrawt	Perquisite of Chummars.
Chonda	Kutcha well where the water is near the surface.
Charaee	Pasture land.
Cheyda	Disease of grain similar to the weevil.
Churroee?	Raising rent.

D

Dabhera	Large ploughshare.
Dowon	Slings in the sling basket in irrigation.
Doogula	Sling basket of small size.
Dhenka	Instrument for pounding rice.
Dorus	Soil in equal proportion of clay and sand.
Dhab	Low ground.
Dhoosee	Reddish sandy . . . [land], quite sterile.
Dhondhee	Reed grass.
Dhurohur	Deposit.
Dhurohur	Field yielding two crops in one season.
Downree	Treading out corn with oxen.
Dahur	Pathway.
Daveys	Road margin.

Deola	Mounds.
Dohur	Old bed of river.
Dubra	Small pond.
Deh	Homestead.
Dabur	Hollow below homestead.
Dughar	Path.
Donghee	Small boat.
Dangur	Superannuated horned cattle.
Dumka	Hillocks.
Dadunee	Advances to cultivators.
Dhadha	Plants running to stalk.
Danth	Refuse of harvest floor.
Dohao	Zamindar's perquisite of milk from ryot's cows.
Dishtbunduk	Mortgage without occupancy.
Deepdan	Land assigned to Brahmins on the banks of rivers, to deprecate river encroachments.
Dheokul	Lever used in drawing well water.
Dabhee	Young shoots.
Dakhilla	Receipt.
Dastoor	Patwaree's wages.
Dhoorkut	Advances paid upon promise of lease.

F

Furkutee	Final receipt.

G

Gou	Pannier.
Goend	Field near the homestead.
Gorhour	Stacks of cowdung fuel.
Gosaul	Stacks of cowdung fuel.
Gharee	Cattle sheds.
Ghorut	Cattle pens.
Ghurdwaree	Illegal cesses from shopkeepers.
Girowee	The weevil.
Gundheya	The arsot(?) in rice crop.
Gandheyla	The weevil in gram and arhar.

Goorduchna	Rent-free land given to spiritual teachers.
Gunowree	Bulrush.

H

Hurwur:	Advances without interest made to ploughmen.
Huris	Plough handle.
Henga	Piece of wood used in crushing clod.
Herrana	Manuring a field by keeping a herd of cattle on it for several hours.
Hurwot	First commencement of ploughing.
Huree	Contribution of assistance in ploughing fields of the zamindar by his ryots.

I

Inglis	Pension [Elliot, p. 480, renders it: 'A pensioner', and suggests that the word is a corruption of 'invalids'. Beames, II, p. 178, retains the meaning but drops the etymology].

J

Jonwra	Payment of service of village servants in kind.
Jat	Revolving beam of sugar mill.
Jhangee	Called also Jhonga—bramble and brushwood.
Jhowo Jhau	Alluvial brushwood.
Jurhun	Species of rice thriving on being transplanted.
Jamog	Transfer of liabilities by mutual consent.
Jagheer jeywa	Service land for service to be performed.
Jeonar	Field left with stubble for one season.
Jharee	Small jungle.
Jaba	Ox muzzle.
Jhootan	First winnowing double crop (?)

K

Kyhun	Provision given to ploughmen.
Koorpee	Hand hoe.
Kuntee	Dibble.
Koraee	Wages paid for digging.
Kola	Ditch for irrigation.
Kolhoo	Sugar mill.
Koond	Earthen pots for raising water from wells.
Kuraila	Tenacious clay soils.
Koowar	Soil when wet soft mud; when dry very hard.
Kishnarpurt	Rent-free land assigned to Brahmins without conditions.
Koorooree	Narrow path through villages.
Kurha	Division of crops in equal proportions.
Khooreyl	Soil broken up for subsequent sowings.
Khanwa	Boundary ditch.
Koonda	Deep pool.
Kuchar	Slope of river banks.
Kohera	Also Kohesa—mist fog.
Karha	Taking advances.
Khurayel	Gum exuding from Sakhoo tree.
Khoont	Tax leviable upon timber.
Kurgyee	Cess illegally taken from weavers.
Kerao	Species of pea.
Koenda	Seed nut of Mhowa.
Kut kunna	Sub-lease.
Khad	Manure.
Kussownja	Rope grass.
Khadur	Low land bordering marsh jheels, etc.
Kharean	Harvest floor.
Khurha	Herd of cattle.
Khalsa	Zamindaree estate in which the Birt tenure does not obtain.
Koroo	Measure of 10 beegahs.

L

Loodhua	Plucking cotton pods.
Lumberdar	Registered maalgoozars.

M

Munda	A measure of 5 biswa 1/4 of a beegah.
Munee	Ploughmen's provisions in grain. ['Mani': an allowance of grain made to a servant in lieu of pay in neighbouring Saran Dist. cf. Grierson, para 1185.]
Moot	First sowings for good luck.
Maner	A measure of weight, 16 seers.
Mutheyar	Clay soil.
Manjha	Alluvial tract between two streams.
Mun	Old bed of a river.
Murleya	Mud pools.
Murwana	Cess taken on marriages.
Murwat	Land assigned rent-free to the heirs of murdered persons. [See para 576 above.]
Muthowna	Kodo crops when injured by excessive rain.
Mussowan	A disease peculiar to all kinds of grains pods from which the latter are enlarged while the former is scanty.
Meynd	Border of a field.
Mahor	Blight.
Mut koovan	Small kutcha well.
Murree	Land assigned in lieu of interest upon loans.
Mokuddum	Manager of cultivation and village matters subject to the zamindars.
Muhto	Head ryot.
Mohraon	Mhowa garden.

N

Nankar	Government assignment of land or money for maintenance.

O

Oodean	Plain tableland.
Osowna	Winnowing.
Ootawon	Process of breaking the soil on young crops and rolling it afterwards.
Oosar	Barren plains.
Ook	Sugarcane in crops [sic].
Oolda	Raising ropes of the irrigation sling baskets.
Oatnee	Gins for separatating the cotton seed of cotton plants.
Owa	Elephant pits.

P

Phulwaree	Garden.
Pala	Frost.
Phar	Ploughshare.
Putowan	Lease of land paying Government revenue of which the profits are earned to credit of the principal and interest recurring thereon.
Pulowtee	Young branches of the date tree.
Poorwat	Drawing water from well by cattle.
Phurwar	Harvest floor.
Pans	Manure.
Patee	Measure of grain in store.
Panja	Rice stalk without grain called also Phurra.
Par	Borrowing plowing [*sic*] in lieu of labour.
Phan	Process of catching wild elephants.
Ponchee	Gratuity to herdsmen paid on sale of cattle.
Putour	Bark rope.
Pursa	Perquisite of grain set aside from the harvest floor to appease evil spirits. The Goseyn gets it eventually.
Pussur	Leading cattle to pasture at night.
Pokrah	A tank.
Purjhowt	Forbidden cess upon residence from the lower classes.

Paleepur	Land tilled three years, and left fallow for one season.
Peree	Land in the preceding season sugarcane, afterwards ploughed up for wheat or barley, etc.
Puthul	Hail.
Pussaree	Spontaneous rice crop in jheels.
Puchdo	Division of grain, 2/5 the zamindar 3/5 the cultivator.
Puchkoor	Division of grain, 1/5 the zamindar, 4/5 the cultivator.

R

Roopnee	Process of transplanting.
Russotur	The ploughman's title of grain.
Rapar	Barren plain.
Rutwa	Called also Rara—long red grass.
Rass	Heap of grain.
Rukwaree	Watch over crops.
Rukhaut	Land set aside for grass to grow for thatching or for cattle.
Rujeya	Measure of grain.
Ramdana	Spontaneous grain, red in appearance, common in Oorid fields.
Rahela	gram.

S

Sawak	Price of bondage. The sum advanced to a ploughman for whom [sic] his labour is rated as interest.
Sohnee	Weeding.
Seyhee [*Sei*]	Measure of grain=88 sicca weight: 16 seyhees make a maund—16 Manees make a Don, or nearly 7 ordinary muns.
Silla	Gleanings in the field.
Seyota	Sowing after the plough.
Sernik	Ledge grass.

Sendooree	The red bolt in wheat and rice.
Seet	Dew.
Sootnee	Sweet potatoes.
Sohee	Streamlet of a river.
Seerwar	Supervisor of zamindar's very jot (?)
Shunkulp	Positive alienation without possibility of recall, to a Brahmin, of any kind of property.
Shoopreet	A gift to a peculiar class of Fakeers.
Salarynt (?)	Report of occurrences.

T

Tuppeh	A Pegunnah subdivision.
Tahpazaree	Illegal cess from vendors at markets.
Tiller	A disease in grain from which it becomes unusually small.
Teeuee (?)	A species of rice grown by the side of jheels.
Tooma	The same as above.
Tanghee	An axe.
Tak	Frost.
Tiree	The locust.
Teerwah	Lowland.
Terkool	The palm tree.
Teesooree	Mode of paying labourers loads of one bundle in thirty bundles.
Teekoor	Division of crop when zamindar gets 1/3, the ryot 2/3.
Teep	Called Kafee, a corruption of "Kafee zamnee": security to pay a sum by a stipulated period.
Teakee	Irrigation stages for irrigating from tanks.
Thak	Boundary mark.

Z

Zerayut	Seer cultivation of zamindar or Birtiya.

Bibliography

Azamgarh Glossary, being Appendix III to the *Azamgarh Settlement Report* (1881). J. R. Reid.

Azamgarh Settlement Report: Report on the Settlement Operations in the District of Aẓamgarh (Allahabad, 1881) J. R. Reid.

Bareilly Settlement Report: Report on the Settlement of the Bareilly District, North-Western Provinces (Allahabad, 1874). S. M. Meons.

Beames, John(ed.), *Memoirs on the History, Folk-lore and Distribution of the Races of the North Western Provinces of India, being an amplified edition of the original Supplemental Glossary of Indian Terms by the late Sir Henry M. Elliot*, 2 vols (London, 1869).

Carnegy, Patrick, *Kachahari Technicalities, or a Glossary of terms Rural, Official and General etc.* (Allahabad, 2nd. edition, 1877).

Colvin, A., *Memorandum on the Revision of Land Revenue Settlements in the North Western Provinces, 1860–1872* (Allahabad, 1872).

Commission Appointed to enquire into the origin, nature, etc. of Indian Cattle Plagues, 1869 (Calcutta, 1871).

Elliot, H. M. *see under* Beames.

Fallon, S. W., *A New Hindustani-English Dictionary, with illustrations [from] Hindustani literature and Folklore* (Banaras: London, 1879).

Gazetteer of the Province of Oudh, i–iii (Lucknow, 1877–78) ed. W. C. Benett.

Growse, F. S., *Mathura, A District Memoir* (1874).

Kerr, Hem Chunder, *Report on the Cultivation of and Trade in Ganja in Bengal* (Calcutta 1877).

Nawādir-ul-alfāz (n.p., n.d.).

Prinsep, James, *Useful Tables* (a reprint of Mr. J. Prinsep's

'Useful Tables,' forming an Appendix to the Journal of Asiatic Society, 3 pts, Calcutta, 1834–6).

Statistical, Descriptive and Historical Account of the North-Western Provinces of India, vols. i–iv (Allahabad, 1880–4).

Wilson, H. H., *Glossary of Judicial and Revenue Terms, etc.* (London, 1855).

Wright, F. N., *Memorandum on Agriculture in the District of Cawnpur* (Allahabad, 1877).*

* The above is a list of sources to which Crooke made repeated reference in his Glossary. In the original text Crooke cites a source for most of the terms and words listed by him. I have dispensed with the detailed footnoting and have provided a complete list of references in this bibliography.

Index

(Paragraph numbers prefixed with a star indicate location in a footnote)